THAILAND

THAILAND

THE WORLDLY KINGDOM

Maurizio Peleggi

REAKTION BOOKS

Published by Reaktion Books Ltd
33 Great Sutton Street
London EC1V 0DX

www.reaktionbooks.co.uk

First published 2007

Printed and bound in Great Britain
by Cromwell Press, Trowbridge, Wiltshire

British Library Cataloguing in Publication Data

Peleggi, Maurizio
    Thailand : the worldly kingdom
    1. Thailand – History 2. Thailand – Social life and customs
    3. Thailand – Civilization
    I. Title
    959.3

    ISBN-13: 978 1 86189 314 7
    ISBN-10: 1 86189 314 0

Contents

Note on Romanization and Lexical Conventions

Various systems are employed to romanize the Thai script, some of which approximate actual pronunciation while others highlight the Pali and Sanskrit etymology of Thai words. Romanization in this book follows the Royal Institute's General System of Phonetic Transcription (1939) with some slight modifications. Personal names too have been transliterated accordingly for the sake of consistency, regardless of the individuals' preference (e.g., Wachirawuth instead of Vajiravudh); however, in the References and the Bibliography names are entered in the transliteration favoured by the individual author. Names are listed in the Index in the romanized form adopted in the book, followed in parenthesis by the individual's preferred form. Following common usage, historic figures and authors are entered in the Bibliography and index by their first name. Italicized Thai words are not pluralized (e.g., *wat* for both singular and plural). Chinese words and names are romanized according to the Pinyin system of phonetic transcription.

Introduction:
Civilization, Globalization and the Thai Nation

Saffron-robed monks, slender dancers, monumental ruins, gilded Buddha images, exquisite handicrafts – here are some of the stereo-typical images of Thailand featured in travel guidebooks and adver-tisements. As always, tourism promotion formats real aspects of a country's physical and cultural landscapes into instantly recogniz-able clichés to allow easy product identification. In the case of Thailand, the appeal of such clichés of exoticism made the country one of the world's most popular tourist destinations over the last two decades or so. This international popularity generated wealth but also fears of an erosion of the distinctive Thai identity, leading academics and bureaucrats to rally behind the *cri du cœur*, 'We love Thai culture!' Concurrently, the national agency for the promotion of tourism reassured prospective visitors about the country's enduring traditions in the face of rapid modernization with the slogan: 'Thailand remembers its gracious past and anticipates its dynamic future.'

Although never formally colonized, Thailand was exposed to Western influences (and interferences) as much as the rest of South-east Asia – if not more, in fact. One aspect of the culture of colonial-ism on which scholars have recently focused is the documentation of the history and archaeology of the subjected countries. In Thailand too, pre-modern narratives of the past, in which the secu-lar and the religious and the mythical and the historical were fused together, were replaced by empirical history, which became an instrument for the legitimization of the modernizing monarchy and later a fundamental ally to the nationalist ideology. Because it had no need to account for the rupture in the traditional political order caused by Western colonialism elsewhere in the region, Thailand's historical narrative could locate the nation's origins in the thirteenth century by virtue of the secular continuity of the two institutions – the monarchy and the Buddhist monastic order – upon which the third pillar of the state's symbolic trinity – the nation itself – is predicated.

This book considers the emergence and consolidation of modern Thailand in the form, not of a diachronic narration of events, but of a thematic examination of the social, political, cultural and intellectual forces that shaped the process of state formation and nation building. To write the history of a country outside the chronological framework that places historical actors and events in a linear narrative may seem unorthodox; but while possibly more demanding on the reader, this approach seeks to highlight the relationship of the forces constitutive of the Thai nation-state to that constellation of phenomena – from imperialism to nationalism, from urbanization to the diffusion of mass media, from the institutionalization of religion to the politicization of youth – characteristic of modernity in both metropolitan and colonial and post-colonial contexts. Situating, historically as well as conceptually, the emergence of modern Thailand in the wider process of the emergence of the modern world is important because of the entrenched view of the exceptionality of Thai nation building in the regional ambit of South-east Asia. This book is thus intended as an introduction (admittedly partial and perhaps even idiosyncratic) as much as a reinterpretation of Thai modern history.

The seven interconnected themes that give the chapters their titles form the set of analytical prisms though which the history of Thailand is reframed in this book. Chapter One, 'Landscapes', describes the geographical, ethnic and cultural features of the kingdom and its inhabitants as they were shaped by the nation building project. Chapter Two, 'Boundaries', examines the delineation and modification of the nation's territorial, social and gendered spaces. Chapter Three, 'Institutions', considers the monarchy, the Buddhist monastic order and the bureaucracy and military as both promoters and products of state formation. Chapter Four, 'Ideologies', analyses the lexical and conceptual adaptation of nationalism, communism and democracy to the Thai political landscape. Chapter Five, 'Modernities', looks at the emergence of the Thai modern in the domains of bodily practice, scientific knowledge and literary production. Chapter Six, 'Mnemonic sites', discusses the role of commemorations, monuments and heritage sites in the production and reproduction of social memories. The last chapter, 'Others', dissects the discursive representation of figures of alterity – namely, the Burmese, the Chinese and the Westerners – as photonegative images of the Thai national self.

This introduction explores the book's central theme of the yearning for association with the dominant world civilization of the day as the leitmotif in the history of Thai society since early times; at the same time, it presents a broad historical overview as a reference for the thematic treatment that follows.

Before moving on, an explanation on the usage of the names 'Thailand' and 'Siam' is necessary. 'Siam' is the romanized form of *sayam*, the name given to the kingdoms of the Chaophraya River valley by their neighbours since the fourteenth century. Adopted by the Europeans in the seventeenth century, 'Siam' became current and was retranslated into Thai in joint diplomatic treaties even though the kingdom's inhabitants commonly referred to the country as *muang thai*. In 1939 the government decreed Thailand to be the country's name in international usage. The new name stuck, except for a brief reversal to 'Siam' after the war. Usage here follows by and large this chronology; the term 'Siamese' is meant as adjectival of Siam, not as a collective noun for its inhabitants (unless when occurring in quotations).

During the decade from 1987 to 1996 Thailand experienced a rate of economic growth among the highest in the world and economists predicted it would soon join company with Japan, South Korea, Taiwan, Hong Kong and Singapore as the next 'Asian tiger'. The boom ended abruptly in the summer of 1997, when Thailand's 'bubble economy' exploded with dramatic consequences. Suddenly, to the new rich created by the boom, globalization appeared a cause of personal destitution and national shaming. But over the previous decade, during which the national media had waxed lyrically on globalization, pundits had often pointed to the assimilation of outside elements as a Thai characteristic. The first to put forth this argument was none other than Prince Damrong Ratchanuphap (1862–1943), the revered 'father of Thai history' as well as the architect of the kingdom's administrative reform at the turn of the last century. Writing in the 1920s on the origins of religious art in Thailand, Prince Damrong stated: 'The Tai [sic] knew how to pick and choose. When they saw some good feature in the culture of other people, if it was not in conflict with their own interests, they did not hesitate to borrow it and adapt it to their own requirements.'[1]

This belief in the ability of the Thais to adopt and adapt whatever element of a foreign culture they see fitting arguably reveals an interest in the origins and uses of civilization. One of the key terms in the vocabulary of modernity, 'civilization' (from the mid-eighteenth century French *civilisation*) recast the individual qualities of civility and self-cultivation inherited from antiquity and the middle ages into the Enlightenment framework of human progress. By the 1800s the meaning of civilization had shifted to denote the ensemble of ordered society, systematized knowledge and technological innovation that set 'civilized' nations apart from 'barbaric' ones.[2] As such, civilization provided the ideological foundation of late-nineteenth-century imperialism under the hypocritical mask of 'the white man's burden'.

Unsurprisingly, attempts to translate into Thai the term and concept of civilization started at the time of the encounter with the West. Its first rendering was in the 1850s by a word, *charoen*, whose meaning of spiritual growth shifted to indicate material progress. The Thai elite's subscription to Victorian societal and behavioural norms was indicated by the transliterated form of 'civilized', *siwilai*, which entered the vocabulary in the last quarter of the nineteenth century. At the turn of the twentieth century, a neologism was fashioned from Pali (the Buddhist canon's classical Indian language), *arayatham*, which compounded the terms 'Aryan' and 'dharma' (in the sense of customs) to express the idea of civilization as ancestral legacy. In the 1920s the vernacular expression *than samaimai* became current to qualify what was up-to-date or 'modern'. In the late 1930s another Pali-based neologism, *watthanatham*, was coined to translate 'culture' with its then prevalent nationalistic connotation. In the 1950s the term 'development', the Cold-War era's equivalent of 'progress', was translated as *phatthana* and made into a keyword of state propaganda. And in the 1990s the latest civilizational trend – globalization – was domesticated by its translation as *lokaphiwat* (yet another archaizing neologism whose etymology evoked the Buddhist notion of impermanence of the physical world).[3]

This lexical review illustrates the shifting meanings that were ascribed to ideas of civilization, progress and development at different stages of Thai nation building. Indeed, the kingdom's rulers – from pre-modern Buddhist sovereigns to British-educated monarchs and from army officers to tycoon-politicians – were never shy in claiming the role of civilizing agents and harbingers of progress. Yet, at the same time, they imagined the sources of civilization to lie in the outside world: India and China in the ancient and pre-modern period, Europe in the nineteenth and the first half of the twentieth century and America in the latter half. Thai understandings of civilization reveal thus a syncretic disposition. As archaeologist Charles Higham has recently proposed, 'The roots of civilization in Thailand were firmly anchored in the prehistoric past, but were nourished by contact with exotic societies'.[4]

Thailand's classic statecraft, religion, literature and plastic and performing arts were based, like those of neighbouring societies, on the cultural practices and materials disseminated by South Asian merchants, artisans and priests along the trading routes of the Indian Ocean. The spatial expansion of Indian civilization into mainland and island South-east Asia resulted in a diffuse geo-cultural space – or œcumene – the legacy of which is still visible today in lexicons and symbols (for example, in the mythic bird Garuda, which adorns the state crests of both Thailand and Indonesia). The doyen of French orientalists, George Cœdès, named this process of dissemination *hinduisation*, which in the English translation of his work was rendered as 'Indianization'.[5] While Cœdès placed emphasis on external agency by highlighting the imposition of a foreign cultural matrix onto South-east Asia, the historian O. W. Wolters emphasized, on the contrary, local agency in the double process of adoption and adaptation of selected Indic materials by the local elites – a process Wolters termed 'localization'.[6] Localized Sanskritic vocabulary, Brahmanic rituals, Hindu myths as well as patterns of urban design and religious architecture provided South-east Asian elites with a social identity that set them apart from their subjects by connecting them to mythical genealogies of gods and heroes.

Along with Hinduism and Brahmanism, another Indian cultural import to South-east Asia was Buddhism. The diffusion of Mahayana Buddhism in the island of Java and what are today lower Myanmar and southern Thailand during the second half of the first millennium AD was followed, in the early centuries of the second millennium, by that of Theravada Buddhism from Ceylon (Sri Lanka). The Theravada precepts of renunciation of the secular world, asceticism and meditation were taken up by monastic communities but made also an impact on local ruling elites, who became great patrons of the religion, as well as ordinary people. Pre-modern polities in Thailand as well as Myanmar, Laos and Cambodia were thus brought together into a Theravada œcumene, within which local populations were bonded by the cult of Buddhist icons and relics and the patronage of the monastic order, or Sangha.[7] Roughly at the same time, proselytizing by Persian and Arab traders brought southern Thailand and the Malay Peninsula as well as the Indonesian archipelago into the expanding Islamic œcumene, as a result of which the pre-existing Indianized cultural landscape was reconfigured without, however, being erased.

From the early thirteenth to the late nineteenth century the Thai world was a mosaic of regional polities (*muang*), whose reciprocal relations were regulated by a precarious balance of suzerainty, alliances and conflict. According to the official historical narrative, the Thai nation originated in the Chaophraya valley in the middle of the thirteenth century, when Sukhothai, a principality under Khmer (Cambodian) suzerainty, proclaimed its independence. In Sukhothai, wrote Cœdès, 'between 1250 and 1350, the Siamese were able to develop their own characteristic civilization, institutions and art'.[8] In the middle of the fourteenth century, Ayutthaya, a kingdom in the lower Chaophraya valley (named after the mythical place of birth of the Hindu god Rama), overtook Sukhothai. Ayutthaya imbibed the Indic culture of its powerful eastern neighbour, Angkor, and over the following four centuries rose to become a regional power as well as a global emporium that, during South-east Asia's 'age of commerce',[9] hosted merchant communities from neighbouring countries, China, Japan, the Muslim world and Europe. The missions of tribute and reciprocation exchanged with the Chinese court assumed a special importance, as did the movements of goods and people between China's southern littoral and Siam as well as the rest of the region, to where Chinese people had migrated in large numbers since the early modern period. Neo-Confucian texts gave ideological formulation to this Sinic œcumene as the area encompassed by the diffusion of 'civilization' (Mandarin: *wenli*) from the imperial centre – Beijing – to the lands of barbarians.[10]

In 1767 the kingdom of Ayutthaya collapsed as a result of protracted warfare with Burma as much as from the disintegration of its administrative structure. A Central Thai polity re-emerged fifteen years later further south, on the bank of the Chaophraya, where a new dynasty, the Chakri, installed itself in a new royal capital: Krungthep ('City of the Gods'), known internationally as Bangkok.[11] In the seventy years since its foundation in 1782, the Bangkok kingdom stood in the cosmological, cultural and trading space at the overlap of the Indic and the Sinic œcumenes. One can find evidence of this double positioning in the realm of cultural production: the composition in the 1790s of a new version of the court epic *Ramakian*, based on the Indian *Ramayana*, was paralleled by the translation of the Chinese historical romance *Three Kingdoms* (*Sam kok* in Thai). Such a situation was typical of what imperial historian C. A. Bayly terms 'archaic globalization', which differed from modern globalization for being multi-centred, driven by ideologies of universal kingship and cosmic religion (often conflated, as in the medieval ideals of Christian and Buddhist monarchy) and characterized by the consumption of diversity in the form of charismatic substances and goods.[12]

As the multi-centric geography of interregional and intercontinental networks of dominance, trade and cultural exchange characteristic of archaic globalization gave way to a unified world system under the hegemony, when not direct political control, of the West, older globalizing centres lost their importance. By the 1850s the

Bangkok court's transnational affiliations to pre-modern œcumenes by way of cosmologies, religious texts and materials, and charismatic goods had considerably weakened; at the same time, Europe had emerged as a civilizational exemplar. The Thai royalty realized that only by becoming part of the fraternity of 'civilized' nations, or 'Victorian œcumene' in Carol Breckenridge's apt definition,[13] they would be able to secure the prestige and authority that they had previously derived from their place in the trading and cultural networks of the Indian Ocean and the South China Sea. During the third quarter of the century, encompassing the reign of King Mongkut (Rama IV, 1851–68) and the minority of King Chulalongkorn (Rama V), the Thai court established close contact with the Western powers that were colonizing the region and adopted many of their civilizational norms. Breaking a secular taboo on the vision of the royalty, King Mongkut had daguerreotype portraits of himself with his queen and their children sent to Queen Victoria, the US president and the Pope. In 1867 Siam was represented for the first time at an international exhibition, in Paris. In 1871, eighteen-year-old Chulalongkorn paid his first visit to Java, where the Dutch colonial authorities took him on a tour of their civilizing institutions (barracks, the judiciary court, the customs house and the museum); the following year the young sovereign acquainted himself with the British colonial project by visiting Burma and northern India.

The latter half of King Chulalongkorn's long reign (1868–1910) saw the implementation of a wide-ranging programme of reforms celebrated by historians as the Chakri Reformation. Education, administration, infrastructure, the bureaucracy, the monkhood and the army were modernized under the direction of Western advisers. Consumption informed by Westernized tastes allowed the Thai royalty to identify with the monarchies of Europe rather than those of the Theravada œcumene, which had been subjugated by colonialism and had lost with their power their mystique as well. By 1880, the court was living in neoclassical and Italianate palaces furnished with imported furniture that served literally as stages for the enactment of civilizing rituals. In the following two decades vicarious knowledge of Europe gave way to first-hand experience acquired through state visits and overseas education. In 1897 Chulalongkorn embarked on an eight-month tour of thirteen European countries

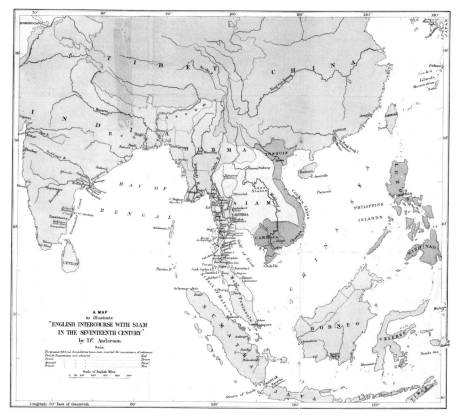

The region in the 17th century, from a late-19th-century British map.

(Russia included), relishing the opportunity to get acquainted with his Western peers and enjoy the honours prescribed to foreign heads of state by diplomatic protocol.

Above all, Siam was incorporated in the modern world system by means of cartography. As British and French surveyors drew the borders of Burma, Malaya and Indochina, they also gave shape – on maps first and eventually in the national consciousness – to Thailand as a territorial entity. The demarcation of the territory also created the conditions for the expansion of Bangkok's political authority at the expense of regional polities, such as the Lanna kingdom of Chiang Mai, that did not fit in the modern world of bounded states (and bounded colonial possessions). As a formally sovereign state whose autonomy in fiscal and jurisdictional matters

15

was curbed by the unequal treaties with Western countries, Siam occupied a liminal space in the political order of the high imperial age – that of a 'semi-colony', according to Marxist historians, or perhaps a 'crypto-colony', as proposed by Michael Herzfeld, whose independence was possible 'at the price of a sometimes humiliating form of effective dependence'.[14]

The populations who were included within Siam's newly demarcated borders were subjected in the intervening years to the state's modern technologies of governance such as censuses, taxation, law enforcement and military draft. These developments followed global trends in the nineteenth century, which 'above all, was the period of the "internationalization of nationalism", when the ideas and practices of the nation-state became rooted among the elites in all major world cultures'.[15] The promotion of a national consciousness, particularly since the reign of King Wachirawuth (Rama VI, 1910–25), followed thus another main vector of global modernity: nationalism as a source of differentiation and competition (and, eventually, conflict) in a world made increasingly uniform by the advent of the nation-state as the basic geopolitical unit. In common with European nationalism and different from nationalism in the rest of South-east Asia, Thai nationalism appeared to be a top-down rather than a bottom-up movement aiming at uniting subjects *around* rather than *against* the ruling elite. Recent historiography has however problematized this assumption by documenting a Thai 'popular' nationalism comparable to the region's anti-colonial nationalist movements in that it was animated by a stratum of educated commoners who endeavoured to overthrow the illiberal rule of the absolute monarchy. Significantly, however, what catalysed the public dissatisfaction against absolutism was the local repercussion of the great economic depression of 1929.

The promoters of the bloodless coup d'état that in June 1932 overthrew the absolute monarchy shared a vision of how to make Siam 'civilized' that was markedly different from the royal elite's; their aims were to introduce individual constitutional rights and bridge class and gender disparities. However, different from the Young Turks' defenestration of the Ottoman sultan in 1908 and the nationalists' disposal of the Chinese emperor in 1911, in Thailand the institution of the monarchy was retained even though King

Prachathipok (Rama VII, 1925–35), unwilling to play a mere symbolic role, abdicated in 1935. The democratic ethos of the early 1930s gave way, by the decade's end, to a more authoritarian and chauvinistic nationalism partly modelled after fascism. Not unlike Italy's *duce*, Thailand's self-proclaimed 'leader' (*phunam*), Marshal Phibun Songkhram,[16] possessed a somewhat schizoid political personality. Strongly anti-monarchist yet illiberal, ardent nationalist yet keen Westernizer, he issued a series of decrees that changed the country's name, instructed men to kiss their wives before going to work and exhorted women to wear hats and gloves in the name of national progress.

Phibun might have followed in the neutralist footsteps of Spanish dictator Francisco Franco had not the Japanese landed in Thailand on 8 December 1941, on the same day as their attack on Pearl Harbor. Phibun's collaborationism caused his fall from power towards the end of the war although *Realpolitik* brought him back in 1947 as an ally of the USA in the Cold War in East and South-east Asia. These were the years when Asia's geopolitics were reshaped by decolonization and the rise of nationalist leaderships; Thailand, instead, was integrated into the post-war American œcumene – the so-called 'Free World'. The establishment in 1954 of the South-East Asian Treaty Organization (the equivalent of NATO), with its head-quarters in Bangkok, underscored Thailand's role as paladin of the 'Free World' in the region. But the antagonist communist œcumene also found support among some Thais (especially those of Chinese ancestry); thus communism was outlawed for being un-Thai and, indeed, incompatible with civilization. When in 1955 recently decolonized Asian and African countries came together in Bandung (Indonesia) in the first conference of non-aligned countries, Phibun made a belated attempt to accommodate Thailand in the changing international scenario; in 1957 he was ousted by a former subordinate, Marshal Sarit Thanarat, whose political style has been aptly characterized as 'despotic paternalism'.[17]

Over the next decade and a half, 'development' (*phattana*) became the catchword for policies seemingly informed by Western liberalism but, in fact, carried out by an authoritarian oligarchy that was the first beneficiary of the massive American military and economic aid (some two billion dollars of the first between 1951 and

1971 and 650 million dollars of the second between 1950 and 1975).[18] Thai politics became dominated by figures of ruthless and corrupt military dictators who enjoyed full US patronage. The Thai government proved a major supporter of international organizations that articulated the ideological principles and economic interests of liberal capitalism such as the World Bank, the Asia Development Bank and the International Monetary Fund; it was also a founding member of the Association of South-east Asian Nations (ASEAN), founded in 1967. At the same time, Thailand became increasingly drawn into the Indochinese conflict: 11,000 Thai troops were fighting in Vietnam alongside the Americans by 1969, while planes on bombing missions to North Vietnam and Cambodia regularly took off from airbases in north-eastern Thailand, where the US air force regional headquarters were moved from South Vietnam after 1973.[19]

In October 1973 a student uprising ended a quarter century of military rule and inaugurated a short-lived experience in 'open politics'. The uprising was the closest Thailand had to a revolution – that is, a 'bourgeois revolution' on the French model of 1789. Mass demonstrations orchestrated by tertiary students in Bangkok convinced the throne to withdraw its support to the military dictators, whose fall coincided with the disengagement of the USA from Indochina. Though inspired by a largely suppressed tradition of local radical thinkers, the Thai student movement was also an off-shoot of the global student revolution that between the late 1960s and early '70s took to the streets of Paris and Mexico City, American campuses and China's countryside. When, after the brutal repression of October 1976, many of the students fled to the jungle and joined the clandestine Communist Party of Thailand, they discovered that the cultural differences with the party's cadres were stronger than ideological affinities. Thus, when a political amnesty was declared in 1979, the students welcomed the opportunity to abandon weapons and return to their books, some eventually assuming prominent roles in academia, the media and company boards.

By 1982, when the bicentennials of Bangkok and the Chakri dynasty were celebrated with great pomp, the bitter political divisions of the previous decade were shelved if not quite forgotten. The incumbent King Phumiphon (Rama IX), who since the 1950s had patiently rebuilt the monarchy's mystique after a long eclipse, was now regarded as the nation's moral pivot – even though universal praise of the king depended on his exceptional charisma as much as on the anachronistic law of lese-majesty. In this regard at least, Thailand was in counter-tendency to other constitutional monarchies in the world, where the media mercilessly demystified surviving royals by exposing even the most private aspects of their lives. The economic boom that started in the mid-1980s and cemented national pacification around the institution of the throne was, however, very much a product of globalization. The boom prompted the rise of a new middle class that, following in the footsteps of the royalty a century earlier, felt modern by consuming conspicuously the status symbols of the globalized marketplace – from German cars to Swiss watches and Italian shoes. Yet, by the turn of the 1990s, urban professional strata were demanding a stake in the political process in order to break free from the bureaucracy's stifling embrace.

A sense of déjà vu was hard to escape when, on 18 and 19 May 1992, scores of demonstrators that had taken to the streets of Bangkok in a challenge to a self-appointed prime minister were shot at by soldiers. Unexpectedly, the outcome of the violent incidents of those days was the turning away of the military from involvement in politics. The 'Black May' of 1992 thus came to stand in public consciousness as a new beginning for Thai democracy after the false starts of 1932 and 1973. The renewed momentum for democratization culminated in 1997 with the promulgation of the sixteenth, and arguably the most liberal, of Thailand's constitutions since 1932. By an unfortunate coincidence, 1997 was also the year of the financial crisis that ended a decade of portentous economic growth and quickly spread to the economies of the region and as far as Japan, Thailand's main foreign investor. Between the start of July, when the Bank of Thailand allowed the floating of the national currency (previously pegged to the US dollar) and the end of 1997, the Thai currency fell by over 100 per cent against the dollar, causing a devaluation of the value of national reserves from US$38 billion to US$2.8 billion; concurrently, the stock market fell by over half, from 800 points to below 400. Saddled with a foreign debt of $89 billion, Thailand saw the collapse of its banking system, widespread bankruptcy and massive retrenchment of workers and employees.[20]

Thailand was eventually bailed out by the IMF, whose concession of a loan of US$17.2 billion was conditional on the acceptance of a recovery strategy based on the principles of economic liberalism that many saw, not without reason, as the root cause of the crisis. Despite evident signs of an economic bubble since the beginning of the decade, the crisis of 1997 was blamed mostly on external forces – capitalism, globalization, the IMF and the West in general   and reinforced the heterogeneous aggregation of socially committed monks, non-governmental organizations (NGOs) and intellectuals who, already in the years of globalization triumphant, had animated the 'communitarian' camp under the ideal aegis of King Phumiphon, a staunch advocate of a self-sufficient economy and sustainable development based on agriculture.[21] In the public debates of the late 1990s the past was often held as a mirror to the present situation. Some commentators fanned the flames of nationalism by comparing the IMF and World Bank's intrusion into domestic affairs to the imperialist advances of the 1890s; others, however, blamed the elitist and authoritarian nature of nation building for Thailand's crony capitalism and inefficient bureaucracy.

At the turn of a century that had radically transformed its physical, economic, political and social landscapes, the dilemma of Thailand lay in reconciling the objectives of, on the one hand, achieving regional leadership by managing globalization and, on the other hand, preserving an assumed national essence – 'Thainess' (*khwampenthai*) – seemingly threatened by globalization. The eventual outcome of the financial crisis was the ascendancy of a new kind of tycoon-politician in the person of Thaksin Chinawat, the very embodiment of globalization as the owner of a telecommunications empire, who became prime minister in 2001. Thaksin's grafting of the corporate jargon onto the political vocabulary and his humongous conflict of interest were by no means unique to Thailand – his closest parallel being Italy's media-magnate-turned-prime minister, Silvio Berlusconi. Thaksin restored national self-confidence after the blow of 1997, but he did so at the cost of polarizing public opinion between ardent supporters and staunch critics. After a long institutional crisis, this polarization eventually led to Thaksin's deposition in a military coup d'état in September 2006.

In this context the notion of local knowledge or native wisdom (*phum panya*, most likely a loan translation of the English expression) acquired great currency. The indigenousness (*phum*, meaning 'earth, soil') that qualifies and gives ideological force to the idea of local knowledge stands as the antithesis to Westernization, modernization and globalization – rejected for trying to impose a foreign, unsuitable mould on Thailand's economic, social and cultural development.[22] In fact, the notion of local knowledge arguably reflected the recent tendency in developmental theory to place emphasis on the agency of subaltern groups as well as the antagonism to economic globalization of grass-root international organizations such as the World Social Forum. Noted public intellectual Sulak Siwarak, a sympathizer of local knowledge, has written of the Thais' relation/confrontation with other cultures in earlier times: 'We had to give up some aspects of our identity for a more universal aspect of civilization not only acceptable to the West, but also . . . according to the Dharma . . . the pristine teaching of the Buddha that predated . . . [that] which mixed Buddhism with Hinduist cosmology'.[23]

A self-proclaimed traditionalist (though not a political conservative), Sulak assumes the existence of a primordial identity that was tainted and eventually thrown into a crisis by interaction with the world. The overarching argument of this book is, on the contrary, that Thai identity was shaped and continuously redefined through such interaction. This argument does not deny social reality to Thai identity nor dismiss it as false consciousness, but holds Thainess to be, contrary to essentialist assumptions, a syncretic product, the result of the translation, assimilation and adaptation of exogenous ideas, practices and materials to the indigenous socio-cultural terrain. Civilization has always implied globalization. Thailand was no exception.

one | Landscapes

Territory, ethnicity and culture are constitutive elements of national identity as much as historical products of state formation. In Thailand this process resulted in uniformity replacing regional diversity: the physical landscape was reshaped by massive agricultural colonization, the ethnic landscape by intermixing and linguistic assimilation, and the cultural landscape by the creation of a 'national' culture.

The pursuit of uniformity responded to a civilizing project informed by nineteenth-century ideas about the moulding, control and management of the physical and social environments. Supporting the agricultural colonization of the territory to boost the country's economy; fostering linguistic, religious and cultural uniformity to instil a common identity in the ethnically diverse population of the kingdom; and modifying social customs so that they befit a civilized nation – these were objectives that both the absolutist regime and the post-1932 bureaucratic governments saw as necessary for the nation's progress. Yet the peoples and environment of Thailand both benefited and suffered as a result. The improvement in living standards, though dramatic, was unequally distributed across the country's regions and ethnic groups and was accompanied by considerable environmental degradation; and local identities were eroded by the diffusion of public education and the irradiation, later in the century, of electronic media from Bangkok.

The examination of the transformation of Thailand's physical, ethnic and cultural landscapes highlights a number of themes – such as the demarcation of boundaries, economic development, Chinese immigration, the institutionalization of the Buddhist monkhood and the promotion of nationalism – that are discussed in detail in the following chapters.

The Physical Landscape

One of the most immediately recognizable images of Thailand's physical landscape is that of emerald-green paddy-fields. Thailand is one of the world's major producers of rice (*khao*), which as a dietary staple and a prime export crop has had a pivotal role in the Thai socio-cultural universe. The stone inscription of King Ramkhamhaeng (AD 1292), reputedly the oldest extant text in the Thai script, reads: 'This Sukhothai is happy: there are fish in the rivers, there is rice in the fields'. Seven centuries later, in the early 1990s, cultivated land covered slightly less than half of the national territory of 513,000 sq. km; conversely, the forest cover was reduced to just a quarter of it. Thailand's extent of land under cultivation, unrivalled even in South-east Asia, is the result of a comparatively recent development fuelled by international demand for rice; in the early decades of the twentieth century as much as 80 per cent of the Thai rice production was exported to Singapore and Hong Kong, and re-distributed from there to British India, the Dutch East Indies, French Indochina and China.

Agricultural colonization gained momentum in the last quarter of the nineteenth century and over the following hundred years literally reshaped the landscape of Thailand's four distinct geographical regions: the central alluvial flood plain, drained by the Chaophraya River; the highlands and valleys in the north, drained by the Chaophraya's tributaries (Ping, Wang, Yom and Nan), and in the north-west (the Tenasserim Range abutting Myanmar); the Khorat Plateau in the north-east, drained by the fluvial system formed by the Chi and Mun rivers (tributaries to the Mekong); and the southern peninsula, divided by the central range in a rocky coastline to the west and a low-lying one to the east. Geographical diversity was reflected in distinct ecosystems that supported a great

Thailand's towns, coastline and neighbours.

floral variety, considerably reduced by the advancement of the agricultural frontier. The central flood plain was covered with freshwater swamp forest, which was almost entirely cleared to make space for irrigated rice cultivation. The higher range of the northern highlands (above 1000m) is still covered by montane evergreen fores, while the lower slopes, which supported semi-evergreen and mixed deciduous forest, were mostly cleared of valuable teak trees and placed under cultivation. While much remains of the semi-evergreen forest on the higher elevations of the Tenasserim Range, the lower slopes were cleared of the deciduous forest or degraded and reforested since the 1980s with bamboo and eucalypt trees. The Khorat Plateau, now largely deforested, supported dry deciduous forest. The southern peninsula was once covered in evergreen rain forest, but its slopes were cleared on the eastern side for rubber plantation and on the western side for oil palms and rice cultivation; coastal mangroves were recently converted into aquacultures.

Agricultural colonization caused not only the disappearance of most of the forest cover but also the advancement of human settlement in the upland areas. The geographical distinction between valleys and uplands historically marked the civilizational boundary between Thai sedentary lowlanders, who practised wet-rice cultivation along with Buddhism, and non-Thai nomadic highlanders, who practised swidden agriculture along with animism. Lowlanders saw themselves as being socialized into the 'cultivated' space of valley polities and perceived hill people as living in a state of nature in the 'uncultivated' forest.[1] In fact, while dangerous because of the presence of wild animals, the forest was an alien space neither for lowland peasants, who fled to it to escape exploitation from their masters, nor wandering monks, who found in the forest the ideal environment for meditation. The forest also integrated the economy of the rice-growing valley polities as a source of game, spices, gems and, especially, wood. Logging was in the long term responsible for deforestation even more than land clearing; indeed, historical evidence indicates that lowlanders were ruthless exploiters of the environment, even though deforestation has been blamed largely on highlanders.

Right before the beginning of extensive agricultural colonization in the last quarter of the nineteenth century, most of the estimated 5–6 million *rai* of paddy land were concentrated in the Chaophraya delta.[2] When the agricultural frontier began to expand in the 1870s, it advanced initially in the delta and the river valleys in the North and the lower North-east. By 1900, paddy acreage had increased to some 7 million *rai* in the delta, by then known as 'the rice bowl of Asia', and to 2.4 million *rai* in the outer regions. By 1950 paddy land covered 17 million *rai* in the Chaophraya basin and 18 million *rai* in the other provinces, where the agricultural frontier had expanded considerably faster than in the basin since the start of the century. By 1990, paddy acreage in the Chaophraya basin had decreased to 12 million *rai* as rice was replaced by other crops, but had more than doubled to 47.5 million *rai* in the Khorat Plateau, the northern valleys and the peninsula's coastal plain.[3] These 59.5 million *rai* (96,000 sq. km) of paddy land constituted more than a third of Thailand's total 150 million *rai* (240,000 sq. km) of the land under cultivation at the close of the century.

Unlike the collective agricultural system of China and Vietnam, the clearing and cultivation of land in Thailand was undertaken on a family basis. Although the sovereign was the titular 'lord of the land' (*chao phaendin*), a land registry was in use in Ayutthaya by the late sixteenth century to record individual families' plots, which were inheritable on condition that the same family remained as occupants. From the seventeenth century to the first half of the nineteenth, rice harvests fed primarily the local population; only a modest amount of surplus was exported to South-east Asia and China's southern littoral. The impetus behind the dramatic expansion of the land frontier was the demand for rice to be exported to Britain's colonies. For a couple of decades after the signing of the economic treaty with Britain (1855), Siam's main export crop was sugarcane, which was grown in the Chaophraya delta. But after the boom of sugar production in Java under the Dutch in the 1870s, the delta's swamps were transformed in the century's last two decades into paddy-fields through projects of canalization and drainage.

The pattern of agricultural colonization in the Chaophraya delta was typified by the Rangsit scheme, which involved the canalization of a vast jungle area north-east of Bangkok in the 1890s by a company whose shareholders were members of the royalty and the

Opening the delta: works of canalization, c. 1900.

nobility; they became the absentee landowners of the large tracts of paddy land which were parcelled out and rented to tenant farmers. However, this was not the pattern of agricultural colonization in the rest of the country. The Rangsit scheme had alerted the throne to the danger of the possible formation of a landed nobility; thus, projects of canalization in the provinces were entrusted to the Irrigation Department, created in 1902 under the supervision of a Dutch engineer. Peasant smallholders settled in newly drained tracts following the customary right of operating an amount of land appropriate to family needs (*chop song*), sanctioned by the Land Act of 1901, which (on the basis of a cadastral survey) introduced property rights that were formalized by title deeds issued in 1908. In 1936 the government fixed the limit of land ownership at 50 *rai* per family.

During the first half of the twentieth century the opening of new land in the Chaophraya basin spread from the lower to the upper delta, then into the jungle on the delta's fringes and eventually advanced north into the valleys of the Chaophraya's tributaries. In the North too, the Chiang Mai nobility was involved in the opening of new land through the realization of works of canalization before Bangkok extended its administrative authority there. The integration of the northern rice industry into the national economy followed the extension of the railway line from Bangkok in 1921. Booming exports caused a second phase of colonization in the lower hillsides and the unpopulated areas abutting the Burmese border by pioneer settlers, while a rice milling industry developed in Chiang Mai. The advancement of the agricultural frontier in the Khorat Plateau also followed the construction at the turn of the 1920s and '30s of the railway line linking the North-east's provincial capital, Nakhorn Ratchasima, to the towns along the river basins. New paddy fields were opened while some tracts growing gluti-nous rice (*khao niao*), the staple of the Isan diet, were converted to white rice for export.[4]

In the post-war period the government for the first time undertook, with the support of international organizations, major infrastructural works in the Chaophraya delta (1950s) and in the Chiang Mai valley (1960s) to increase surplus extraction by intro-ducing new cash crops (cassava, maize, soybean, tobacco and commercial trees). The extension of the road network and the con-struction of highways linking Bangkok to the North-east and the eastern seaboard, built for strategic reasons by the USA, paved the way for the colonization of the highlands, where the acreage of cultivated land tripled (from 43 million *rai* to 128 million *rai*) between 1950 and 1990. Following the pattern of the agricultural colonization of the lowlands during the first half of the century, the highlands were colo-nized by pioneer farmers who settled in the wake of the construction of roads and dams; but exploitative cultivation methods coupled with the destruction of the forest cover caused quick soil erosion and declining fertility.[5] After the extension of cultivation was brought to a halt by the closure of the land frontier in the early 1980s, the inten-sity of land use increased due to the adoption of seasonal crop rotation and the diversification of agricultural activities.

As a result of long-term clearing for agriculture and commer-cial logging, deforestation emerged in the 1980s as a grave environ-mental problem. The forest became a site of conflict between the state and rural settlers. At the start of the colonization of the uplands in the 1950s the forest still covered over 60 per cent of the national territory; by 1961 it had been reduced to 53 per cent. Although the National Forest Reserves Act (1964) stipulated that the forest cover must not decrease to less than 40 per cent, the govern-ment continued over the following two decades to promote agricul-tural colonization by allowing farmers to settle into areas officially designated as forest reserve without, however, granting them occupancy titles, setting the path for subsequent disputes. By 1985 the forest cover had decreased to a third of the national territory. At that juncture, the land frontier was declared officially closed and reforestation initiated in the North-east, the region that had suffered the worst environmental degradation. However, this reforestation scheme (called 'Green Isan') led to violent opposition from villagers because it provided for the long-term lease of degraded forest areas to agribusinesses, which planted water-draining commercial tree species (such as eucalyptus) and encroached further on forest reserve. At the same time, legislative ambiguities over the definition of 'reserve' led to the planned resettlement of around a million forest dwellers under an army scheme that was eventually dropped. The king himself called attention to the illegal dealings between logging companies and local politicians by according special funerary honours to a Forestry Department official, Sob Nakhasathian, who committed suicide in 1990 in protest against logging in the Thung Yai forest sanctuary, a UNESCO World Heritage Site. From the mid-1980s the rate of deforestation slowed down dramatically but did not cease; by 2000, the forest cover had been further reduced to one quarter of the national territory.[6]

The closure of the land frontier was counterpointed by the acceleration in the industrialization of the landscape. Thailand's industrial landscape was characterized by small and medium-size enterprises (whose principal products were processed food, textiles and garments, and electrical, electronic and automobile parts), which were concentrated mostly in the Bangkok Metropolitan Region, comprising the capital and its five adjacent provinces, and in the Eastern Seaboard (along the Gulf of Thailand), which in 1983 was designated an industrial region. The Board of Investment attempted from the 1970s to orient industrialization towards peripheral regions by offering investment incentives to companies based on the division of the territory in a three-zone system (attracting low, intermediate and high incentives), but this policy had only a modest success. At the century's close, the spatial imbalance in the distribution of industries across Thailand was reflected in a marked regional sector orientation: agro-food industries dominated in the South, while the North and the North-east presented some degree of diversification (wood and agro-food industries as well as minerals and machinery). But only in the Bangkok Metropolitan Region and the Eastern Seaboard did new industries (metal, plastic and chemical industries, car manufacturing) flourish alongside traditional ones (food processing, textile manufacturing).[7]

Thailand's rapid industrialization had a serious impact on the environment. Industrial waste dumping, including both hazardous and biodegradable wastes, polluted the country's waterways, particularly the lower Chaophraya and its system of tributaries in the highly industrialized Bangkok Metropolitan Region. The massive increase in the output of solid waste was also an issue, both because of the insufficient number of waste treatment plants and because of public opposition to the construction of such plants near cities and towns, with the result that a significant amount of waste was dumped into canals, illegal landfills, at isolated sites and even on farmland. Possibly the most dramatic problem was that of air pollution due to dust and vehicle exhaust; the Thai Ministry of Public Health estimated in the mid-1990s that around 900,000 Bangkok residents were suffering from respiratory illness. Efforts to tackle the consequences of industrialization were weakened by the conflict of interest between the government agencies in charge of industrial development and of safeguarding the environment.[8]

At the close of the twentieth century, after four decades of ongoing urbanization and industrialization, 69 per cent of Thailand's 60 million inhabitants were still living in the countryside.[9] Conversely, about a third of the country's urban population of 18.5 million lived in Bangkok, whose concrete jungle of high-rises enshrouded in a permanent smog haze is the most recurrent image of the Thai urban landscape. Bangkok's transformation during the twentieth century was possibly even more dramatic than that of the countryside. From its foundation in the 1780s to the middle of the nineteenth century, Bangkok was largely a riverine settlement, where people dwelled in floating houses along the banks of the Chaophraya and its network of canals. The maze of waterways and the gilded spires of temples emerging from the thick foliage unfailingly struck Western visitors as they approached Bangkok cruising the Chaophraya upstream

View of the Chaophraya with Bangkok and Thonburi, *c.* 1900.

from the Gulf of Siam. The Western appellation of Bangkok as 'the Venice of the East' is revealing of the mentality of European travellers, who tended to read foreign landscapes through the lenses of familiar spatial images, but captured also the similarity in the role that waterways played in both Renaissance Venice and early Bangkok as a means of communication as much as channels for the importation of exotic goods and as the setting for pageants staged to enhance the ruling elite's charisma.

Up until the 1850s the main terrestrial settlements were the royal citadel on Rattanakosin Island (which was artificially created by digging a canal around the river's bend), and the Chinese settlement east of it. Rattanakosin Island's topographical configuration replicated that of Ayutthaya, which was situated on a natural isle at the confluence of two rivers, and so did its royal and religious buildings, which were built not just in the style of Ayutthaya's but by recycling bricks from its damaged edifices and transporting them downriver to Bangkok. By articulating spatially a direct continuity with Ayutthaya, the founder of the Chakri dynasty attempted to claim the role of restorer of the kingdom and put aside as a dynastic interlude the reign of King Taksin (1767–82), who had reestablished Thai control over Siam after the fall of Ayutthaya from his headquarters on the Chaophraya's left bank, Thonburi. The construction of Chakri's citadel on the opposite bank was justified on strategic and logistical grounds, but the symbolic significance of installing the new dynasty in a virgin space was obvious, especially

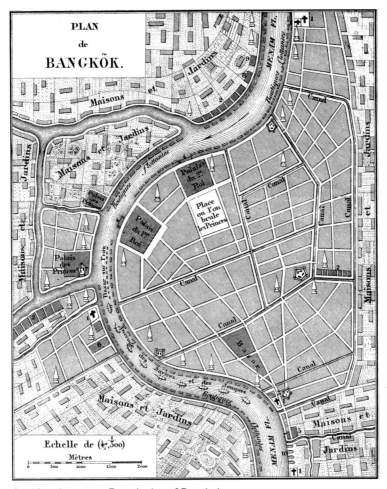

A mid-19th-century French plan of Bangkok.

since General Chakri's accession to the throne carried the stigma of usurpation and regicide (after deposing King Taksin, Chakri had him executed on charges of impiety).

The growth of Bangkok in the second half of the nineteenth century paralleled that of other colonial port cities in the region, such as Batavia (Jakarta) and Singapore, since it reflected the needs of the world economy as much as the dynasty's designs. Population density increased considerably as artisans and shopkeepers took up residence around the royal palace as well as in the Chinese district (Sampheng). A third area of terrestrial settlement, occupied by

Outside the walls: commoners along a canal in the Dusit district, c. 1900.

Western consulates and trading firms, formed between the royal citadel and Sampheng along Bangkok's first thoroughfare – aptly named Thanon charoen krung ('the Road that Extends the City'), though known most prosaically in English as New Road. The construction of roads suitable for carriages during the 1860s took up the recommendation by a well-regarded resident missionary, D. B. Bradley, for more such arteries if Bangkok was to join the club of the capitals of the 'civilized world'.[10] In the Western district, perpendicular streets flanked by blocks of multi-storey buildings in neoclassical styles created a novel urban landscape that was represented in the temple murals of the period's leading artist, Khrua In Khong.

At the turn of the century Bangkok acquired the appearance of, if not a metropolis, a colonial capital like Rangoon or Hanoi. The court moved out of the overcrowded Grand Palace to a new suburban palace, Dusit Park, built to the north of Rattanakosin Island on an area of paddy-fields and linked to it by a European-style boulevard, Ratchadamnoen ('Royal Progress'). King Chulalongkorn's stay in the country residences of the European royalty in 1897 is often regarded as the inspiration behind the construction of Dusit Park, which was designed by Italian and German architects employed by the Public Works Department. If the architecture of the Grand Palace and the layout of Rattanakosin Island had restated the Thai royalty's place in the Indic œcumene at the moment of foundation of the Bangkok kingdom, Dusit Park and the other princely palaces

33

built in the eponymous district (many of which were transformed into government offices after the change of government in 1932), proclaimed the court's new location in the Victorian œcumene by appropriating some of the prominent features of *fin-de-siècle* urbanism: tree-lined rectilinear avenues, monumental bridges and a wide open space centred on the king's equestrian statue. At the same time, Dusit's walled compounds bespoke an idea of civilization as the preserve of an elite and offered no public spaces or amenities to the ordinary population.

In the 1930s and '40s Bangkok expanded along a grid of thoroughfares (Silom, Ploenchit and Witthayu) that intersected in the downtown area and linked it to three outbound arteries (the eastbound Sukhumwit, the northbound Phahonyothin and the westbound Phetkasem). New roads were built by filling the canals and the cityscape was dotted with modernist monumental landmarks. In the 1950s a shopping and entertainment district was built in the downtown area along Silom and Ploenchit Roads; and in the next decade suburban housing sprawled along Sukhumwit Road and its maze of side lanes (*soi*). Between 1850 and 1950 Bangkok's population had doubled from around half to one million; from the 1960s it grew exponentially as a result of internal migration, especially from the impoverished North-east.

By 1982, when Bangkok celebrated its bicentenary, the consequences of two decades of unplanned urban growth were becoming apparent. The limited surface area of the road network in the inner city, due to its former aquatic topography, coupled with the increase in the number of privately owned motor vehicles (from around 5,000 in the late 1940s to two million half a century later) resulted in chronic traffic congestion. To escape increasing population density in the inner city districts the middle class moved to new residential suburbs. Many also continued to reside in slums that, unlike in Jakarta and Manila, were small and scattered throughout the city, except for the large Khlong Toey slum located near the port. By the 1990s, the capital and the five adjacent provinces forming the Bangkok Metropolitan Region accounted for just over half of the country's entire urbanized population; Bangkok's population alone was twenty times as large as that of Thailand's next most populous city, Nakhorn Ratchasima.

Bangkok's demographic, administrative and economic primacy over the rest of the country rested on the system of rail, road and air transportation radiating from the capital. Railway construction began at the end of the nineteenth century to link Bangkok to the North-east (the first railway track, Bangkok–Ayutthaya, was opened in 1897); the train was intended to transport neither passengers nor goods but troops, as Isan resisted integration under the kingdom's central administration. The southern line was developed in the 1930s in conjunction with the British Malayan railway to provide a connection between Bangkok and Singapore via Butterworth (on Malaysia's west coast), while the northern line never extended beyond Chiang Mai. During the Pacific War the Japanese notoriously tried to link western Thailand to Burma by cutting a railway line into the malaria-infested jungle (the so-called 'Death Railway') using Thai peasants and Allied prisoners of war as workforce. After the war, further development of the railway network was neglected in favour of the construction of the road network with the support of American and international aid.

Thailand's first highway, the Friendship Highway, was built in the mid-1950s to link Bangkok to the North-east following US strategic interests; but with the extension of the road network to the provinces north and south, new bus services, whose stations became the landmark of every provincial town, afforded the cheapest means of transport for both goods and passengers. After facilitating seasonal migration to the capital in the 1960s and '70s, roads provided in the 1990s the means for the expansion of Bangkok business interests into Myanmar, Cambodia and Laos (linked to Thailand in 1994 by the Friendship Bridge, spanning the lower Mekong). Since 1960, when the national air carrier, Thai Airways International, started operations, Bangkok has also developed into an international air transportation hub second in South-east Asia only to Singapore. By the 1990s Bangkok's airport received almost all of the seven million annual tourist arrivals – holiday-goers who, arriving in search of pristine beaches and forests, stepped instead into 'non-places' such as airports, hotels and shopping malls, which had turned the 'Venice of the east' into yet another globalized cityscape.[11]

The Ethnic Landscape

The change in the country's name from Siam to Thailand decreed in June 1939 has been generally regarded as an assertion of Thai chauvinism over the other ethnic groups in the kingdom, particularly the immigrant Chinese. This reading overshadows the continuities with the policy of the absolutist era on ethnic minorities, which was developed in response to the racial policy of colonial states. The Ministry of Interior recommended as early as 1899 the replacement of regional ethnonyms with the uniform *thai*. Not only did this nominalistic policy reflect the imposition of Bangkok's political authority over outlying provinces; it also reacted against colonial ethnographic classifications of Central Thais ('Siamese') as descending from the Tai/Thai race,[12] along with the Shan and Lao people, but distinguished by intermixing with the Chinese. Continuing opposition by some to the name 'Thailand' for conflating nationality with ethnicity highlights the lasting import of Western ethnic categories in the construction of the Thai identity.

The history of Thailand before the settlement of speakers of Tai languages in the twelfth and thirteenth centuries has only recently begun to be unravelled. Systematic investigation into Thailand's prehistory started only in the 1960s; and while a considerable amount of data has been gathered since then, reconstruction of the history of human settlement in the region before the Christian era is often speculative and consensus is yet to be achieved among scholars on several key issues. The presence of sedentary communities of tool-making hunter-gatherers in the upland regions of mainland South-east Asia is presently dated from *c.* 15,000 to 5000 BC. Traces of hunter-gatherer settlers, named by archaeologists Hoabinhians (after the Vietnamese province where evidence of their presence was first discovered), were found in a number of rock shelters in the area of present-day Thailand – notably, Spirit Cave in Mae Hong Son, a province bordering with Myanmar's Shan State. These communities were characterized by widespread adaptation to the ecology of the region. They survived thanks to fishing, hunting, trees, plants and possibly domesticated root crops, although no evidence of a transition to agriculture has been found in Hoabinhian settlements.

The first farmers in the region were most likely migrants from the Yangtze valley, where the oldest evidence for rice cultivation (dating to *c.* 5000 BC) has thus far been discovered. The linguistic affinities noted across the area from Vietnam to north-eastern India has been explained as the result of the gradual expansion of early Austroasiatic speakers of southern Mongoloid stock into upper mainland South-east Asia from the fifth millennium BC – a theory that finds support in the roughly contemporary colonization of the Pacific Islands by Austronesian speakers, possibly the descendants of the Hoabinhians pushed east by the southern advance of Mongoloid peoples. Some linguists think, however, that both Austronesian and Austroasiatic languages shared a common origin in an ancestral super linguistic family (called Austric). What does seem certain is that by the third millennium BC rice was grown in the seasonally flooded valleys of mainland South-east Asia by sedentary agriculturalists who also raised domestic stock. The best known of these settlements is the village of Ban Chiang, in the Khorat Plateau (a region rich in copper and tin), where a large amount of locally manufactured ceramic, bronze and iron artefacts were excavated, including adze blades, spearheads, vessels, burial jars and figurines, bangles and bracelets.

The discovery in the late 1960s of the prehistoric culture at Ban Chiang caused considerable controversy among archaeologists. The initial dating of bronze findings to the fourth millennium BC (roughly contemporary to Mesopotamia's Bronze Age and much older than China's) suggested that the Khorat Plateau had been among the earliest metallurgical centres in world civilization. However, the subsequent later dating to 1500–500 BC reopened the question of whether metallurgy was a local innovation or the result of technological transfers along river routes from the Yangtze Valley to the Huanghe Valley, now in northern Vietnam (where the highly accomplished Dongson culture flourished in the Bronze Age), and the Khorat Plateau. The variety in the design and decorative patterns of the artefacts excavated and, conversely, the absence of monumental sites suggest a sparse pattern of settlement during the Bronze Age, when villages housed two to three hundred people and the excess population lived in satellite villages (such as Ban Nadi, a village some twenty kilometres from the older and larger site of Ban Chiang). The technical advances of the

Iron Age, whose advent in Ban Chiang culture is dated to the middle of the first millennium BC, supported a crucial development in the social and political organization of sedentary communities: the formation of chiefdoms ruled by hereditary elites that competed with each other for power and status.

Culturally Indianized polities emerged in mainland South-east Asia around the beginning of the Christian era. The earliest one, Funan, was centred in the area of the Mekong River's delta, in southern Vietnam, but its authority extended as far as the territory of present-day Cambodia, Laos, Thailand and the Malay Peninsula. At the beginning of the seventh century AD, Chenla, a vassal of Funan, over took its master and drew the centre of power westward towards the plain of the Tonle Sap (Great Lake). The Mons, an Austroasiatic speaking group of Central Asian origins that had adopted Buddhism, took advantage of the power vacuum determined by Chenla's overthrow of Funan to expand their settlements from the lower basin of the Salween River (in present-day lower Myanmar) into the river valleys of the Chaophraya and the Mun (in the Khorat Plateau). Epigraphist George Cœdès derived from numismatic evidence the Sanskrit name Dvaravati (Krishna's capital in the Indian epic *Mahabharata*) as that of the Mon settlement of the Chaophraya valley centred in the modern province of Nakhorn Pathom. Dvaravati interacted with other regional centres through the network of overland and maritime trade routes that linked the eastern coast of India to the Indochinese peninsula and south-western China.

Around the turn of the first millennium, the Mons were pushed westward and southward from the Central Plain by the expansion of another Austroasiatic group: the Khmers. After conquering Chenla, the Khmers had formed early in the ninth century a territorial empire with Angkor as its capital. From the plain of the Tonle Sap and the Khorat Plateau, the Khmers extended their dominion further west during the twelfth century and the first half of the thirteenth by conquering the Mon cities and holding under their sway the upper valley of the Chaophraya. In the same period the peninsula, which during the first millennium had been drawn into the trading routes spanning the Indian Ocean and the South China Sea, was incorporated in the insular empire of Srivijaya, with its centre in Sumatra (or, according to some historians, in the peninsula itself). The first coastal settlers were overtaken by Austronesian people coming from the Indonesian archipelago, who later inter-mixed with the Austroasiatic (Mon) populations from the north as well as Indian colonists.[13]

The origins of Thailand's majority ethnic group are still a matter of debate. The diffusion of Tai languages across southern China, northern Vietnam and north-eastern India, first noticed by ethno-graphers in the 1920s, is the main evidence behind the theory of the southward migration of Tai populations and their settlement in the upper valleys of the Salween, Mekong and Chaophraya rivers (an area in between the Burmese kingdom of Pagan and the Khmer empire of Angkor), possibly as a result of the massive population movements caused by the Mongol invasion of southern China. Tai groups in the Khorat Plateau and the Chaophraya valley were ini-tially subjected by the Khmers – a situation depicted in a bas-relief in Angkor Wat, in which mercenary troops of *sayam kuk*, recogniz-able by their distinctive outfit and slack regimentation, are repre-sented marching ahead of the Khmer troops. The Tai chiefs of Sukhothai proclaimed their autonomy around the middle of the thirteenth century; a century later, the lower valley kingdom of Ayutthaya imposed its authority over Sukhothai and expanded its dominion over the Central Plain by launching a series of attacks on the Khmer empire and eventually forcing the court to flee Angkor in 1432. In the late thirteenth century Tai chiefs overtook also the northern Mon centre of Haripunchai, which became (as Lamphun) the capital of the kingdom of Lanna until the foundation in 1296 of Chiang Mai ('New City'), as well as the peninsular Mon settlement of Ligor, which was renamed Nakhorn Sithammarat.

The newcomers' political assertion set in motion a process of assimilation of earlier settlers that French ethnologist Georges Condominas has termed 'irreversible Thai-ization'.[14] Numerically inferior when they burst onto the scene, the Thais reversed the unfavourable demographic balance over the course of the follow-ing centuries by intermixing with other ethnic groups and appro-priating their social and cultural practices. An important tool for the assimilation of Mon and Khmer elites was the creation in the thirteenth century of the Thai alphabet, based on the Khmer cur-sive script but modified to suit the tonal and monosyllabic nature of the Thai language; through the Mon and Khmer languages, Thai also assimilated a large number of Pali and Sanskrit words. At the end of the 1980s, Tai speakers accounted for 83 per cent of Thailand's population. The great majority of these (around 80 per cent) spoke one of the four Thai regional idioms: the northern idiom (*kham muang*), that of the north-east (*isan*), Central Thai (*phasa klang*) and the 'southern tongue' (*pak tai*); a further 3 per cent included Tai and Tai-Lao speaking groups (such as the Phu Tai and Lao Phuan). The remaining 17 per cent of the population included speakers of languages other than Tai: tribal languages (less than 1 per cent), residual Mon and Khmer (2.3 per cent), Malay (3 per cent) and immigrant speakers of southern Chinese languages (about 11 per cent).[15]

The ethnic minorities in the north and the south that account for some 4 per cent of Thailand's total population of 63 millions are geographically, as well as culturally and economically, at the margins of the modern nation-state. Their marginality is rooted not only in demographics but also in government policies that made them second-class citizens at best, when not denying them citizenship outright. Karen-speaking populations constitute slightly more than half of the kingdom's 550,000 or so 'peoples of the mountains' (*chao khao*). The Karens, who live today in the highlands along the northern and the western borders, were possibly among the earliest migrants to reach the Irrawaddy and Salween valleys from south-western China; pushed uphill by the later migrations of Mons and Burmans, the Karens continued however to identify themselves as lowlanders rather than highlanders. In the nineteenth century the majority of the Karens were converted to Christianity by American Baptist missionaries. The remainder of Thailand's tribal population is constituted in almost equal shares by Tibeto-Burman groups (Akha, Lahu and Lisu) and the two related ethnic minorities of Mien (or Yao) and Hmong (called derogatively Meo by the Thais), who migrated from southern China and Laos as recently as the latter half of the nineteenth century.

The Hmongs in particular had a difficult relationship with the central government as cultivators of opium and destroyers of the forest due to slash-and-burn agriculture. The boom in opium production in the 1970s, which was fuelled by increasing international demand for heroin, brought prosperity to the Hmongs but also made

Staging ethnicity: studio portrait of Karen women, 1923.

them into the *bêtes noires* of drug enforcement agencies. And while the common interests linking drug dealers, sectors of the Thai army and police and the CIA hampered efforts to eradicate opium production (see Chapter 2), the Hmongs bore the brunt of the failure and were denied land entitlement deeds and nationality. Agricultural colonization of the highlands and the consequent privatization of land since the 1950s considerably reduced the space for swidden cultivation by ethnic minorities and brought them increasingly into the orbit of the market economy. Their recycling as living attractions in the circus of ethnic tourism gave them international visibility but,

41

Facing the camera: studio portrait of Akkha woman, 1923.

Documenting ethnicity: Lao women in northern Thailand, mid-1920s.

as with the opium trade, the profits generated by the Thai-operated tourism industry largely escaped them.

Central Thai perceptions of minority ethnic groups are exemplified by the designation of the Malays as 'guests' (*khaek*) by reference to the Indian and Arab traders that spread Islam in the peninsula, in spite of the fact that the Malays are indigenous to the southern region. Some two million Malay citizens of Thailand, almost all of them Sunni Muslims, are concentrated in the three provinces bordering Malaysia (Satun, Yala and Narathiwat) and that of Pattani. These provinces were created in 1933 by the administrative regrouping of sultanates that, though nominal vassals to central Thai kingdoms since the sixteenth century, enjoyed semi-autonomous status until the end of the nineteenth century, when Bangkok and the British negotiated the border between Siam and the Straits Settlements (see Chapter 2). Their integration within the Thai nation-state has never been easy, however; Pattani in particular was ruled for centuries by a lineage of Muslim queens whose recorded history continues to be the source of great local pride. After the transitional decade that followed the administrative centralization of 1892, local rajas were replaced by Bangkok-appointed governors and Islamic law (Sharia) by state legislation even though Malay customary right (*adat melayu*) that adjudicated family matters was retained (temporarily abolished in 1944, the *adat* was reinstated at the end of the war). Buddhist missionary undertakings and the settlement of Thais caused frictions between the central government and the ethnic Malays. Education was another major source of tension; the implementation of the Compulsory Education Act (1921), which made proficiency in Central Thai mandatory, resulted in local uprisings in 1922–3.

Malay separatism emerged during the Second World War, when a local leader, Tengku Mahmud Mahyuddin (the son of the last raja of Pattani), struck an alliance with the British hoping that, in the case of an Allied victory, Pattani would become independent. After the comeback of Marshal Phibun Songkhram in 1948, the government responded to the local Malays' demands for cultural autonomy within the Thai nation-state (notably the permission to teach in schools Yawi, the vernacular script) by forcing assimilation; and in 1961 Koranic schools (*pondok*) were subjected to the legislation on private education. The launch of the Pattani United Liberation Organization in the late 1960s heightened Thai perceptions of the Malay minority as a threat to national security and strained diplomatic relations with Malaysia, which was seen to back Malay separatism. After the suppression of the insurgency along the border, the central government took steps to appease the Malay minority by creating the Office of Islamic Affairs and increasing the number of ethnic Malays in the ranks of the provincial administration. Despite the expansion of the regional economy since the late 1980s and the enshrinement of religious liberty in Section 38 of the constitution of 1997, the early 2000s saw a recrudescence of separatist violence that has caused close to two thousand deaths in the context of the international rise of Islamism and Thailand's support of the us-led 'War on Terrorism'. Government buildings, military installations and schools as well as soldiers and even teachers and monks were targeted by the separatists; the government's heavy-handed response (in particular the allegedly accidental death by suffocation in October 2004 of 78 arrested rioters who were being transferred in police trucks from Narathiwat to Pattani) attracted a royal admonition and led to further clashes. Thus, in 2005, prime minister Thaksin advocated emergency laws to deal with the insurgency despite the earlier appointment of the National Reconciliation Commission tasked with finding a political solution to the Malay unrest.

One critical factor in shaping Thailand's ethnic landscape was the immigration of people from southern China (*chin*, derogatory *chek*). Most arrivals were recorded between the 1880s and the 1940s, but the Chinese presence in Thailand dated as far back as the fifteenth century, when Chinese merchants settled in Ayutthaya and Chinese admirals commanded the Thai royal fleet. The defeat in 1661 of the Ming loyalist armies that had waged a war of resistance against the Manchurian Qing dynasty caused a flow of refugees from the empire's southern provinces to the countries of the 'southern ocean'. In Siam they settled mostly in the south – Pattani, Songkhla, Nakhorn Sithammarat and the island of Phuket, where the Chinese developed tin mining. Some settlers and their progeny were even appointed provincial governors with semi-autonomous status up until the administrative reform of the 1890s. Important

Chinese merchants (*chaosua*) prospered through intermarriage, court connections and reliance on the trading network of the South China Sea, and were able to obtain titles of nobility through the patronage of senior officials and members of the court, whom they propitiated with gifts and daughters given as brides (a custom that persisted throughout the nineteenth century). Both in Ayutthaya and early Bangkok the Chinese community enjoyed an uncommon degree of autonomy; internal policing was entrusted to a *chaosua*, who settled disputes and administered fines and punishment.

Estimates of the number of Chinese in Siam in the first half of the nineteenth century vary between 200,000 and 300,000 from a total population of four to five million. The deterioration of living conditions in the southern provinces of China as a consequence of protracted political unrest and famines determined the start in the latter half of the century of mass immigration, made easier by the repeal of the imperial ban in 1893. Between 1882 and 1950, almost 3.5 million people arrived in Bangkok from China by steamship while others headed directly to the southern provinces; close to 2.3 million returned home after working for a few years, mostly as coolies, while the rest settled in Thailand. Even after the imposition of the annual capitation tax on the Chinese (who had previously paid a negligible triennial tax) and the promulgation of the Nationality Act (1913), whereby those born in the kingdom were registered as Thai subjects regardless of their father's nationality, Chinese arrivals continued to grow. The collapse of the Qing dynasty in 1911 opened the door to female emigration, which accounted for about one-fifth of the more than one million arrivals of the 1920s. The principal immigrant groups were Teochiu speakers from eastern Guangdong, followed by Hakka speakers from north-eastern Guangdong and north-western Fujian, Hokkien from Fujian, Hainanese from Hainan Island and a small number of Cantonese from western Guangdong. Between 1877 and 1919, all five ethno-linguistic groups established self-support societies.[16]

Due to the imperial ban on female emigration in force until 1911, Chinese settlers intermarried widely with Thai women. Intermarriage did not result in a hybrid Sino-Thai identity, such as that of the Peranakans (locally born Chinese of mixed parentage) in Malaya and Singapore. Instead, the adoption of Thai names, the observance of local customs (e.g., funeral cremation rather than burial as practised in China) as well as of Buddhism (with the devotional forms of the Mahayana accommodative of ancestor worship) determined the remarkable degree of assimilation of the Chinese in contrast to neighbouring countries, also due to the absence of colonial racial policies. The beginning of female immigration modified the established pattern of assimilation, but the determinant factor in modifying the relationship between immigrant community and the Thai authorities was the emergence of Chinese nationalism. The spread of Chinese education as well as the support to the nationalist and communist factions worried the government, which in the 1930s adopted economic nationalism followed by more openly discriminatory measures at the end of the decade. However, the Chinese in Thailand were neither the object of wartime racial persecution, as in Malaya and Singapore during the Japanese occupation, nor of pogroms initiated by the local population, as in Indonesia. In the immediate post-war period there was a reprise of Chinese emigration that came to a halt in 1950, when the newly installed communist government imposed its control onto China's southern provinces.

At the close of the century the number of ethnic Chinese in Thailand was estimated at 6.5 to 7.5 million, but this figure varies considerably according to whether children of mixed marriages (*luk chin*) are counted as Thai or, rather, Chinese. If one assumes half or even a third of Bangkok's population to be Sino-Thai, then the figure above is obviously an underestimate. In fact, besides the ability to speak to some degree a southern Chinese language, for many a second- and third-generation Sino-Thai to identify oneself as Thai or Chinese is very much a personal choice. Throughout the 1970s flaunting one's Chinese lineage was not expedient socially, despite (or, more precisely, because of) the preponderance of *luk chin* in industry, finance and commerce. Rather, economic capital was converted into symbolic capital through the patronage of Buddhist monasteries and religious ceremonies (most typically funerary rituals for the victims of violent death, discarded in the Thai worldview as evil spirits possessed of negative karma) as well as charitable works, such as the construction of hospitals and schools. The economic boom of the late 1980s prompted a re-evaluation of the Chinese contribution to nation building. This shift in social perception (discussed in Chapter 7) pointed to the continuing redefinition of ethnic identities alongside the ongoing transformation of Thailand's cultural landscape.

The Cultural Landscape

A fundamental aspect of nation building was the standardization of a cultural landscape characterized until the early twentieth century by great regional variations. Practically since coming into being the modern Thai state has endeavoured, through government agencies and the institutionalized monkhood, to efface distinctive regional traditions with a 'national' culture befitting universal standards of civilization. The state was not, however, the only agent of cultural transformation; the capitalist market too affected definitions of culture, especially in the last quarter of the century by spawning a Bangkok-centred media culture and, conversely, reviving obsolete cultural practices (and occasionally inventing them anew) for tourist consumption. Because the process of state formation and nation building was initiated by the Bangkok monarchy, what became the hegemonic 'national' culture was patterned largely after the culture of the Central Thais. The Thai cultural landscape was originally composed of three distinct zones, each centred on a distinct social space: aristocratic culture, centred on the court; monastic culture, centred on the monastery; and peasant culture, centred on the village.

Courtly culture in the Ayutthaya and early Bangkok period was moulded in the Indic stamp derived from the empire of Angkor. Its main features were a Brahmanical liturgy, which asserted the divine nature of the sovereign and connected his worldly realm to the cosmic order; a royal idiom (*ratchasap*), whose vocabulary was rooted in the scriptural and liturgical languages of Pali and Sanskrit rather than the vernacular Thai; a Hindu mythology, versified in the court epic *Ramakian* and performed in court spectacles such as the *khorn* (a masked performance) and the *lakhorn* (a danced drama); an architecture redolent of Indian styles assimilated via the Khmer; and regalia and status symbols (such as crowns, jewels, ritual vessels and fabrics). This Indic legacy was periodically revived during the Bangkok dynastic era: at the start, by the naming of Krungthep in honour of Indra, the purification of Brahmanic rituals and the composition of a new version of the *Ramakian* by the king's order; in the middle of the nineteenth century, when King Mongkut, a Buddhist reformer, had the court Brahmans reformulate the capital's horoscope and re-found the shrine that housed its guardian spirit; at the turn of the century, when King Chulalongkorn, an avid Europhile, recorded in a treatise the liturgy of rites in the Brahmanic calendar; and again, in the late 1950s, when the court rituals scrapped after the change of government in 1932 were reintroduced in connection with the resuscitation of the monarchy.[17] These periodic revivals of the court's Indic heritage can be seen as an indication of its loss of relevance in the dynastic transition from Ayutthaya to Bangkok, whose upper classes possessed, according to historian Nithi Iaosiwong, a 'bourgeois' taste characterized by the realistic representation of urban life in literature and painting, and the 'readiness to accept strange, new and exotic cultures'.[18]

The boom in tributary missions and junk trade with China during the third Bangkok reign (1824–51) was reflected in the court fad for Chinese novels, architecture and decorative arts. In this context the Indic heritage survived but in museified form, as demonstrated by the early touristification of *lakhorn* in the reign of Mongkut, who abolished the royal prerogative on the court's female dancers so they could perform for Western envoys.[19] During the last quarter of the century the court absorbed a great deal of Western influences in clothing, architecture, entertainment and pageantry. New royal palaces in Bangkok and the countryside, built and furnished in a variety of European styles, served literally as sites for the domestication of Western culture and stages for the enactment of civilizing rituals. In 1880, Norwegian naturalist Carl Block noticed in the palace's library 'all the leading European and American periodicals and newspapers'; and Florence Caddy, an English socialite who attended a court reception in 1889, recounted: 'Dinner was served in European style, the glass and porcelain [were] all from Europe ...'. Rama v even reconciled the monarch's traditional role as patron of Buddhism with the dominant Empiricism by providing financial

Female court dancers.

support for the translation of the Pali Buddhist canon under the editorship of Oxford University's renowned Indologist, Fredrick Max Müller. Still, the Thai court did not engage in a wholesome purchase of colonial modernity; rather, not unlike the primitive *bricoleur* of Lévi-Strauss, they fashioned their modern selves by negotiating personal inclinations and external expectations about civilized behaviour.[20]

Central Thai Buddhist monasticism was grounded in the doctrine of Theravada, or Way of the Elders, which is espoused in the 'three baskets' of the Pali canon (*Tipitaka*). From about the middle of the thirteenth century, ascetics roaming the forest areas that were being progressively incorporated into Thai chiefdoms embraced Theravada Buddhism, whose diffusion also contributed to the cultural assimilation of the Mon and Khmer population to the Thais. Thanks to the support of local rulers as well as the ordinary population, itinerant monks were able to form permanent chapters and live in monasteries where they devoted their time to meditation and the study of the scriptures. While the strict moral code and asceticism of the monastic community was reserved for the disciples, the laity (who must observe five basic precepts against the 227 of monastic rule)[21] took advantage of the Sangha as a 'field to accumulate merit' by offering monks food, clothing and shelter, and supporting the faith by building and repairing monasteries. The ritual offering of robes to the monks (*thot kathin*) at the end of the

49

rainy-season retreat assumed a central function in the Thai social experience; but it was above all the period that young males spent in the monkhood as novices, marking their maturation from the state of 'raw person' (*khon dip*) to that of 'ripe person' (*khon suk*), that made the Sangha an active shaper of society.

As a social space, the monastery (*wat*) constituted a *trait d'union* between the court and the village by providing a common cultural ground made of religious objects (texts, relics and icons) and practices (worship, pilgrimage and patronage). Indeed, monasteries until recently served as places of education – the only one in most provinces until the 1930s – and entertainment – temple fairs being a typical aspect of Thai social life in both urban and rural areas – as much as of worship and meditation. At the end of the 1990s there were 30,678 registered *wat* in the kingdom (an average of one for every 2,000 inhabitants).[22] The compound of Thai monasteries typically includes an ordination hall (*ubosot*), a meditation hall (*wihan*), a reliquary (*chedi*) enshrining relics and a repository of sacred texts and objects of worship (*mondop*); larger compounds may also house an open-air assembly hall (*sala*) and a library (*hotrai*). A notable feature of many *wat* were mural paintings that, similar to frescoes in medieval and Renaissance churches, illustrated the tenets of Buddhist cosmology and episodes from the Buddha's past lives (*jataka*) in settings reflective of contemporary customs and material culture and that, given the lack of written documentation about the commoner class, constitute a major source for social historians quite apart from their artistic value.[23]

The life of rural communities converged on the social space of the village (*ban*, meaning also 'house'), at the spiritual centre of which stood the *wat* and the guardian spirit's shrine (*ban phi*). Buddhist religious practice syncretized with animism, kinship ties (which were patrilineal in the Central Plain and matrilineal in the North and the North-east) and basic literacy skills imparted by the monks to male villagers bounded rural communities socially as well as culturally in a context in which hierarchical and normative rules had little space. The material culture of rural communities was mostly limited to domestic architecture and utilitarian objects, among which textiles had a special value both as exchange goods and products of a technology that was in the hands of women.

After the start of agricultural expansion in the 1870s, the village was brought into the orbit of the world market even though some historians argue that the economy – and the underlying cultural values – of rural communities remained self-sufficient well into the early twentieth century. Even so, the administrative and educational reforms of the turn of the century reshaped village culture to a significant degree, particularly through the establishment of government schools distinct from temple schools (though often located until the 1950s within monastery compounds).

Significant regional variations characterized literary traditions, domestic and religious architecture, and folk performances. To the four regional dialects corresponded as many writing systems: interactions between the northern Thai kingdom of Lanna and the Lao kingdom of Lanchang (which included Isan) resulted in the transmission from the former to the latter of the two orthographic systems employed, respectively, to transcribe Buddhist texts from Pali and compose poetry. In the southern peninsula, which prior to the Thai expansion had assimilated Hinduism and Mahayana Buddhism along with their artistic and literary forms, a distinct alphabet based on Khmer was devised to transcribe Pali while the Central Thai script was used for the composition of non-religious texts, such as poems and medical treatises. Distinct geographical and climatic conditions accounted for regional variations in domestic architecture. Houses in the Central Plain sat on stilts to avoid seasonal flooding and included one or two steep-roofed structures surrounded by a central veranda; in the cooler northern regions, houses had small windows and slanted side walls to better support a high roof. Religious architecture too presented significant regional variations. *Wat* in the Central Plain were stylistically derived from Khmer architecture, built with bricks and characterized by multi-layered roofs, colonnade porticos and richly ornamented doors and window frames; *wat* in the North were built in the architectural tradition of the Tai people of Yunnan and Laos and used wood for both structure and ornamentation. Other regional cultural forms were the folk dances in the North (*sap*) and the North-East (*ramnon*), the folk music of Isan (*molam*) and Malay shadow puppetry (*nang thalung*) in the South.

A national culture based on a common language, uniform religious practice and shared historical memory began to be promoted at the start of the twentieth century with a number of initiatives taken during the last decade of King Chulalongkorn's reign, including the creation of the precursor of the National Library in 1905. Culture, rather than politics, was the cornerstone of King Wachirawuth's solipsistic nationalism, which rested on the four pillars of Buddhism, history, literature and the arts. Fearing the erosion of Thai culture as a result of the imitation of the West, he established in 1912 the Fine Arts Department (*krom sinlapakorn*) to promote the revival of court craftsmanship on the model of the art schools in British India. The court's pre-eminence as a centre of cultural production was challenged during the 1920s by the emergence in Bangkok of a public sphere animated by writers and journalists who addressed a new middle-class public, also targeted by the nascent film industry. The first feature film produced in Thailand (in 1922) was a Hollywood co-production with the Royal Railway State Department, which in the same year, also produced a documentary on traditional Northern festivities to promote train transportation. The first film entirely produced in Thailand, *Chok song chan* ('Double Luck') hit the screens in 1927. From then until 1932 sixteen more films were produced, including the first Thai sound film, *Long thang* ('Gone Astray'), which premiered on the occasion of the dynasty's one hundred and fiftieth anniversary in April 1932.[24]

The constitutional government inherited the absolutist regime's penchant for monopolizing culture and assigned to it a prominent role in the nation-building project. This was particularly true in the period of heightened nationalism at the turn of the 1930s, when the Thai neologism for 'culture' (*watthanatham*) was coined. The chief state ideologue, *Luang* Wichit Watthakan (a figure discussed later in the book), explained that the term 'culture' carried two meanings: a tangible one, meaning artefacts that 'demonstrated the national achievements or progress . . . to other countries'; and an intangible one, referring to the moral and behavioural bases for 'national progress and stability'. Between 1939 and 1942 the government issued twelve state edicts (*ratthaniyom*, sometimes translated as 'cultural mandates'), which prescribed, as Marshal Phibun Songkhram himself explained, 'the proper type of etiquette to be observed by all civilized people'.[25]

The first edict changed the country's international name from Siam to Thailand. Those that followed prescribed a public conduct protective of national security; the designation of individuals as Thais regardless of ethnic origins; obeisance to the national flag and anthem; the purchase of local produce and goods; knowledge of the correct tune and lyrics of the national and royal anthems; the holding of a regular employment; the proper use of the Thai language and the observance of civic duties; neat or Western-style dress; the division of the day into working, personal and leisure activities; and the proper treatment of children, elderly and handi-capped people. The texts of the twelve edicts were distributed to schoolchildren while the National Cultural Maintenance Act (1940) and the Royal Decree Prescribing Customs for the Thai People (1941) enforced legally the prescriptions on dress and public conduct.[26] Along with behavioural norms, linguistic usage was given special emphasis as an index of the nation's civilizational attainment. Reforms drawn up in 1942 stressed Central Thai as the medium of instruction; individuals were required to adopt gender-specific names; a Western-style pronominal structure with three singular and three plural pronouns was adopted in lieu of the Thai system, which denoted the status of the speaker and addressee vis-à-vis each other; the expressions *sawaddi* and *khopkhun* were introduced for greeting and thanking (traditionally Thais expressed them through body language); and orthography was simplified by reduc-ing the number of letters in the alphabet.[27]

The National Institute of Culture (comprising the five bureaus of Spiritual, Customary, Artistic, Literary and Women's Culture), established in 1942, bureaucratized cultural management through decrees and initiatives such as the dispatch of mobile units to the provinces in order to make the rural population conform to rules of orderly and civilized behaviour.[28] During his post-war term as prime minister, Phibun revived the bureaucratic management of culture by creating a ministry in charge of it. Marshal Sarit Thanarat abolished it upon seizing power in 1958 and created in its place the Ministry of Development. Even though state rhetoric during the 1960s emphasized modernization over culture, the bureaucracy continued to police it through the publication of the 'Thai Cultural Magazine' (*Warasan watthanatham thai*) and especially the further expansion of national education, which took on a distinctive spatial dimension in the provinces with the construction outside *wat* compounds of school buildings whose architectural uniformity – in addition to the pupils' uniforms – bespoke the cultural uniformity pursued by the central government. Phibun's state management of culture was revived in the late 1970s by the National Culture Commission (under the Ministry of Education) in the wake of the deep political divisions, military repression and communist insurgency that had characterized the decade. 'Thai culture' and its virtual synonym, 'Thai identity' (*ekkalak thai*), were itemized, iconized and brandished as ideological weapons in the fight against radicalism and the quest for a renewed political consensus.[29]

The impact of the market on the cultural landscape, especially in the last quarter of the century, produced a schizophrenic situation: on the one hand, the transformation of crafts and performances into commodities having profit as their only *raison d'être*; on the other hand, a Bangkok-centred metropolitan culture characterized both by cosmopolitan tastes and the manipulation of the icons of Thainess in film, music and advertising.[30] The Tourism Authority of Thailand (TAT, founded in 1959 as Tourism Organization of Thailand) affected considerably the external perception of Thai culture through its promotional campaigns and the organization of festive events. National celebrations became occasions to promote tourism, as in the case of King Phumiphon's sixtieth birthday and the Visit Thailand Year (1987), the Year of the Longest Reign (1988) and the Thailand Arts and Crafts Year (1989). Using the cliché of 'the Land of Smiles', the TAT launched a series of unabashedly Orientalistic campaigns that depicted the country as the meeting place of opposites – at once exotic and cosmopolitan, ancient and developed. With tourism as the prime foreign exchange earner since the mid-1980s, commercialization involved not only 'traditional' craftsmanship and the very people – the ethnic minorities along the Northern border – who practised it, but even embodied expressions of Thainess, such as the greeting gesture with conjoined hands (*wai*). Thailand's international popularity as a tourist destination increased, however, the visibility of its culture abroad; this was especially true of cuisine, which in the 1990s became the latest fad in the international food industry from London to Sydney and Los Angeles.

The rural migration to the city that had accompanied the economic development of the 1960s had spawned a country music genre called *luk thung* ('children of the fields'), which expressed the peasant experience of displacement in the urban context. The popularity of *luk thung*, broadcast on AM radio, grew steadily in the following decades by grafting onto its harmonics the instrumentation and theatrics of Western folk-rock and surged to national prominence in 1992, when the premature death of *luk thung* star Phumphuang Duangchan attracted hundreds of thousand of mourners (including a princess) to her hometown of Suphanburi. Another bottom-up phenomenon was the celebration of North-eastern culture, particularly folk dance and spicy cuisine – a trend that was all the more remarkable given the long-standing disdain of Central Thais for the allegedly uncouth Isan population. Isan cultural regionalism was driven, in fact, by a two-way dynamic that converged on Bangkok – one vector being the mass migration of North-easterners to the capital, where Isan culture achieved 'national' visibility; the other vector being the urban strata's perception of Isan as the last bastion of authentic 'Thai' culture despite the region's predominant Lao identity. The paradox of the metropolitan rehabilitation of provincial culture was redoubled by the deep social anxiety caused by the spread of global consumer culture among the new urban middle class, an anxiety that – despite token gestures to local customs – was behind growing social nostalgia for the rural way of life and bureaucratic initiatives such as the Year to Campaign for Thai Culture (1994).

Thailand's culture industry, whose products throughout the 1980s were deemed both inferior to 'high culture' (i.e., the remnants of the court tradition) and unable to compete with US and Hong Kong imports, had grown sophisticated enough by the late 1990s to satisfy the full gamut of urban taste – from local TV soap operas (known as *lakhorn tiwi*), derivative pop music and a stream of comedy and horror films targeting low and middlebrow audiences to Thai rap, hip-hop and avant-garde films, such as Wisit Sasanatieng's *Tears of the Black Tiger* (*Fa talai chorn*, 2000) and Apichatphong Wirasethakun's *Blissfully Yours* (*Sut sanaeha*, 2001), whose poor performance at the local box office was counterbalanced by the

Golden Arches in Bangkok: middle-class consumerism today.

accolades gained on the international film festival circuit. These and other young Thai directors (including Nontri Nimibut and Pen Ek Ratanaruang) were not only leading a cinematic new wave, evidence of cultural self-assurance, but also securing a place for Thailand in the cultural landscape of the global œcumene.

two | Boundaries

Thai modern identities at the national, collective and individual levels resulted from the delineation and modification of territorial, social and gender boundaries. Traditionally, social and civilizational boundaries separated the aristocracy from commoners, commoners from slaves, town dwellers from villagers, villagers from hill people – and, more fundamentally, men from women. In the transformation from Buddhist kingdom to modern nation-state (to paraphrase the title of Charles Keyes's book), Thailand acquired national boundaries, which demarcated its newly mapped territorial space, and underwent shifts in the boundaries that delimited social and gendered spaces as a result of the incorporation in the world economy and the emergence of a bourgeois public sphere.

The concurrent establishment of territorial boundaries and the centralized system of administration at the close of the nineteenth century brought Siam in line with modern patterns of statehood and governance by means of technologies of cartography, census and surveillance. The modernization of the polity was followed by the redefinition of social hierarchies, understood as 'systems of subordination legitimated by cultural values'.[1] The bureaucracy, which was originally created as 'the king's servants', inherited after 1932 the aristocracy's symbolic capital and placed under its patronage the ethnic Chinese capitalists while peasants and urban labourers were unable to break free of their subaltern role. Shifts in social

boundaries went hand in hand with the modification of the boundaries that presided over gender relations. These latter boundaries
were historically more marked among royalty and nobility than
among commoners and the peasantry. The rise of Thai women's
status in society was the result of education among the upper
strata and internal migration among the lower ones, but was not
uniform across the population reflecting distinctions of class,
ethnicity and locality.

Territorial Boundaries

The pre-colonial polities of South-east Asia attached little importance to the demarcation of boundaries. Boundary stones and
watch houses intermittently placed at passageways and strategic
points marked the extension of the sovereign's authority but did
not delimit his realm. The sovereignty of one kingdom 'blurred'
into another's according to the changing allegiances of the smaller
polities at the margins. Conflict in pre-colonial South-east Asia
revolved around the control not of land, which was abundant, but
of people, who were scarce and hence a precious resource. The
common outcome of wars was the forced transfer of captive populations, one of the latest examples of which was the mass resettlement of Lao populations to the Khorat Plateau following Bangkok's
defeat of the king of Vientiane in the 1820s.[2] The historian O. W.
Wolters has described the spatial dimension of South-east Asian
statecraft with reference to the Hindu-Buddhist cosmographic
design of the *mandala* as 'a particular and often unstable political
situation in a vaguely definable geographical area without fixed
boundaries and where smaller centres tended to look in all direc-
tions for security'.[3]

In the regions of Thai settlement, the orbit of the *mandala* was
composed of unbounded polities centred on the main royal town,
or occasionally a smaller town under a viceroy (Lopburi had this
function in the kingdom of Ayutthaya) and the surrounding countryside, which produced the agricultural supply needed to support
the court and the nobility. More than as a defined geopolitical entity,
the traditional Thai polity, called *muang*, is better understood as
the spatial configuration of a hierarchical relationship of power;

the rulers of smaller *muang* subjected themselves to the authority of the overlord of larger *muang* by accepting tributary status. The absence of fixed territorial boundaries between *muang* underscored the fluidity of sovereignty in the frontier regions, where tributary lords switched allegiance from one overlord to another if the former failed to protect them, and even submitted to two or more overlords at the same time if they were deemed equally powerful.

Cartographic and topographic techniques, which had been developed on the oceans and perfected on the battlefields since the 1500s, became crucial tools of the modern state as a result of the political importance that boundary demarcation acquired in Europe after the Thirty Years War (1618–48). The French and the British, who had conducted exhaustive topographical surveys of their own countries in the second half of the eighteenth century, were well equipped to undertake the mapping of their overseas empires: Egypt was surveyed in the first decade of the nineteenth century during Napoleon's occupation, while between 1818 and 1840 the British carried out the so-called Great Trigonometrical Survey of India. After the British occupation of Lower Burma in 1824, topographical surveying came to intersect, literally as much as metaphorically, with the formation of the modern Thai state.

The British first raised the issue of the border between Lower Burma and Siam with Bangkok in 1824, but the Thais refused to be drawn into negotiation. Ten years later the British approached the king of Chiang Mai and proposed that the Salween River be regarded as the natural boundary between the Tenasserim Province and the Lanna kingdom (a Thai *muang* tributary to Bangkok). Chiang Mai's ruler accepted and even gave to the British some territory under his control as a goodwill gesture but declined to participate in the demarcation of the boundary, which the British undertook with the assistance of Karen elders in 1849. This boundary was ratified in 1874 by the first treaty stipulated between Siam and the viceroy of India. In 1880, the authorities of British India requested Bangkok's permission to let surveyors into its territory in order to complete the triangulation of Lower Burma from the Siamese side. Despite initial concerns, the Thais eventually consented to the request and ended up employing an English surveyor, J. F.

McCarthy, to initiate at the same time triangulations for a map of Siam. The Royal Survey Department under the Thai Ministry of the Interior was founded five years later, in 1885. That same year the British conquered Upper Burma; subsequently, a team of British and Thai officials conducted a joint survey along the northern frontier, which resulted in boundary demarcation in 1893.[4]

Misplaced hopes of turning Britain into an ally against France were probably behind the Thai eagerness to cooperate in the delineation of the boundary with British Burma, notwithstanding the considerable commercial value of the teak forests along the frontier. The British intervention in the conflict among the Malay sultanates and the consequent creation of the Federated Malay States in 1895 provided Bangkok with the opportunity to establish direct control on its tributary principalities in the peninsula. In 1909, however, Bangkok ceded to Britain four Malay principalities (Kedah, Perlis, Kelantan and Trengganu) because of their resistance to incorporation into the Thai state in exchange for diplomatic and financial concessions; negotiations for the demarcation of the boundary between Siam and British Malaya were initiated soon after.[5]

By contrast, the demarcation of boundaries between Siam and the neighbouring protectorates of Laos and Cambodia, which were now French protectorates, involved a dispute that spanned four decades – from 1867, when a Thai envoy signed in Paris a treaty recognizing France's exclusive authority over the kingdom of Cambodia (a tributary to Bangkok), to 1907, when King Chulalongkorn ratified the treaty that settled the border dispute, again in Paris. In between, the Thai and French armies clashed in 1888 at Dien Bien Phu, where they had converged to suppress an itinerant gang of Chinese bandits, the Ho; and, more famously, in July 1893 at the mouth of the Chaophraya River, where the French had organized a blockade by gunboats. This episode occupies a pivotal place in Thailand's national historical narrative as an act of imperialist aggression that eventually led to the mutilation of Siam's territory. Yet, historian Thongchai Winichakul has argued controversially that Thailand as a geopolitical entity was actually engendered by colonial cartography, and that the real loser in the struggle for the demarcation of boundaries was not Siam but the semi-autonomous *muang*, whose ambiguous status under the pre-colonial regime of multiple sovereignty was no longer viable in the modern world order of bounded national and colonial states.[6]

The French and the Thais had been competing since the mid-1880s in exploring and mapping the northern region of the Lao kingdom, which both aimed to incorporate in their domains. Thai surveyors under McCarthy's guidance accompanied the troops dispatched to fight the Ho rebels and drew topographical maps as they advanced in the uncharted region of the upper Mekong valley. Collected data were used to draw what is considered the first modern map of Siam (today in the British Library), which was printed in 1888; significantly, it depicted a boundary between Siam and northern Laos before negotiations about it had even started. Instead, on the map drawn by French explorer Auguste Pavie in 1902, the only boundary lines shown are those between Siam and British Burma according to the demarcation of 1893. An updated version of Pavie's map showing all the territorial boundaries in the region was published in 1909, two years after the treaty by which Bangkok had agreed to the retrocession of Cambodia's western provinces (Battambang, Sisophon and Siamreap) and the withdrawal of its troops to a distance of twenty-five kilometres from the Mekong's left bank, which came under French jurisdiction. Ironically, Pavie's map was subsequently reproduced in Siam as the kingdom's official map.[7]

The shift from a relational to a territorial concept of sovereignty underpinned the centralization of the provincial administration, which was instituted in 1892 but had been tested as early as 1874, when Bangkok sent a commissioner to oversee the affairs of the kingdom of Lanna. The same procedure was followed in the 1880s, when Bangkok tried to reassert its authority on the Lao kingdom of Luang Prabang, which was seeking the protection of the French. The administrative reform of 1892 made the central government responsible for the safeguard of the territory, as spelt out in the system's designation (*thesaphiban*), and of the people who had become Siamese subjects as a result of boundary demarcation. It also centralized, through the Mining Act (1898), the exploitation of natural resources. In the first stage of the reform, a four-tier administrative system was created, in which provinces (as the larger territorial unit) were placed under governors appointed by the Ministry of the

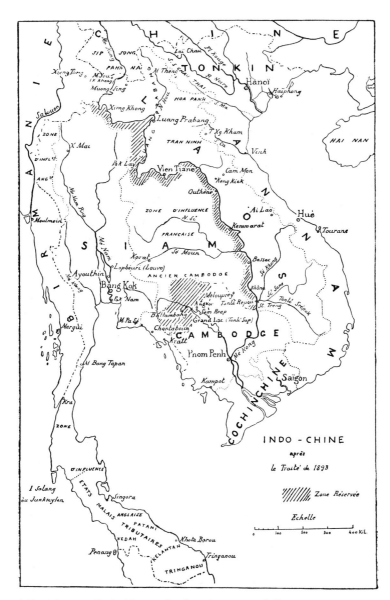

A French map of Indochina made after the treaty of 1893.

Interior. In 1899, centralization was strengthened by grouping provinces into regions that were however abolished in 1933; provincial courts' judges and provincial comptrollers were also appointed by the ministries of justice and finance.[8]

Administrative centralization made possible the implementation of the mechanisms of any modern state, whether national or colonial: the registration of households, the collection of taxes and universal military conscription. It also redefined communal bonds within the administratively defined village (*muban*) under the authority of the centrally appointed village head (*phuyaiban*), who replaced the council of village elders. In the central provinces the administrative reform was hardly noticed. In the northern provinces a degree of continuity was allowed by co-opting local lords into the new system (thus divesting them of personal power) and later replacing them with government officials. In the southern provinces the demotion of local sultans was initially counterbalanced by the institution of Islamic courts (on the model of the British Federated Malay States), whose judges were nominated *in loco* with Bangkok's approval; in 1902 state legislation replaced the Sharia except for Malay customary law (*adat*). The north-eastern provinces, where the majority of the population was ethnically Lao, were instead subjected to a drastic pattern of administrative assimilation owing both to Thai prejudices and the tensions with French Indochina over the legal status of Siam's Lao subjects even after France's renunciation to the extraterritorial rights of its Asian subjects in the 1907 treaty.[9]

The Western concept of national sovereignty as bounded territoriality had a peculiar reverse in the legal notion of extra-territoriality, whereby the nationals of European states, the USA and Japan (as well as the Asian subjects of colonial governments) were not subject to the fiscal and juridical authority of their state of residence. Extraterritoriality was imposed through the so-called 'unequal treaties' to countries like China and Siam, which had not been reduced under direct colonial rule. The clauses on extraterritoriality contained in the commercial treaties that Siam had concluded with Western countries in the 1850s and '60s curbed its sovereignty even before this acquired territorial form at the century's end. Even afterwards, the recruitment by European consulates of protégés among wealthy Chinese immigrants and ethnic minorities in border areas was a thorn in the side for the Thai authorities. Only in the second half of the 1920s, partly as a result of Siam's symbolic participation in the First World War on the Allies' side, did some Western countries agree to revise the commercial treaties in order to write off extraterritoriality rights.[10]

Historians have long debated whether Siam's administrative centralization was a major step in state formation or, rather, a tool of internal colonization by the Bangkok monarchy. Yet, this may not be a productive question, after all, because if the *thesaphiban* was modelled on colonial administrations, these were in turn moulded on metropolitan systems. Insofar as the Thai state emerged from the Chakri's project of self-strengthening and territorial aggrandizement, dynastic and national objectives tended to overlap. An instructive comparison can be made here with the creation of the unitary Italian state in the 1860s as the result of the piecemeal annexation of regional states by Piedmont's House of Savoy. Both the modern kingdoms of Siam and Italy were indeed, like several other instances of nineteenth-century state building, the outcome of top-down political projects. So, while there is some truth to the argument that governors dispatched from Bangkok to administer peripheral provinces were no less foreign to the local populace than British and Dutch colonial commissioners were to the Burmese and the Javanese, the same could be said of a Piedmontese police superintendent sent to impose law and order in Sicily in post-unification Italy. Indeed, they all met with popular resistance – in Siam by self-proclaimed 'holy men', leaders of a rebellion in Isan in 1902; in Burma and Java by proto-nationalists; and in Italy's South by 'brigands'. However, it was only in Siam (and Italy) – and not, of course, in colonial states – that after the modern state came into being, the ruling elites assiduously fostered a sense of nationality through the promotion of a standard language, the creation of national symbols and the public commemoration of historical figures and events.

To return to the main theme, one can note the twentieth-century legacy of the unbounded *muang* in the territorial disputes and the permeability of national frontiers to the movement of peoples and goods, which made border surveillance paramount to the Thai state's rhetoric on national security. In 1941 and 1942 Thailand, bolstered by Japan's support, re-annexed Cambodia's western provinces and then occupied allegedly lost territories in the Shan states – all of which were returned at the end of the war. But conflict resulting from unclear boundary demarcation lingered on in the post-colonial era. In 1962, after a protracted dispute, the Cambodian government requested the International Court of Justice in the Hague to arbitrate on the sovereignty of a spur along the Dongraek Range (marking the natural border with Thailand), which is notable for the presence of the hilltop sanctuary of Preah Vihear (Thai: Phra Wihan) and which Bangkok claimed as part of its national territory. In late 1987 and early 1988, Thailand and Laos fought a three-month war, which resulted in some seven hundred casualties, for the control of an 80-square-kilometre patch of forest-land rich in teak wood.

Even more destabilizing for national security was the function of border areas as a sanctuary to drug dealers, insurgents and refugees. Poppy cultivation and the refinement of opium came to be concentrated in an area across the frontiers of Thailand, Myanmar and Laos – the so-called Golden Triangle. Opium, which the Hmongs introduced in the mid-nineteenth century, was grown largely for local consumption until the end of the 1940s, when culti-vation was expanded with the consent of the Thai government, partly in order to sustain the disbanded 93rd battalion of the Chinese nationalist army (Guomindang), which had settled in Burmese territory and the CIA intended to use for an invasion of Communist China. Both the Thai army and police became involved in the opium trade and their rivalry even led to internal clashes. The head of the police, General Phao, gained control of the trade from the Thai end but his rival Marshal Sarit Thanarat, who also had greatly profited from the opium revenues, abolished the still exist-ing state monopoly on opium after seizing power in 1958. The Thai police continued to profit from the opium trade even more so when, at the start of the 1960s, Rangoon forced the Guomindang and its drug operations out of Burma into northern Thailand. On the east-ern border too, opium provided a major source of revenues for the Hmong mercenaries enlisted by the CIA to fight the Phathet Lao revolutionary army. By the 1970s, as consumption of heroin in the Western world boomed, the Americans started exerting pressure on the Thai authorities to eradicate opium production through pro-grammes of settlement and crop substitution.[11]

Insurgency along the borders included the clandestine army of the Communist Party of Thailand, whose main army division was stationed along the frontier with Laos but also had troops on the western border; the Shan United Army and the Karen National Liberation Army along the north-western border; and, in the south, the armed Muslim separatists, occasionally allied to the Malayan Communist Party (which the Thai authorities long tolerated and at times covertly supported as a source of disturbance for the Malaysian government). An ad hoc paramilitary corps, the Border Patrol Police (BPP), was created in the early 1950s with the patronage of the royal family and training and assistance from the CIA and the US Army Special Forces advisers. The BPP quickly became 'a primary counterinsurgency force because of its training, motivation and unique skills.' It co-opted villagers into counterinsurgency through construction projects and the formation of the Volunteer Defence Corps, a civilian militia designed to maintain law and order in the provinces at the border with Laos, Cambodia and Malaysia. The BPP also collaborated with the Narcotics Suppression Centre to stop the opium trade across the western border.[12] Perversely, the BPP acquired national notoriety for storming, on 6 October 1976, the campus of Thammasat University – in the middle of Bangkok and hence a long distance from any border. Another paramilitary organization, the 'forest soldiers' (*thahan pa*), with around 14,000 irregular combatants, was created in the late 1960s to carry out counter-attacks across the borders with Myanmar and Cambodia.

As political insurgency waned in the early 1980s, the issue of refugees became prominent. An estimated 1.3 million people were displaced in the second half of the 1970s as a consequence of the Second Indochina War (1964–75). South Vietnamese, Laotians and Cambodians as well as hill people sought refuge in Thailand's territory. The Thai government's classification of foreign nationals and stateless people into four categories ('immigrants', 'illegal immigrants', 'displaced people' and 'refugees') subsumed ethnicity to the policing of borders. Hmong refugees fleeing the reprisal of the authorities of the Lao People's Democratic Republic (PDR) found shelter in Thailand's North-east. Cambodians displaced by Vietnam's overthrow of the Pol Pot regime at the end of 1978 sought refuge in Thailand's eastern provinces, but their camps were infiltrated by Khmer Rouge resistance forces who used them as bases to attack the Vietnamese troops stationed along the Thai-Cambodian border throughout the 1980s. The Burmese military too repeatedly infringed Thailand's sovereignty by raiding Karen and Shan sanctuaries across the border and causing retaliations by the Thai army. By the 1990s, however, Yangon and Bangkok were working together to halt the cross-border movement of ethnic minorities; and only in 1998 did the Thai government allow the UN High Commission for Refugees to come to their aid, though still refusing to become signatory to the UN Refugee Convention. By the close of the century, most refugees in Thailand had been repatriated or relocated overseas (mostly to the USA); the number of those remaining was 217,000 – more than half of which were Karens and most of the rest Shans.[13]

With the beginning of the economic boom, a wave of 'economic refugees' from Myanmar, Cambodia, Laos and southern China came to Thailand following on the trail of earlier political and ethnic refugees. The majority of immigrants were Burmese, as they were able to access several entry points along the northern and western border. Illegal immigrants escaped the political and economic conditions of their own countries with the hope of taking advantage of Thailand's booming economy. However, in Thailand they ran the risk of exploitation, deportation and – for young females and also males – the contraction of fatal disease as sex workers. In the mid-1990s the presence of illegal immigrants came to be regulated by a permit system and by the end of the decade they constituted a sizable segment of the workforce in the agricultural and the informal industrial sectors.[14]

Social Boundaries

Historically, Central Thai society had a hierarchical structure even though it lacked the rigid boundaries of the Indian caste system that, through the Khmer mediation, constituted its original model. The royalty occupied the top of the social ladder, nobility and court officials the upper and middle ranks, and commoners and bonded serfs were at the bottom. Due to polygamy, royal princes (*chao*) bore different ranks according to their mother's status. The nobility (*khunnang*) was composed of families related to the royalty as well as officials ennobled as a reward for their services to the crown.[15] Commoners (*phrai*), who made up the great mass of the population, enjoyed the status of 'free men' and hence the right to occupy land, which belonged nominally to the king; however, they were subject to an annual corvée of several months for royal projects and to army service during wartime under the command of a master in the nobility, to whom they also consigned a share of the family's crop. Serfs (*that*) were generally debtors bonded to a noble household or a monastery while actual slaves (*kha*) were mostly non-Thai war prisoners; while they had no right to own land, their living conditions could be better than indigent peasants' since they were not subject to levies and corvée.

This pattern of social organization, which persisted throughout the end of the nineteenth century, was rooted in a ranking system called *sakdina* (literally, 'power over fields'), which had been instituted in the fifteenth century with the aim of concentrating power in the crown on the model of the centralized Khmer empire. The lexical hybridity of the term *sakdina*, combining the Sanskritic *sakdi* with the vernacular *na*, underscored the localization of a foreign practice of social distinction. The *sakdina* accorded every man in the kingdom a 'dignity mark', from 100,000 marks for a royal prince to five marks for a court serf, corresponding (at least in theory) to their endowment of paddy-fields measured in *rai*. In practice, though, while in the lower levels of the social hierarchy the mark corresponded to the acreage of land assigned to commoners (usually between 10 and 25 *rai*), at the higher levels (400 marks and above) the mark corresponded to the number of commoners assigned to the nobleman's service.[16]

The *sakdina* system, which Thai Marxist historians have assimilated to feudalism in Europe, institutionalized the exploitation of the peasant population by the nobility as well as the king's ultimate authority to determine princes' and nobles' access to wealth. This dimension of royal authority required emphasis because, not unlike the absolutist monarchies of early modern Europe, the Thai kings' maniloquent claims to divine and absolute power were often challenged by other princes. Political stability thus resulted from a balance of power between the king, court factions and the provincial nobility. From this perspective, the *sakdina* was a means to create a hierarchic and self-reproducing social order organized around a chain of patron-client relations in which the king himself represented the first link as supreme patron, guarantor of individual power and wealth – a prerogative underscored by his appellation as 'lord of life' (*chao chiwit*). The fall of Ayutthaya in 1767 was largely the result of the loosening of the *sakdina* as a mechanism of social organization founded on reciprocal obligations: the noblemen, whose status rested on the control of commoners, failed their obligation to protect the court in time of war. The practice of tattooing on a commoner's wrist the name of his patron suggests the stiffening of the *sakdina* when the system was reconstituted after the re-establishment of Thai political authority over the Chaophraya basin in the 1770s.

From the 1820s onwards commoners could avoid the levy by paying a tax equivalent. The crown responded to the decline in corvée labour by using increased revenues to employ Chinese immigrant work in building and canalization projects – a practice that expanded in the course of the century. But it was the reforms of Chulalongkorn's reign, designed to integrate Siam in the international capitalist economy, which determined the demise of the *sakdina* even though the system was officially abolished only in 1938. To begin with, the abolition of bondage, passed as law in 1874 and effected in stages over the next twenty years, freed the economically unproductive serfs to boost agricultural production.[17] Next, all levies in labour and kind were replaced by a capitation and a land tax (by the 1910s, revenues from these two taxes amounted to 20 per cent of the total annual revenues). Of major consequence was also the creation of a salaried bureaucracy that, within one generation, came to represent a social group of its own. However, the bureaucracy (whose characteristics as an institution are discussed in the next chapter) was not homogenous, being sharply divided between high-ranking officials, who bore nobility titles and wielded considerable personal power, and low-ranking officials in need of their superiors' patronage to advance their careers.

By the end of the Fifth Reign (1910), three broad social strata could be discerned in the capital: the numerically marginal but politically dominant bloc composed of royalty, the nobility and ennobled officials, and their Sino-Thai business associates; the demographically preponderant but powerless urban proletariat, made up of wage labourers (largely, though not exclusively,

69

Chinese) and street vendors and domestic servants (mostly Thais); and an embryonic (and ethnically Sino-Thai) middle class, which was the social outcome of the administrative and educational reforms of the turn of the century. This latter stratum, numbering in the region of several thousand by the 1920s, was employed in the bureaucracy's lower and middle ranks, in Chinese and Western commercial and industrial enterprises, education and publishing. Unsurprisingly, it was this intellectual elite, who lacked status and economic capital but possessed cultural capital, that opened fire on the old order by denouncing in cartoons and editorials the ineptitude, arrogance and corruption of nobles and government officials, and that started agitating for the redrawing of social as well as gender boundaries. According to historian Scot Barmé, 'this sociological process of redefinition sought to establish order through the creation of a new contemporary morality that was seen as fundamental to the nation's progress and prosperity'.[18]

Resentment towards the old regime found muted support among the middle and lower middle ranks of the civil bureaucracy and the army, who had been dismissed or had their salary cut in the wake of the economic depression of 1929–30. However, the post-absolutist period did not see the assertion of an urban middle class championing the bourgeois values of justice, political freedom and free enterprise. Because the middle class was dominated throughout the 1960s by the civilian and military bureaucracy, its values perpetuated the ethos of the *sakdina* aristocracy, such as personal status and respect for authority and hierarchy. At the same time, by representing its class interests as coinciding with the 'public good' and co-opting the ethnic Chinese business elite, the bureaucracy was able to gain (in an analytical perspective informed by the theory of political thinker Antonio Gramsci) the hegemonic position in the social bloc that was politically dominant until the early 1990s.[19] Twice over this period of time the socio-political status quo was disrupted by seismic societal movements: in 1973, when the largest generation ever of university graduates, who were the product of the growth of tertiary education in the 1960s in a context of declining social mobility,[20] rose to challenge bureaucratic rule and ushered in the brief period of 'open politics'; and in 1992, when the professional strata outside the bureaucracy that had expanded since the mid-1980s staked a claim in the political process by orchestrating street rallies to demand the resignation of the unelected prime minister.

The successful resolution of the 'Black May' crisis, dubbed by the press the 'hand-held revolution' (with reference to the widespread use of cellular phones to mobilize protesters), transformed the 'Thai middle class' in a category of socio-political analysis despite the fact that its heterogeneous composition made its use highly problematic. Different educational and income levels distinguished the 'old' (occupational) middle class, made of public servants and military officers, blue collar workers, small entrepreneurs and shopkeepers, from the 'new' (consumer) middle class, formed by managers, executives and professionals who tended to be foreign educated, cultivate an international outlook and pursue a consumerist lifestyle.[21] While even after 1992 some commentators continued to doubt the long-term commitment to democratization of the new middle class, the financial crisis of 1997 dealt it a heavy blow. In its aftermath the capital's outskirts saw the mushrooming of 'weekend markets of the formerly rich', where second-hand items for sale included portable phones, golfing gear and German sedans – the status symbols of the affluent urban strata as much as social boundary markers whose repositionability underscored the relative fluidity of such boundaries.

A class of ethnically Chinese capitalists began to emerge in Thailand in the middle of the nineteenth century following the establishment of commercial relations with Europe. In the early Bangkok period (1782–1851), Chinese merchant lords (*chaosua*) had accumulated considerable wealth through tax farming, royal monopoly and the junk trade in association with the court and the nobility, in which they were often incorporated as ennobled officials. The third reign (1824–51) saw the peak of *chaosua* power before the commercial treaty signed with Britain in 1855 set the stage for the transformation of the Thai economy. Because of available capital and reliance on overseas trade networks, Chinese merchants were in the best position to invest in industrial and commercial ventures (milling, mining and import-export) when the opportunity arose. In the last quarter of the century the rice industry became the biggest area of economic growth and most Chinese capital was invested into milling and trading (in 1912, 47 out of the 50 rice mills in Siam were owned by Chinese), despite the fact that the rice market was subject to dramatic fluctuations. Some rice merchants, known by the old term *chaosua*, acted simply as middlemen between local producers and foreign exporters, but the most successful ones competed with European entrepreneurs by forming business partnerships, such as the Siam Commercial Bank (founded in 1906), with members of the royalty and the nobility. At this stage, the social boundary between the Thai aristocracy and the big Chinese merchants on the one side and Thai peasants and recent Chinese immigrants working as coolies on the other side was far more marked than the ethnic boundary between Thais and Chinese.

The years immediately after the First World War saw the emergence of a new generation of Chinese rice merchants, descendants of migrants who had settled in Siam since the 1850s. They formed integrated business groups that dealt with the various aspects of the rice trade and diversified their capital by investing in parallel activities. By the 1920s five families (Wangli, Lamsan, Bulasuk, Mahbunkrong and Iamsuri) dominated the rice trade; 'family capitalism' would become the trademark of the Thai economy. The retreat of Western investors as a result of the Great Depression created a space for investing in the manufacturing sector the capital accumulated in the rice trade. The wartime closure of the local branches of European banks also offered new opportunities for the Sino-Thai trading families that had emerged in the 1930s. They founded new banks, such the Bangkok Bank (established in 1944 by a consortium of nine families), which financed industrial ventures in the post-war period. High inflation and infrastructural damage plagued the Thai economy after the war but by 1947, when the military returned to power, booming exports of primary goods led to a quick recovery.[22]

The loosening of the Chinese migrants' ties to the motherland after the rise to power of the Communist Party and the restrictions placed by the Thai government on remittances also diverted surplus capital from overseas to local investments. The leading Sino-Thai business families began to forge connections with the bureaucracy by inviting high-rank army and police officers to join the boards of directors of banks and firms. Mutual interest was behind the alliance between entrepreneurs and the bureaucracy that formed during the 1950s: the first offered chairmanships, payouts and commercial networks in exchange for political protection and patronage. This partnership was reinforced by the restructuring of the economy under the Sarit regime (1958–62) by redeploying government funds to develop infrastructure and promoting foreign investment according to the recommendations of the World Bank report (1959) and US strategic demands in the Cold War.[23]

In the early 1960s a younger generation of foreign-educated technocrats, such as the one-time director of the Bank of Thailand Puai Ungphakorn, was put in charge of macroeconomic management, which ensured fiscal stability and the inflow of foreign capital (mostly American and Japanese). The developmental strategy set up by new agencies, such as the National Economic ('and Social' was added later) Development Board, the Board of Investment and the Budget Bureau, was implemented in five-year plans starting in 1961. These policies, coupled with the massive US grant and military aid, determined the full expansion of agriculture in response to rising international demand as well as the growth of an import-substitution industry and the banking sector. Between the late 1950s and the early '70s, when the Thai economy grew on average 7.2 per cent per annum, local entrepreneurs were able to move from trading to manufacturing (primarily in agribusiness and the textile industry) by gaining access to capital and technology through joint-ventures, to financial backing from commercial banks, and to government contracts and monopoly concessions from the generals sitting on their boards of directors. At the same time, a limited number of Sino-Thai commercial groups (who, besides the 'big five' of the rice industry, included the Sophonpanich, Thechapaibun and Rattanarak families) further reinforced their grip on the increasingly intertwined industrial and banking sectors.[24]

The overthrow of military rule and the first oil crisis in 1973, followed by the decline in crop exports, altered the landscape in which the Sino-Thai capitalist class had flourished. By the end of the 1970s, when the second oil crisis hit the global economy, the balance of payments was in deficit and Thailand had to borrow money from the World Bank. In the first half of the 1980s Thailand faced its worst economic crisis in three decades: inflation was rampant, industrial and financial profits in decline, and retrenchment in the private sector widespread. From that low ebb, the Thai economy picked up again and went on to experience a spectacular ten-year boom between 1987 and 1996, during which the Thai economy grew at an average rate of 8 per cent. From manufacturing, banking and services (notably tourism), entrepreneurs moved in the early 1990s into high-tech industries and global finance. The socio-ethnic boundaries between Thai bureaucracy and Sino-Thai capitalists, which had started blurring in the 1960s, had become even looser by the 1980s, as the new entrepreneurial class forged an alliance with the technocratic elite in the government to promote market-oriented reforms.[25]

Conditions were thus ripe for the transmutation of businessmen into politicians (nearly half of the cabinet ministers in the coalition governments of the 1980s had business backgrounds), which elevated their status from 'ethnic pariah' to policy makers. The irresistible ascent of businessmen to positions of power was epitomized by Thaksin Chinawat. Born to a Sino-Thai family of Chiang Mai silk traders turned bureaucrats and provincial politicians, Thaksin began his career in the police force. In the mid-1980s he started a private business thanks to a government concession for operating a cable TV and paging service and later went on to launch Thailand's first satellite to run a mobile phone service. After the incidents of May 1992, Thaksin joined the political arena, first as an MP elected within the ranks of the Democrats and then as founding leader of the Thai Rak Thai party, with which he won the general elections in January 2001.

The social bloc formed by the alliance of the bureaucratic and capitalist classes had no counterpart at the opposite end of the social spectrum. The failure of peasants and urban workers to develop a class consciousness depended at least in part on the ethnic division between Thai rural labour and Chinese industrial labour that persisted until the 1960s and the different worldviews inherent in this division. But a much more decisive factor was the state's consistent repression of labour activism – from the policing of Chinese associations and working-class districts in the 1920s and the anticommunist legislation of the 1930s to the nationalization of trade unions in the 1940s; and from the assassination of farmer and labour leaders in the 1950s through the '70s (and not unheard of even in the 1990s) to the fragmentation of the workforce according to sector, level and gender in the 1980s and '90s. The disempowerment of Thai industry workers paradoxically mirrored their massive growth from the 1960s onwards, which underlay the shift from agriculture to the manufacturing and service sectors as the prime contributors to Thailand's gross domestic product.[26]

The pioneering role assigned to small landowners in agricultural colonization meant that, although Thai farmers gained little from the massive expansion of the rice industry, they fared considerably better than peasants in colonial societies. The Thai state's investments in agricultural development were limited through the 1940s to canalization work, but taxation and surplus extraction were also lighter than under colonial governments. Because of low capital requirements, Thai peasants were able to start smallholding activity with relatives' support without the need for borrowing from money lenders, as was generally the case in Burma and Vietnam. The recession of 1929–30, when the price of rice fell by half in the wake of the global depression, badly affected peasants in the Chaophraya delta (partly also because the central bank's clinging to the gold standard until 1932 depressed rice export in favour of Burma). A third of the rural population of the delta became indentured farmers after selling land titles to repay debts to the advantage of big landholders. Yet, partly as a result of the curtailment of the land tax (eventually abolished in 1938), tenancy and landlessness were confined to the delta; in the rest of the kingdom peasant livelihood was still sustained by the continuing availability of new land, limited indebtedness to Chinese traders and light state taxation.[27]

This situation changed dramatically in the post-war period. First, in 1955, the government introduced the tax on rice exports to finance infrastructural development; in the late 1950s, following the advice of the World Bank, it also imposed higher duties on seeds and fertilizers and increased the acreage limit on land ownership. These policies set in motion the capitalist transformation of the countryside, as a result of which distinct social formations emerged in the countryside: tenant peasants and smallholder farmers, well-to-do farmers and agribusiness entrepreneurs. The introduction of new cash crops and technologies in the 1960s increased further the gap between wealthy farmers, who could afford farming products and machinery, and poor peasants; agricultural mechanization in the Central Plain allowed landlords to dispense with tenant farmers altogether and rely exclusively on wage labour. Pioneer farmers who had colonized the uplands faced high rates of crop failure due to soil degradation, and eventually they left cultivation in the hands of agribusinesses. According to the agricultural census of 1978, the top 16 per cent of the farmers operated 44 per cent of the land, while the bottom 44 per cent operated only 13 per cent of it. The closure of the land frontier in the early 1980s caused impoverished farmers, largely in the Northeast, to migrate to Bangkok, where they became waged labourers, as well as to foreign countries, especially in the Middle East.[28]

At the beginning of industrial development in the early decades of the twentieth century urban labour was done mostly by immigrants from southern China. Chinese workers in Bangkok were organized in *angyi*, a combination of welfare society, political association and protection racket. The government relied on *angyi* to settle labour disputes yet, at the same time, took repressive measures to curb labour disruption in the port, rice milling and construction industry by promulgating the Secret Societies Act as early as 1898. Despite Chinese labour organizations supporting the demand for political reform on the eve of the overthrow of the absolute monarchy, tensions increased in the post-absolutist period due to the proselytizing by nationalist and communist activists among immigrant workers and the government's economic nationalism. During the recession of the early 1930s, Thai farmers migrated to the city looking for jobs taking advantage of the opportunities created by the imposition of ethnic quotas in the rice industry. To the growth of ethnic Thai urban labour in the 1930s and '40s, especially in government enterprises such as transportation and public utilities, corresponded ironically the curbing of the nascent working-class consciousness, since rural migrants tended to approach labour relations as 'peasants in disguise' through the paternalist framework of the master-client relationship. Trade unionism gained pace only briefly after the Second World War with the foundation in 1947 of the Central Labour Union.[29]

The return to power of the military in 1947 saw the revival of the pre-war corporatist approach to labour relations. A nationalized union, the Thai Labour Union, was founded while the Central Labour Union came under attack for being dominated by Chinese communists and hence purportedly contrary to the interests of Thai workers. Labour politics became even more repressive in the first half of the 1950s, only to be reversed briefly by Phibun's tactical appeasement of the left in 1956–7, when new labour legislation (providing for a 48-hour working week, paid holidays and health and safety coverage) was passed. The transition from the Phibun to the Sarit regime saw, however, a policy reversal: the law of 1957 was abrogated, trade unions outlawed and labour leaders incarcerated. The management of labour relations by the Labour Department (founded in 1965) favoured the expansion of private capital in the industry since the 1960s. This development divided the labour force between workers in the public sector, who enjoyed better pay and conditions, and those in the private sector; among the latter, those in capital-intensive multinationals and joint ventures enjoyed similar conditions to state employees, while those in the informal sector (such as small garment factories) were regularly exploited and often unfairly dismissed, their employers relying on an abundant labour supply.[30] The ethnic composition of urban labour also changed due to the end of Chinese immigration and three decades of continuous demographic growth beginning in the mid-1950s.

The democratic interlude of 1973–76 saw a dramatic surge in labour unrest: the total number of strikes staged in those four years (1232) was more than five times that of the strikes that had taken place since 1956 (219). Labour actions by peasant and worker organizations, such as the Farmers' Federation of Thailand and the Thai Federation of Labour Unions, often co-ordinated by the student movement, achieved some important successes, including the creation of a farmers' welfare fund, the passing of the Land Reform Act and the Labour Relations Act, and the doubling of workers' minimum wage despite the recession and high inflation that plagued the Thai economy in the mid-1970s. The intensification of industrial actions caused the brutal reaction of factory owners, especially in the textile industry, while the state enterprise unions distanced themselves from the radical politics of some labour activists. After the counter-revolution of October 1976, the government broke the alliance between farmers and urban workers by fragmenting their aggregate power not through suppression but co-option in a multitude of corporatist unions under the umbrella of the state labour federations. After a brief return to industrial actions during the recession of the first half of the 1980s, unionization declined steadily as the economy started its recovery in the middle of the decade.[31]

The workforce behind the industrial boom of the second half of the 1980s, when the value of manufactured exports surpassed that of agricultural exports, was constituted by young villagers, the majority of them women.[32] Rural migration to the cities, compounded in the 1990s by immigration from neighbouring countries, blurred the conventional social and ethnic boundaries between villagers and city dwellers, and sedentary/Thais and migrant/non-Thais. Internal migration was induced not only by the scarcity of farm land and the economic decline of agriculture but also by the appeal of higher factory wages and the desire to escape pre-ordained village life for financial independence, blue-collar status and the buzz of city life. Even seasonal migration during the off-farm period affected the identity of rural communities by undermining communal practices such as courtship and temple festivals; on the other hand, villagers who were permanently urbanized did not necessarily acquire the identity of city dwellers, for their place of residence and employment in the industrial suburbs were detached from urban socio-cultural dynamics.[33] The social heterogeneity of the labour force combined with bureaucratic control to discourage unionization: in the mid-1990s, less than 5 per cent of an industrial workforce in excess of six million was unionized, the government had signed none of the conventions of the International Bureau of Labour, and most employers in the informal sector evaded contractual obligations such as minimum wage and working hours, breached safety regulations and made use of child labour (estimated at the close of the century in the region of one million children working).[34]

Mobilized by the increasingly numerous and influential non-governmental organizations (NGOs), peasants achieved more negotiating power than industrial workers on the issues of rural poverty, development and environmental degradation. Vocal opposition to government plans for the construction of the Nam Choan dam in the 1980s and the resettlement of forest settlers in the early 1990s led in both cases to their repeal. Subsequently, the Assembly of the Poor, a network of rural associations founded at the end of 1995, organized massive demonstrations to negotiate compensation and relief packages for farmers hit by natural disasters and the fall in crop prices. The open articulation of social conflict was a novel feature of the Thai social landscape, its only precedents being in the mid-1970s, and provoked mixed reactions among the urban middle class: the intelligentsia hailed it as a form of resistance to global capitalism rooted in local wisdom and Buddhist ethics; the technocratic and business elites criticized it as a misguided rejection of globalization. But the economic crisis of 1997 complicated this juxtaposition.

The dramatic rise in rural unemployment and the consequent prospect of social unrest led Thaksin Chinawat's Thai Rak Thai party to give a prominent place in its electoral platform to measures in support of rural communities (a debt moratorium, a cheap health scheme and a one-million baht loan scheme for every village), which were endorsed by grass-root leaders. The party's landslide victory in the general elections of 2001 revealed a novel consensus that cut across traditional social boundaries by bringing together domestic capitalists and the peasantry, the two classes that had been most affected by the crisis.[35] The realization of the electoral programme during the legislature broadened further the rural base of the Thai Rak Thai and led to its triumph in the elections of 2005. Still, the Thaksin government was far from attempting to redraw the social boundaries. For once, the failure to institute a progressive system of taxation underscored the unwillingness to touch the entrenched interests of the wealthiest classes. At the same time, the government support of rural communities, though effective to a certain extent, aimed at neutralizing the NGOs' discourse of social justice and sustainable development by urging farmers to be active participants in the global economy.

Gender Boundaries

Thai folklore and popular wisdom are notorious for emphasizing women's subordination to men.[36] The cultural and historical roots of Thai patriarchy have been identified both with Buddhism, which placed women in an inferior position to men in the chain of rebirth and forbade their ordination, reserving for them the role of lay ascetic (*maechi*); and with the *sakdina* social order, in which women were considered under the law to be male property. Women were also commonly given as tribute by peripheral rulers to valley overlords to cement alliances. The peculiarity of such a 'gift system' was not the use of women as means of court alliances, which was practised in Europe throughout the nineteenth century, but the fact that polygamy made possible multiple contemporary allegiances that underpinned the pre-colonial regime of relational sovereignty. The Thai institution of the royal harem, which persisted until the early twentieth century, was a means to regulate the women's gift system, in which court officials and Chinese merchants with connections to the Crown too participated.

Nevertheless, women in the Central and Northern Thai kingdoms generally enjoyed, as in other South-east Asian societies, a better condition than in imperial China or the Christian and Muslim worlds. Status was critical in demarcating boundaries between the sexes, which were more rigid the higher a woman's social position. Royal wives and concubines resided in isolated quarters in the inner palace, from which male children were removed upon reaching puberty. Palace women were trained in the bodily skills (crouching, crawling, sitting, walking and dancing) prescribed by courtly culture. Even among the nobility, women's sociability was mostly confined to the domestic sphere and the household constituted the space within which their authority was exerted. By contrast, as noted by seventeenth-century European visitors to Ayutthaya, women from the commoner stratum enjoyed considerable autonomy, both in rural areas, where they operated the land and market stalls, and in the city, where they ran stores, manufactured crafts and animated the bourgeoning sex trade.[37]

Ayutthayan laws regulating marriage and the status of women were re-codified at the beginning of the Bangkok era in a law included in the Code of the Three Seals (1805). The law recognized three basic categories of female conjugality: major wife (*mia luang*), minor wife (*mia noi*) and slave wife (*mia that*). Nubile women were considered the possession of their parents, who had the authority to choose a spouse for them; after marriage, they became the property of husbands, who could sell them into serfdom or prostitution. This provision was modified in 1867, when it was decreed that the sale of any young woman above fifteen years by parents and of wives by husbands necessitated their consent, and was made obsolete by the abolition of serfdom in 1874. Illicit sexual intercourse attracted a range of penalties (execution, flogging, imprisonment or monetary compensation to fathers or husbands) depending on the rank of the man and woman involved and their mutual relationship. In 1865 Rama IV had also decreed that female commoners over twenty were free to marry whomever they wanted; yet the same decree restated paternal authority over spouse selection among the nobility. This royal proclamation thus granted legal protection to peasant women, who were often sold as brides, but also tightened social boundaries to prevent the loss of rank of noble families as a result of their daughters' marrying below status.[38]

During the Fourth Reign, Western missionaries foregrounded polygamy and female education as the future battlegrounds for the redefinition of gender boundaries. Their attacks on polygamy as unbecoming a civilized nation prompted a court official to write an articulate defence of it in 1867.[39] In fact, polygamy not only thrived under the successive Fifth Reign, in counter-tendency to the cultural Westernization of the court, but was also accompanied by increasing endogamy among the royalty. The three highest-ranking royal consorts – Sunantha, Sawang and Saowapha – were sisters among themselves as well as half-sisters to Chulalongkorn himself (King Mongkut being the father of them all). Rama V fathered 76 children from 36 mothers and some of his minor wives, in a harem of some 70 women, came from the queens' own households.[40] However, in the famous group portrait of Chulalongkorn, Saowapha and their five sons (including the future Rama VI and Rama VII), painted by the Italian artist Edoardo Gelli (1899), polygyny and endogamy were seamlessly elided from the court's official representation by depicting the royal family according to the monogamous Western format.

Another idiosyncrasy in the Fifth Reign's civilizing drive was the lack of concern for female education. King Chulalongkorn openly admitted that 'whenever suggestion is made that a girls'

The beginnings of female education: a girls' school, c. 1900.

school be founded, I am quite annoyed'. But Queen Saowapha, who was elevated to the position of regent during the king's visit to Europe in 1897, actively promoted female education by establishing a number of girls' schools both in Bangkok (including the Sunanthalai School in 1893, the School of Obstetrics and Nursing at Sirirat Hospital in 1896 and the prestigious Queen's School in 1904) and the provinces. The queen's initiatives followed the pattern of charitable social work that European royalty embraced to justify their privilege in the age of elective government, yet generated a momentum that led to the creation of private girls' schools both in Bangkok and provincial towns to obviate the exclusively male education offered by temple schools. The number of female students increased sharply after the beginning of state education in 1921: from 5,396 in 1915 (against some 115,000 males), their number had jumped to 235,465 ten years later. Almost all (232,120) were enrolments at the primary level, 3,277 at the secondary level and 68 at the tertiary level.[41]

Along with education, the social practices of arranged marriage and polygamy were increasingly debated in the last decades of the absolute monarchy. As early as 1890 an article in the literary review *Wachirayanwiset* criticized arranged marriage by positing a remarkably modern parallel between mate selection and consumer choice: 'If we want to buy something, which is the better way: let other people choose for us or decide for ourselves? . . . Selecting a spouse is more difficult than picking any other thing. It is not proper to allow senior relatives to choose a spouse for us.'[42] Proto-feminist views were aired in new periodicals that targeted a specifically female readership: *Kunlasatri* ('Sophisticated Lady') and the more progressive *Satriniphon* ('Lady's Magazine'), in which an article of 1915 claimed: 'These days the position of women is much improved. They study the same things as men and most of them are educated. They are coming out of the dark.' At the start of the Sixth Reign (1910–25), a French legal expert was appointed to advise the royal cabinet on the revision of the family law in the Code of the Three Seals, but the initiative had no outcome.[43] King Wachirawuth's position in the public debate about gender relations was significant; while the demise of the royal harem arguably depended more on his homosexual leanings than his progressive views, the king published a piece on 'The benefits and disadvantages of marriage' (1921), in which he acknowledged, 'there are many couples who do not live happily together. The husbands take minor wives and the wives have to stand the suffering.' A landmark court ruling in 1925 reflected growing social censure of polygamy by acceding to the plaintiff's request to divorce her husband after he had taken a minor wife.[44]

Early social critics blamed the patriarchal attitudes that hindered Siam's progress along the lines of Western nations on aristocratic culture, and thus sought the concurrent redefinition of class and gender boundaries. Printed media played a crucial role in popularizing bourgeois notions of monogamous marriage and romantic love. Thai classical literature contained a fair share of romantic and erotic tales but their mythological setting and poetic language heightened detachment from the realities of modern life. The new literary realism, instead, provided urban readers with both a mirror to contemporary social trends as well as behavioural models. The new forms of popular culture localized during the 1920s not only expressed the values and aspirations of the emerging middle class but were also consumed in modern public spaces, such as restaurants, ballrooms, tennis courts and cinemas, in which nubile women were able to socialize with the opposite sex even if under the supervision of a chaperon(e). For upper-class youth, who were increasingly educated abroad, 'love marriage was the way of civilized people'.[45]

The last absolute king, Prachathiphok, and his consort, Queen Rambaibarni, formed a monogamous couple in public as well as in private life. But although notions of romantic love, monogamy and gender equality had acquired a certain currency, cross-class marriage remained anathema among the elite. If Prince Mahidon, King Phumiphon's father, had caused a sensation by marrying a commoner, Sangwalya Chukramon (later to become the Princess Mother), up until 1932 the law forbade princesses from crossing social boundaries. Even outside the circle of royalty, prevailing class barriers prevented marriages between upper-class women and men from the middle strata.

Immediately after coming to power, the constitutional government implemented a number of legal measures to eliminate the gender boundaries of the old regime; both men and women were granted voting rights in 1932 and three years later the Civil and Commercial Code instituted monogamy by allowing the registration of only one marriage. The new civil code also abolished legal parental authority over the selection of the spouse, set the legal age of consent at seventeen for men and fifteen for women (raised to seventeen in 1976) and forbade marriage between blood relatives.

The new government also embarked on an ideological campaign to extol the moral and even martial virtues of women as fundamental national assets. Legendary figures of female warriors were accorded the status of national heroines and celebrated by monuments and on stage. Beauty too was celebrated as a quintessential female virtue by the institution of the Miss Siam beauty pageant, first held in December 1934 as part of the celebrations for the inaugural Constitution Day. In the markedly more nationalist climate of the Phibun era (1938–44), the state actively promoted family and motherhood. Group weddings were celebrated in Bangkok and in the provinces under the auspices of the government, which presented wedded couples with gifts and money; and a 'mother of the year' competition was instituted, on the model of Fascist Italy and Nazi Germany, to achieve the demographic target of a population of 40 million (it was only 17.4 million in the 1937 census). State propaganda instructed men to be attentive to their wives and compliment them as 'flowers of the nation', and wives to enhance sartorially their feminine appeal.

The loosening of social boundaries that occurred after the change of government reflected the novel democratic ethos as much as changes in class stratification. A combination of egalitarianism and social readjustment was behind the increase in cross-class marriages in the 1930s and '40s, when aristocratic and noble families that had lost status and wealth resigned themselves to marrying their daughters to members of the new bureaucratic elite. By the 1950s, the phase of shifting social and gender boundaries had come to an end and marriage connections were commonly used to cement alliances between important business and bureaucratic families. The growth of tertiary education introduced a new element in gender relations; the predominant male ratio of university graduates in the 1960s was reversed over the next two decades. Students' politicization in the 1970s was common to both male and female undergraduates, who participated in equal measure in the demonstrations that brought down the military regime. In the words of a female student leader, 'Thai women must find their own identity, must really examine the injustice in our economic, social and political systems, which oppress the people and Thai women.'[46] Thammasat University students ran a feminist periodical, *Lep* ('Fingernails'), and women's associations endeavoured to localize the politics and vocabulary of Western feminism. In fact, the gender politics of the student movement were shaped more by Mao's puritanical idea of women as aides to the male-carried revolution than by the anti-patriarchal and sexually liberating agenda of the feminist movement in Europe and America.

The social norms regulating gender relations within rural communities tended to be more relaxed than among urbanites and, as such, evolved according to a distinct pattern. The need for a workforce in the fields made female segregation untenable in the countryside. Young males and females could get to know each other at festivals and temple fairs, and parental authority was less pervasive than among the urban elites. Folk culture was characterized by a strong sentimentality evident in poems and songs: serenading was a traditional form of courtship in both the North and the North-east. Love marriages were thus not uncommon in rural communities. Elopements often took the place of formal marriages, especially when parents disapproved of the union or the groom could not afford to pay for a wedding ceremony or the 'bride price' to compensate her family (a custom which had spread from the urban upper class to wealthy peasants in the early part of the century). Monetary compensation also occurred in cases of manifest transgression of the interdiction on premarital sex, which in the symbolic order of peasant society was codified as an offence to the ancestral spirits watching over a woman's chastity. In Central Thailand the custom of matrilocality, whereby newly wed couples resided initially in the bride's family house, was observed as late as the 1960s; even the couple's own house was often built in the family grounds or its proximity.[47]

The relaxation of the boundaries preventing rural women from engaging in work away from the family field underpinned the surge in female migration to provincial towns and the capital since the 1960s (in the mid-1980s, 65 per cent of rural migrants in Bangkok were women). Internal migration had a twofold impact on gender relations. While separation from family and friends was a cause of emotional distress, a separate place of residence and salaried employment gave both men and women greater autonomy in choosing a spouse. Shifts in gender roles were reflected in legislation and government policies. The Family Act of 1976, which amended the Civil Code of 1935, granted women equal rights in divorce proceedings. As women came to constitute a significant segment of the industrial workforce and also made significant inroads in top bureaucratic and managerial positions, they were given special attention in the fourth National Economic and Social Development plan (1977–81) and the long-term Women's Development Plan (1982–2001). More than from government initiatives, however, improvements in the condition of women in the countryside and urban slums were the result of the activity of NGOs, which the authorities tended to regard with suspicion because of their perceived links to Western feminism.[48]

No discussion of Thai women's status can avoid the subject of prostitution. Throughout the nineteenth century brothels were staffed largely by female slaves. The release of debt slaves, the formation of a male salaried bureaucracy and the boom in Chinese immigration at the turn of the twentieth century were factors that contributed to the expansion of the sex trade both in Bangkok, where brothels were concentrated in the Chinese district, and in provincial towns. In 1909 Crown Prince Wachirawuth remarked sarcastically on the situation in Ranong, a peninsular town that was a pole of Chinese immigration: 'in the market they have beautiful ladies on sale. Doesn't this indicate that Ranong is civilized? Maybe not as civilized as Bangkok, since the "mansions of paradise" down there are not yet adorned by lanterns . . .'. The display of green lanterns outside brothels was one of the requirements introduced by the Prevention of Contagious Disease Act (1908) along with licensing, the payment of taxes and the registration of prostitutes, who needed to be at least fifteen years of age and undergo regular health checks. The coercion of young Chinese females into the transnational prostitution network that mirrored that of male emigration led to the promulgation of the Trafficking of Women and Children Act in 1928. By then, the number of prostitutes was estimated at 20,000 in Bangkok and 10,000 in provincial towns. Following the 1928 Act, procurers, often themselves women, started travelling to northern rural areas where indigent families sold their daughters into prostitution, known by the euphemism 'going south' (pai tai). The luring of country girls into prostitution figured also as a theme in one of the earliest Thai novels, Ying khon chua ('A woman of loose morals', 1937).[49]

It was the American military presence in the kingdom that gave international notoriety to Thai prostitution. The Act on Prostitution (1960), introduced by Marshal Sarit in his pursuit of 'propriety' (khwamriaproi), hypocritically outlawed brothels but channelled prostitution into alternative venues such as bars, nightclubs and massage parlours, whose activity was regulated by a subsequent act in 1966. After the end of the Vietnam War in 1975, international tourists replaced military personnel as main patrons of the sex trade, which expanded into a dominant sector of the informal economy despite remaining formally illegal. Thai women became sought-after commodities even in the international network of prostitution and brides-on-order extending from Japan to Europe.

Still, commonplace denunciation of poverty as the reason for women's embrace of prostitution was problematized by some researchers, who pointed to a more varied range of motivations as well as the fact that family shame was eased by the status that some households achieved within village communities thanks to the acquisition of consumer goods purchased with the remittances of prostitutes who acted as 'dutiful daughters'.[50]

The spread of HIV/AIDS since the late 1980s rendered prostitutes the segment of the population most exposed to the risk of contracting the fatal disease. Besides the dramatic impact it had on public health (estimates of the number of Thais infected by the late 1990s ranged between 500,000 and one million), the epidemic also brought to the fore the contradictions in gender identities that had been moulded on bourgeois notions of romantic love and sexual respectability in a context where polygamy was widespread and gender boundaries rather fluid. In 1929, on the eve of the fall of the old regime, a sex advice column in a Bangkok newspaper opined: 'it is the duty of the husband to learn about his wife's feelings and how to satisfy her'.[51] This open invitation to explore sexuality within the boundaries of monogamous marriage was indicative of egalitarian aspirations, but in the end the middle-class idea of moral respectability was focused on women and thus reinforced the double sexual standard that alimented polygamy and prostitution. Sexual orientations too were subjected to the new bourgeois morality; thus homosexuality, which had long been tolerated as a choice pertaining to an individual's private sphere, was pathologized as a sexual perversion in accordance with contemporary Western psycho-medical theories.

Since the 1970s, but mostly as a result of the HIV/AIDS pandemic, which was initially presented in Thailand as a homosexual disease in order not to jeopardize the preponderant share of the sex trade, most Thai homosexuals have been identifying themselves through the imported categories of gay, tom (shortened from 'tomboy') and di (shortened from 'lady'). Imported forms of identification allowed the Thai homosexual community to come out as a single bloc and thus engage in sexual politics, yet at the same time demarcated forms of sexuality according to the Judaeo-Christian binary gender system at the basis of post-classical Western civilization. In fact, northern and central Thai cosmogonies and folklore attest to a tripartite system that included the androgynous gender, that of *kathoei* (male transvestites and transsexuals), also known as 'the second type of woman' (*sao praphet ying*).[52] While the localization of cosmopolitan homosexual identities in the 1980s and '90s rendered *kathoei* almost folkloric, their exaggerated femininity was commodified in extremely popular beauty contexts, television programmes and stage shows that toured even overseas. But if the ample visibility of *kathoei* attested to the survival of a sexual identity seemingly out of touch with modernity, it also reinforced Thailand's international image as an exotic land where conventional sexual and gender boundaries are more easily transgressed.

three | Institutions

The monarchy, the Sangha and the bureaucracy (both civil and military) have been commonly regarded as, respectively, the nation's moral leader, the source of its spiritual well-being and the guardian of its territorial and cultural integrity. Major agents of the nation-building project (often but not always allied), the monarchy, the Sangha and the bureaucracy were also shaped as national institutions by that project. The monarchy and the bureaucracy both sought to mould the Sangha and make it organic to their political designs; and both the monarchy and the Sangha were successfully mobilized at times by social forces that opposed bureaucratic rule.

The monarchy, after extending its power and visibility at the turn of the twentieth century, experienced a decline that led to its demotion and near obliteration in the quarter century from 1932 to 1957. Under the incumbent sovereign the throne's aura was slowly restored, achieving by the early 1980s an unprecedented degree of popularity and, indeed, veneration, which increased further during the next quarter century. Given Thailand's historic constitution as a Buddhist polity, the Sangha had long played a political as much as a spiritual role by legitimating the power holders. Yet, only at the beginning of the twentieth century was the Sangha institutional-ized and put in the service of nation building. While the Sangha's authority was never challenged from without, by the 1980s its ossification opened a space for the proliferation of 'protestant' sects pandering to the spiritually needy new middle class while more or less heretical monks advocated a socially committed Buddhism. A professional civil service and armed forces were set up in the 1890s as the administrative and coercive pillars of the royal absolutist state. After the change of government in 1932, the bureaucracy assumed a more marked political role while the military rose considerably in influence within its ranks. By the late 1950s the military-bureaucratic apparatus had become an obstacle to nation building by inhibiting, through co-option and outright repression, the development of civil society. The removal of bureaucrats and generals from power in the early 1990s by an alliance of businessmen and politicians marked a momentous political transition even though the legacy of the bureaucratic regime lingered on.

The discussion of Thai institutions in this chapter is closely linked to that of ideologies in the next since both are premised upon common political events that are reviewed from different perspectives according to the two chapters' primary concerns.

The Monarchy

A fundamental chapter of the history of Thailand in the second half of the twentieth century concerns the reconstitution of the monarchical institution under the incumbent sovereign, King Phumiphon Adunlayadet (Rama IX), who officially ascended the throne in 1946. Following the abdication of Rama VII in 1935, the throne was but a nominal institution for a decade and a half. Similar to the monarchies of several countries in both Europe and Asia in the period between the First and the Second World Wars, Thailand's might have ended up in history's dustbin or survived as a purely ceremonial institution. Instead, the concomitance of political circumstances and the personal aspirations of a monarch who at the start of his reign was the embodiment of the elite's worldliness (born in 1927 in Cambridge, Massachusetts, to parents who were studying at Harvard University, he was educated in Switzerland, where he resided until 1951), involved the throne in nation building well beyond the institutional boundaries commonly associated with the system of constitutional monarchy instituted in 1932.

When the monarchical institution was re-founded in 1782, seventeen years after the collapse of the kingdom of Ayutthaya, it largely conformed to the Brahmanic model of divine kingship that had been favoured since the fifteenth century. Following the defeat of Angkor in the 1430s, the monarchs of Ayutthaya had fashioned themselves in imitation of the Khmer sovereigns as avatars of Hindu gods, semi-divine kings who exercised absolute power on their subjects as 'lords of life' (*chao chiwit*) and were removed from the secular domain by arcane rituals and taboos. This autocratic trait was partly tempered by the Buddhist notion of the 'righteous king' (*thammaratcha*) possessor of the ten virtues (*barami*). An illustration of the syncretic formulation of Thai kingship is found in the late fifteenth-century poem, *Khlong yuan phai* ('The defeat of the Yuan'):

> The king can create and protect the world like Brahma
> The king can rule and care for the people like Vishnu
> The king can destroy like the God Shiva
> The king possesses loving kindness like the Lord Buddha.[1]

The reality, of course, was quite different from such grand claims. Frequent challenges to royal authority by usurpers within the aristocracy caused chronic political instability and dynastic downfalls in the Ayutthaya period. Court politics in the Bangkok period were stable by comparison, although as late as 1875 factional struggles almost resulted in the deposition of the recently enthroned Chulalongkorn.

The Khmer-derived Ayutthayan model of kingship was matched in the nineteenth century by an alternative, paternalist model rooted in the ancient Thai past. Drawing from the stone inscription of King Ramkhamhaeng of Sukhothai, which he had allegedly discovered in 1833 when still a monk, King Mongkut configured the monarch as 'the father of the people' (*pho khun*). Mongkut even instituted some practices of direct government mentioned in the inscription, such as the submission of popular petitions to the throne. Regardless of doubts over its authenticity that were raised in the 1980s, the inscription furnished the authoritative source for the re-validation of the monarch as the guarantor of fair rule and public welfare in the face of

King Chulalongkorn,
the *modern* monarch.

the looming threat of Western colonialism. Indeed, during the four decades from Mongkut's accession in 1851 to the French blockade of the Chaophraya River in 1893, the Thai monarchy confronted both internal and external weaknesses. Internal weakness stemmed from the lack of control over aristocratic families that held offices, conducted trade and appropriated a large part of the revenues. External weakness resulted from the new colonial order imposed in the region by the British, the French and the Dutch. On several occasions during those forty years the Thai monarchy could have been abolished or reduced to a mere façade institution.

Eventually, the monarchy survived thanks to the combination of commercial and territorial concessions to Britain and France, the buffer role Siam came to play between their empires and apt Thai public relations. Despite the limitations imposed on Siam's tax and legal systems by the unequal treaties, the cabinet composed by King Chulalongkorn and his half-brothers, particularly the highly capable Damrong (minister of the Interior) and Thewawong (minister of Foreign Affairs), instituted the administrative reform that imposed Bangkok's control over the kingdom's outlying provinces. Because of the overlap of dynasty and government, state formation and the consolidation of royal power proceeded hand in hand in the second half of the Fifth Reign. The conflation of dynastic and national interests did not go uncontested; as early as 1885, a group of princes in the diplomatic service petitioned the sovereign for a constitution, but Chulalongkorn rejected the petition on the grounds that the uneducated masses placed their trust in the sovereign.

Even though absolute power could not be fully achieved because the unequal treaties with the West curbed fiscal and jurisdictional sovereignty, the monarchy came close to it precisely when its public image was being refashioned along the lines of national, demystified monarchy. Indeed, the Thai monarchy took on the mantle of civilizing institution while entrenching its own power and economic interests. Indic costumes and regalia were shelved in favour of sabres, sashes and Western uniforms, while state pageants in the global imperial style of the *fin de siècle* celebrated the monarchy as an institution in the service of the nation's progress rather than the conservation of the cosmic order. The modernization of the Thai monarchy contrasted with the colonial preservation of demoted South-east Asian royalty, whereby European officials sought to enshroud their 'rational' authority in the trappings of local tradition. Overseas education, mainly in England but also Prussia and Russia, provided royal princes with a worldly outlook; the last two absolute monarchs, Wachirawuth and Prachathipok, displayed many of the traits and mannerism of upper-class Britons – the former in the eccentric variant and the latter the conservative one.

Behind the public celebrations of Chulalongkorn's jubilee in 1908, the reiteration in royal allocutions of the need for 'unity' (*samakkhi*) highlighted increasing anxiety over the future of the absolute monarchy. From the Sixth Reign the monarchy's popularity underwent a steady decline, which many historians have blamed on King Wachirawuth's profligacy (royal expenditure averaged 10 per cent of the state revenue in his reign) and eccentric personality, especially his escape from state affairs into a make-believe world of thespian activities and his familiarity with male commoners, which alienated the old guard of princes (in 1915 Damrong resigned from the position of minister of the Interior he had held since 1892 after an argument with the king). Yet, an equally critical factor behind the decline of public favour towards the throne was Wachirawuth's open dismissal of constitutional government, which appeared increasingly anachronistic after the nationalist revolutions in Russia (1905), the Ottoman Empire (1908) and China (1911). Symptomatic of the declining popularity of the absolute monarchy were two aborted military coups, in 1912 and 1917, which however did not prompt any reform. Instead, Wachirawuth's successor returned senior royal princes to the government and instituted, in addition to the ministerial cabinet, a Supreme Council of State composed of five of his uncles and half-brothers, and a Privy Council, whose forty appointees all came from the royal family and the upper ranks of the officialdom.

King Prachathipok's initiatives won the monarchy little popular support. Half-hearted plans of introducing a constitution and a house of representatives were being entertained at the end of the 1920s when the Great Depression hit the Thai economy, then on a slow recovery from the budget deficit inherited from the previous reign. At that juncture, the hesitant Prachathipok became the focus of increasing public concern. The king relied on British financial advisers, who proposed higher taxation of salaried officials and a reduction in government spending for the 1931 budget; besides, the retention of the gold standard until May 1932 worsened inflation and depressed rice exports. In a speech given to a group of senior military officers in February 1932, Prachathipok admitted his shortcomings in the management of the crisis: 'I myself do not profess to know much about the matter and all I can do is listen to the opinions of others and choose the best . . . if I have made a mistake I really deserve to be excused by the officials and people of Siam'.[2]

With hindsight, it seems natural that such humbling statements by a monarch who still exercised absolute power should precede by only four months the bloodless coup d'état staged, on the morning of 24 June 1932, by a group of around sixty people who called themselves the People's Party (*khana ratsadorn*). Forty members of the court were apprehended and locked up inside the throne hall in the Dusit district; the king, who was away at his summer palace on the Gulf of Siam, returned to Bangkok two days later after being promised immunity. The leader of the People's Party, Paris-trained lawyer Pridi Phanomyong (1900–83), penned a rousing message to the nation: 'It is proven that absolute monarchy as a form of government has failed to restore the country's economy. It is so because the regime has never treated the people as human beings'.[3] However, despite such inflammatory rhetoric, the People's Party refrained from drastic action. The monarchical institution was retained and even granted some prerogatives under the permanent constitution that was drafted in the following months and promulgated by Rama VII in a solemn ceremony on 12 December 1932. Yet considerable tensions between the royalty and the new political leadership characterized the next couple of years.

In 1933 Prince Boworadet organized a royalist rebellion in which the king himself was allegedly implicated. In 1934 Prachathipok left for England, officially in need of ophthalmic treatment; in March 1935 he abdicated after the government rejected his request to have more power under the constitution. A few months later the government passed the Crown Property Act, which nationalized a share of the royal estates, replaced the Privy Purse with the Crown Property Bureau and limited the king's access to the properties under the purview of the Royal Household Bureau. In 1939, following two assassination attempts on the prime minister, Phibun Songkhram, which were blamed on a royalist conspiracy, King Prachathipok was formally upbraided for embezzlement of royal funds, his personal property confiscated and the display of his portrait prohibited. Given that he was childless and his brothers all dead at the time of his abdication, the line of succession had switched to the eldest son of the late Prince Mahidon, ten-year-old Anantha (Rama VIII). However, because of his youth and the political situation in Thailand, Anantha continued to reside with his mother and his younger brother Phumiphon in Switzerland, where the two were at school. Thus for more than a decade, including the crucial wartime period, Thailand had no resident monarch and the one living abroad was only a boy.

Anantha arrived in Bangkok with his mother and brother at the end of 1945. Six months later, on 9 June 1946, on the eve of their return to Switzerland, Anantha was found dead with a bullet through his head. The mysterious circumstances surrounding his death were never clarified even though three palace attendants charged with the king's murder were executed as scapegoats in 1955. While Pridi Phanomyong, the civilian leader of the 1932 revolution who was then prime minister (after serving as royal regent for the absentee Anantha during the war), was accused of regicide by his opponents, eighteen-year-old Phumiphon was declared king and immediately rushed back to Switzerland with his mother on a RAF plane amid fears that their lives were at risk.[4] Phumiphon returned briefly to Thailand in the spring of 1950 for his coronation and wedding ceremony, and permanently the following year; upon his return, he was tutored in courtly etiquette and the archaic royal language. Meanwhile Phibun, who had seized power in 1948, tried unsuccessfully to appease Rama IX by restoring the sovereign's constitutional prerogative of appointing the senate as well as royal offices (the Privy Council, Privy Purse and the Royal Guards) that had been abolished in the early 1940s. The confrontation climaxed in 1956, when Phibun took on himself the organization of the twenty-fifth Buddhist centenary and the king responded by distancing himself from the ceremonies.

Phibun's downfall marked the beginning of the royalist revival that restored the throne to the centre of the Thai political universe under the military's vigilant gaze. Historian Thak Chaloemtiarana has suggested that behind the apparent continuity of military rule, there was a profound difference between men like Phibun, who in their youth had been exposed to republicanism in France, and Sarit Thanarat and the officers of his generation, who had been educated entirely in Thailand and looked with deference to the throne. Sarit's deference towards the monarchical institution may have been sincere, but his eagerness to give it greater visibility was designed to obviate his own lack of legitimacy. Both in 1957, when he ousted Phibun (who fled to Japan), and the next year, when he replaced his own figurehead, Sarit made a public display of the king's endorsement. As noted by Roger Kershaw, this course of action, whereby the successful promoters of a coup paid formal obeisance to the throne and obtained in exchange the validation of an illegal act along with a royal decree that sanctioned the temporary closure of parliament and the suspension of the constitution, set a vicious pattern that has characterized Thai politics ever since.[5]

The royalist revival under Sarit bore more than a parallel to the colonial patronage of demoted South-east Asian monarchies. A major aspect of the royalist revival was the reconstitution of the aura of kingship through the reinstatement of Brahmanical ceremonies that had been scrapped after 1932. In 1960 the young royal couple undertook a tour of Europe and America, where they met with Western royalty and heads of state and even popular idols such as Benny Goodman and Elvis Presley. On their return, royal visits to the provinces and royal audiences to influential officials became a regular feature of the Ninth Reign. Radio and television, which started broadcasting in Thailand in 1955, played a crucial role in the monarchical revival by providing daily coverage of the royal family's activities, which opened the evening news bulletins, broadcast at the same time on every TV channel. Sarit also managed to forge a close connection between the throne and the military

Royals and Stars: Elvis Presley with Queen Sirikit and King Phumiphon in the USA, 1960.

King Phumiphon
surveys the Thai
countryside.

by having King Phumiphon assume honorary command of the
cadet academy and Queen Sirikit become honorary colonel of
the army regiment assigned to royal duties. A more sinister aspect
of the military patronage of the throne was the manipulation of
lese-majesty as a tool to silence political opponents. Under Sarit,
lese-majesty was transformed from an offence against the monarchy
to a much graver offence against national security.[6]

The royalist revival concerned the institutional as much as the
symbolic dimension of the monarchy. At the start of his reign King
Phumiphon's public image was that of a worldly Asian monarch
(not too different from the Shah of Iran, Reza Pahlevi), who divided his time between family and hobbies. From the mid-1960s
onwards, he took on a gravitas more appropriate to his maturity
and growing political role. Hedonistic activities were played down in

favour of the display of concern for the welfare of the rural population, whom the king and the royal family met in frequent visits
even to the kingdom's most remote provinces (some of which, like
Mae Hong Son, had never before been visited by a sovereign).
Phumiphon's persona in these tours – military uniform or fatigues
later replaced by plain clothes, a map of the visited area outspread
in his hands or folded in his pocket and a camera dangling from his
neck, to record the state of the countryside – became iconic of the
extra-constitutional authority that palace advisers such as Prince
Thaniniwat had been advocating for the throne since the late 1940s.[7]
Several 'royal projects' were initiated in the countryside, divided
between Queen Sirikit, who sponsored the revival of village crafts,
and King Phumiphon, who experimented with innovative agricultural techniques in the palace's orchards.

During the decade of rule by Sarit's associates that followed his
death in 1963 the throne continued to legitimate authoritarian governments, yet also tried to reach out to emerging social groups. The
whole royal family participated in the task of establishing a special
relationship with tertiary students – the sons and (increasingly) the
daughters of the provincial middle strata engendered by the economic growth of the 1960s – by presiding over degree convocations
in the capital's two universities and the new provincial universities
established in that decade; the King's Scholarship was also established in 1965. By the early 1970s the institutional re-foundation of
the monarchy had made considerable advances and Rama IX had
started to voice criticism of the military in his public speeches. In
October 1973 massive street demonstrations led by the student
movement demanded the resignation of the junta that two years
earlier had dissolved parliament and suspended the constitution.
The generals attempted to repress the protest and killed some
eighty demonstrators but failed to obtain the support of the
army commander and the validation of the throne; instead, King
Phumiphon requested the government's two strongmen to leave
the country and appointed a caretaker prime minister.[8] The students, who had rallied in the streets behind giant photographs of
the king and the queen, used as symbolic shields against the
charges of the army and the police, hailed Rama IX as the nation's
saviour.

If impatience with fifteen years of military rule and sympathy for the students' idealism had motivated the king's intervention in favour of constitutional rule in 1973, domestic and regional political developments over the next two years modified the throne's stand. The elected government's apparent inability to control social unrest, along with the American defeat in Vietnam and the overthrow of the Lao and Cambodian monarchies by communist armies, led the Thai monarchy to support the military reaction. It was no accident that the impetus behind the storming of Thammasat University by police and paramilitary forces on 6 October 1976 was the artfully spread rumour of lese-majesty involving the mock hanging of a puppet of Crown Prince Wachiralongkorn. But the extreme brutality of the backlash dissipated the popularity the throne had acquired with the students and intelligentsia over the previous decade. Thus, as early as 1977, Rama IX took steps to mend the monarchy's tarnished image by elevating his much admired daughter, Princess Sirinthorn, to the special rank of Maha Chakri, understood to be her de facto investiture as next in the line of succession to the crown prince (then lacking a male heir), whose private life and close association with the military were the cause of much rumour.

At the turn of the decade, in the context of a cautious political liberalization, the motto 'nation, religion and monarchy' was glossed over with the formula 'and democracy with the king as head of state'. Concurrently, a long series of royal celebrations started with the twin bicentenary of Bangkok and the Chakri dynasty (1982) and continued with the king's sixtieth birthday (1987) and the longest reign in Thai history (1988). The celebrations originated a hagiographic literature, such as *A Memoir of His Majesty King Bhumibol Adulyadej of Thailand* (1987), which articulated an extra-constitutional theory of kingship premised upon the oneness of the sovereign's sacred body and the nation's body politic:

Wherever there is joy or celebration, the King is there to bless the joy and share in the celebration. Wherever there is a problem, the King is there to look for a solution. Wherever there is distress or sorrow, the King is there to soothe, to assist, to strengthen. People thus become used to feel his presence in all instants of life. The King and the People become one.[9]

By the early 1990s there were plenty of signs of King Phumiphon's imminent apotheosis but none more eloquent than the televised royal audience, on 20 May 1992, with the two political contenders – unelected Prime Minister Suchinda Kraprayun and his opponent Chamlong Simuang – behind the bloody clashes of the previous days. Kneeling at the king's feet in front of 50 million viewers, the two humbly received his admonition to take a step back and stop the violence in the streets. Two days later Suchinda resigned, opening the way for a royally appointed caretaker prime minister and King Phumiphon, who had defused Thailand's most dramatic political crisis in years as a veritable *deus ex machina*, was again hailed as the nation's saviour as in 1973. For the rest of the 1990s, punctuated by the celebrations for his golden jubilee (1996) and astrologically auspicious seventy-second birthday (1999), Rama IX spoke openly against the 'money politics' that sustained the rise to ministerial offices of corrupt politicians and formulated a vision of sustainable development and economic self-reliance that the financial crisis of 1997 made especially compelling. The virtually unanimous consensus about the monarchy's institutional centrality was underscored by the constitution of 1997, which reaffirmed the sacredness and inviolability of the sovereign and shielded him from possible criticism.[10]

'Deus ex machina' – King Phumiphon granting audience to generals Suchinda Kraprayun (left) and Chamlong Simuang (centre), 20 May 1992.

Following the appointment of Thaksin Chinawat as prime minister, open contrasts emerged for the first time since the post-war Phibun regime between the throne and the head of government. On more than one occasion King Phumiphon openly criticized Thaksin, who had no choice but to bow to royal admonitions. In June 2006 Rama IX celebrated his sixtieth accession anniversary in the presence of royal guests from twenty-five countries and amidst much public jubilation. One of the country's most respected papers wrote that the jubilee 'had an enormous impact on the Thai people. It has created a long-lasting spiritual bond between them and their monarch in a way that people from other cultures may find hard to understand'.[11] The celebrations took place, however, in the tense climate of confrontation between government and opposition, of which the monarchy was not a neutral spectator. When in September Thaksin was ousted by a coup, the throne promptly legitimated an action that marked an unwelcome return to the interference of the military in the political process. Indeed, the coup demonstrated the throne's willingnesss to exploit its moral authority to act politically in the nation's alleged interest. But while King Phumiphon's personal charisma may make such a role palatable to the majority of Thais, the future of the monarchical institution will clearly depend on his successor's ability to tap into the immense symbolic capital that Rama IX accumulated in his far from ordinary reign.

The Bureaucracy

The backbone of the monarchy's project of state formation initiated in the last decade of the nineteenth century was a modern bureaucracy organized along functional lines and staffed by salaried officials. Traditionally, the administration of the kingdom was based on a territorial system in which two departments (the *mahatthai* and *kalahom*) were in charge of the northern and the southern regions respectively. In the reign of King Trailok (1448–88), a reform patterned after the Khmer empire placed the capital and the surrounding region under the administration of the treasury department (*phraklang*). The eventual outcome of this reform was an overlap of territorial and functional responsibilities.[12] Princes and noblemen, who formed the upper ranks of the bureaucracy, were remunerated by the treasury; local officials, instead, appropriated part of the revenues from the provinces under their authority and extracted fees in kind and service from the local populations – a practice that was termed, with an apt verbal imagery, 'eating the country' (*kin muang*).

The creation of a professional bureaucracy capable of separating personal interest from public office was part and parcel of the localization of Western technologies of governance informed by what sociologist Max Weber termed 'instrumental rationality' (*Zweckrationalität*). Training of civil officials started in the 1880s at the palace's Royal Page School, which at the turn of the century gave way to the Civil Service College; this, in turn, formed the core of Chulalongkorn University, whose function as a hothouse for the cultivation of future civil servants continued throughout the twentieth century. The bureaucracy's *ésprit de corp* was given sartorial configuration by a civilian uniform, comprised of a buttoned-up white jacket worn over a folded black sarong (called *ratcha patten*, 'royal pattern'), which in the 1930s was replaced by a military-style white uniform. In 1887 a Royal Cadet Academy was also founded on the model of the Prussian military school to train a professional body of officers. Although only princes and the scions of the higher nobility were initially admitted to the Civil Service College and the Cadet Academy, their doors were soon opened to young men from the lower nobility and wealthy families in order to satisfy the needs of the new centralized administration (Sino-Thai were, however, prevented from enrolling in the military academy until the mid-1970s). From the early 1900s commoners also started to be recruited, on the interior minister's recommendation, to be trained as clerks and district officers. As a result, the ranks of the bureaucracy expanded between 1890 and 1919 from around 12,000 to 80,000 employees, the largest concentration being in the Ministry of Interior, which already by 1910 counted some 15,000 employees.

Civil officials were, and still are, known as 'servants of the crown' (*kha ratchakan*); but with the massive expansion of their ranks in the early decades of the twentieth century, the principle that their authority stemmed from the sovereign was challenged by the modern, rational principle that it stemmed from the law. This

'Instrumental rationality': civil servants and officers with foreign advisers, c. 1900.

contrast in defining the source of bureaucratic legitimacy mirrored the social distinction between officials of high rank, colloquially known as 'big people' (*phu yai*), and of middle and lower rank, or 'small people' (*phu noi*). The latter's resentment at the pre-eminence of birth and social connections over individual capability in determining ranks and salaries within the bureaucracy became a major cause of dissatisfaction in the final years of the old regime, when the Civil Service Act (1928) was enacted. The new initiative of sending middle-rank officials to study abroad on government scholarships fed the expectation that they would attain relatively high positions upon their return, with the ironic result that existing inequities were highlighted. Class-based exclusion was even more apparent in the army, where the resentment of junior army officers at royalty's monopoly of high ranks and their abuse of power was behind the aborted anti-monarchical plot of 1912. Ironically, it was a small group of young civil and military officials, who had met in Paris while studying on government scholarships and founded while there the People's Party, which finally put an end to royal absolutism.

If from the 1890s to the 1920s the bureaucracy had been an instrument of nation building in the service of the monarchy, after 1932 it continued to carry out that project according to its own political designs. Governments from 1932 to 1992 – except for the period 1973–6 – were the expression of the military-bureaucratic apparatus rather than the parliamentary system; and, indeed, were put in

'His Excellency's Relatives'
(*Sayam rat*, 15 September 1923).

ลูกหลานว่านเครือของท่าน

power by putsches more often than elections. Under the paternalist cloak inherited from the monarchical regime, the bureaucracy was able to domesticate civil society by permitting or disallowing political parties, barring student and labour unions, controlling the media through ownership and censorship, and neutralizing the judiciary (itself a rather conservative institution) through the periodical imposition of martial law and rule by decree. The bureaucracy and the military came to be structured internally by vertical patron-client relations as well as by horizontal peer ties. The latter were especially strong among same-year graduates of the Royal Cadet Academy, which was re-founded in 1948. The armed forces, in charge of national security and the maintenance of law and order, assumed the principal role within the military-bureaucratic apparatus (between 1938 and 1988 the office of prime minister was held by military officers for all but eight years). Within the armed forces, which even during the Pacific War were hardly ever engaged in combat action, the army dominated over other corps; however, rivalry with the police was intense, especially in the 1950s when the police chief, General Phao, vied for US military aid with the army commander, Marshal Sarit. Though at the top of the bureaucratic pyramid, the army was fragmented among competing factions that were behind the sequence of coups and counter-coups that characterized Thai politics from 1947 to 1992.

In the 1960s American political scientists working within the framework of modernization theory dubbed Thailand a 'bureaucratic polity' and argued that the bureaucracy there governed independently of the legislature and the judiciary by virtue of the parcelling of power among rival cliques. In this perspective, the civil service's apparent inefficiency responded to an unofficial 'operational code' designed to reduce the officials' workload as well as tensions with the ordinary population while extracting wealth from them. Rather than following the principle of 'instrumental rationality', the Thai bureaucracy was said to pursue 'patrimonial' values: inflation of one's personal status, enjoyment of legal impunity and pursuit of conspicuous lifestyle.[13] The notion of the Thai bureaucratic polity as a hindrance to political democratization became hugely influential in academic discourse. In fact, such a notion was also functional in the US Cold War strategy of 'democratizing' Thailand – that is, render it politically stable in order to prevent a possible communist takeover. Perversely (as so often in US foreign policy), the meritorious objective of democratizing Thailand was pursued by bolstering unelected, authoritarian governments, with the result that the bureaucratic polity was consolidated and the process of democratization delayed until the 1990s. Besides, training and graduate education of Thai civil and military officials in the USA, while designed to expose them to a professional and technocratic outlook, ended up boosting their rank and, hence, their individual power as patrons upon their return home.[14]

During the parliamentary interlude of 1973–6, the relationship between the military-bureaucratic apparatus and the national assembly were tense. Provincially elected members of parliament, who lobbied on behalf of their constituents for the realization of infrastructures and restraints on local officials, were resented for undermining centrally planned projects and the unwritten principle of the bureaucracy's impunity.[15] Defending the country against the communist threat provided the military-bureaucratic apparatus with a convenient mask for the protection of self-interest. Thus, when the ideological furore of the reactionary backlash abated, the main political priority became re-establishing the paternalist basis of bureaucratic rule. In the early 1980s the armed forces defeated the communist insurgency and re-asserted their institutional mission as 'the defence of the nation, the protection of national independence and democracy with the king as head of state'.[16] At the same time, the newly established National Identity Board and National Culture Commission did the state's hegemonic work by promoting Thai identity and the nation's cultural unity.

As the emergence of new social formations – the new middle class and provincial capitalists – modified the social landscape, the bureaucracy saw fit to co-opt them into a tactical alliance that ensured political stability until the early 1990s. Analysts with a penchant for the jargon of political science termed this alliance 'liberal corporatism' and conceptualized it as the overcoming of the bureaucratic polity.[17] In fact, the alliance, colloquially termed 'money politics', from the open exchange of emoluments for electoral support, came to depend increasingly on provincial power-brokers or 'godfathers' (chaopho). It thus antagonized the higher echelons of the military, who in February 1991 tried to rectify the situation by resorting to an old-style coup. The initial response to the coup from the capital's business and professional elites as well as the throne was favourable, especially because the military junta moved swiftly to appoint a cabinet of technocrats; it was the thirst for power of the coup's leader, General Suchinda Kraprayun, that ignited public protest. The violence of 'Black May' did considerable damage to the military's claim to be the institution in charge of the protection of Thai citizens and arguably marked the definite demise of the bureaucratic polity.

The quick disappearance of generals from the public scene after May 1992 was followed by the new army commander's pledges of professionalization and non-intervention in the political process; however, in the tradition of bureaucratic impunity, the officers responsible for the killings were granted amnesty. Parliament, for its part, abrogated the legislative provisions that validated the army's coercive power and cut the share of the national budget spent on defence; the military's sources of income, both legal (ownership of land and radio and TV channels) and illegal (smuggling and protection), also shrunk considerably.[18] This trend was partly reversed from 2001 by the Thaksin government. The military were rehabilitated by increasing their procurement budget and restoring their influence over the media and foreign policy; the civil bureaucracy, on the other hand, was repeatedly chastised for its torpor and ignorance of the globalized economy and pressed to adopt a managerial ethos. The ministerial structure was streamlined, senior bureaucratic appointments made directly by the cabinet and provincial governors instructed in managerial skills. Above all, it was Thaksin's reiterated denigration of civil servants as incapable of generating wealth that signalled, at the level of public rhetoric at least, the transition to the post-bureaucratic polity.[19]

The Sangha

The institutionalization of the Thai Sangha at the turn of the century had a double inspiration: a reformist one, grounded in religious modernism; and a political one, designed to create a Buddhist ecclesia as a pillar of the nascent nation-state. Late nineteenth-century religious modernism imposed uniformity across faiths worldwide through the establishment of centralized ecclesiastic hierarchies, the systematization and mechanical reproduction of scriptures, and doctrinal and liturgical formalization – and in so doing tied religions intimately to nation-building projects. The Sangha Act of 1902 (revised by the acts of 1941 and 1962 and the amendment to the latter in 1992) put the monkhood in the service of state formation by undermining the religious legitimacy of local lords whose domains were incorporated in the kingdom's territory, and of nation building as the provider of basic education.

Throughout the nineteenth century Buddhism in Siam was characterized by scriptural and liturgical variations. One major difference concerned the vernacular scripts employed in the transcription of the canon and commentaries in Pali. In the central region and the South, Pali texts were transcribed using a script (*khom*) derived from ancient Khmer; instead, the script used in the North and the Northeast (*tham*) was based on the Mon alphabet. Monks (*phra*) able to read the Pali scriptures were celebrated for their learning and were granted titles by local rulers, who appointed the abbots of the main monasteries within their domains from within the ranks of the royalty and the nobility. After the fall of Ayutthaya, the Sangha was refounded by Rama I, who issued various decrees to discipline monastic practice and reorder the system of clerical ranking that was the counterpart to the *sakdina*. The Sangha's refoundation was sealed by the organization in 1788 of the ninth Buddhist council.[20]

In the 1830s the future King Mongkut, then abbot of the prominent Wat Boworn Niwet, set his mind on purifying Buddhism from doctrinal and liturgical corruption. Mongkut's rationalist approach stemmed from scriptural observance and empiricist leanings but was also a response to the Christian missionaries' dismissal of Buddhist rituals and metaphysics as superstitious. Mongkut's reformation eventually led to the institution of the Thammayutnikai ('order of the adherents to the dharma'), which created a division with the rest of the Sangha, the Mahanikai ('great order'). Thammayut monasteries were founded in Bangkok under the patronage of the royalty and their abbots selected among Mongkut's disciples. Although Thammayut monks were a minority, their higher educational levels and royal connections placed them on the forefront of the institutionalization of the Sangha under the lead of Prince Wachirayan, a son of Mongkut, who in 1892 (the same year as the institution of the centralized administration) was appointed head of the Thammayut. Soon after he started compiling with Prince Damrong, the interior minister, the curriculum for novices and monks. Their exercise was the basis for the introduction, as part of the Sangha Act, of standard textbooks, written mostly by Wachirayan himself, which promoted doctrinal orthodoxy, further reinforced by the subsequent introduction of a national system of clerical examinations.[21]

The reform of 1902 had two objectives. The first was the subordination of the entire monkhood to a new figure of royally appointed religious leader, the supreme patriarch, himself an agent of the state. Prince Wachirayan, as the head of a Supreme Council of Elders and first supreme patriarch, oversaw the creation of a centralized Sangha that mirrored closely the four-tier system of territorial administration instituted in 1892. The second objective was to promote general education in line with the Provincial Education Act of 1898. Schools were built inside many monasteries in both towns and villages and pupils schooled in the Central Thai language as well as in history, geography, science and religion. Among other provisions, the reform restricted the ordination of monks and novices to senior monks who had the supreme patriarch's authorization. The reform also placed the Mahanikai and Thammayut orders under a common hierarchy, although ecclesiastical offices were generally entrusted to Thammayut monks.[22]

While Buddhism had long represented in the Thai polities a source of political legitimization, the 1902 Act made the Sangha an instrument of ideological indoctrination. Prince Wachirayan emphasized at the start of his pontificate that monks, while subject to monastic discipline, 'must also subject themselves to the authority which derives from the specific and general law of the state'.[23] When in 1918 Siam joined the Allies in the First World War, the Prince Patriarch sanctioned the intervention as conforming to Buddhist teachings. Also critical was the continuing role of temple schools throughout the 1920s, since government schools were established in most provinces only a decade after the promulgation of the Compulsory Education Act (1921). The regimentation of the Sangha under the Thammayut order created, however, also resentment and opposition among monastic communities at the periphery of the modern state that drew their identity from regional religious traditions, such as the merit-making public recitation of the Vessantara Jataka (the tale of the Buddha's life before his last incarnation). In the North and the North-east in particular, monks sympathetic to animistic beliefs resisted the religious modernism of the zealous and city-educated Thammayut reformers as a challenge to their status. Thammayut monasteries tended to be established on the outskirts of villages, at the centre of which stood the main

Mahanikai monastery. But other monks, following the example of the highly respected guru, *Achan* Man Phurithat (1870–1949), practised meditation in forest retreats, attracting for this the suspicion of the state authorities until they acquired fame as being endowed with thaumaturgic powers.[24]

The fall of the old regime also affected the monkhood, but the whole decade of the 1930s was necessary for a generational change to take place and shift the Sangha's internal balance of power from Thammayut to Mahanikai. In 1941 the government passed an act that reorganized the Sangha according to the constitutional political system by demoting the supreme patriarch to titular head of the Sangha and replacing the Council of Elders with a larger legislative body, the Sangha Council (mirroring the national assembly), in which the numerically preponderant Mahanikai held the majority of the seats. The 1941 Act resulted in a protracted sectarian conflict within the Sangha instigated by the demoted Thammayut order, whose supremacy was finally restored in 1962 by yet another Sangha Act, promulgated by Marshal Sarit Thanarat. This act recentralized the administrative and legislative authority in the office of the supreme patriarch and reconstituted the Council of Elders; it also ratified the administrative separation of Thammayut and Mahanikai, ending earlier attempts to reunify the Sangha. Even as the act made defamation of Buddhism and the Sangha prosecutable under the law, the Sarit regime harassed socially progressive monks such as *Phra* Phimontham,[25] while it enlisted others in the government's campaigns of development and the fight against communism through the newly created Religious Affairs Department. Under the scheme of 'ambassadors of the dharma' (*thammathut*), monks educated in Bangkok's Buddhist university, Mahachulalongkorn, were sent to preach state-endorsed Buddhism to North-easterners and ethnic minorities in the border areas, who were deemed especially vulnerable to communist propaganda.

The royalist revivalism initiated at the turn of the 1950s and '60s was mirrored by a reversion among the urban elite and middle strata to ritualistic and metaphysical forms of religiosity, which further marginalized those monks who espoused a rationalist and socially progressive Buddhism. However, the growing political conflict in the country brought to the fore the divisions within the

Sangha and produced fractures along doctrinal as well as ideological fault lines. On the one hand, the ecclesiastical hierarchy showed open support to the dictators who had been ousted in 1973 (the temporary ordination of one of them, Thanom Kittikhachorn, upon his return from exile in September 1976 unleashed the chain of events that culminated in the student massacre in October). In his sermons the infamous monk Kittiwuttho went as far as inciting the killing of leftist activists, depicted as demonic beings intent on destroying nation, religion and monarchy, as a way of accruing merit. On the contrary, the prominent monk and theologian Phutthathat (better known in the Pali form Buddhadasa, 1906–93), denounced the US aerial bombing of Vietnam and considered a possible communist takeover of Thailand less deleterious than the destruction of Buddhism by Western materialism. Phutthathat upheld Buddhism as a vehicle for political democratization, espoused the notion of 'dhammik-socialism' and emphasized morality as the essential quality of political leadership.[26]

The middle class's thirst for spiritual fulfilment spurred in the 1970s the birth of new religious movements that challenged the Sangha's authority. Phutthathat's critique of the national Buddhist ecclesia was the main inspiration behind the foundation in 1975 of the puritanical sect Santi Asok ('Peace, No Sorrow') by Phra Phothirak, a former television entertainer who had been previously ordained in both the Thammayut and Mahanikai. Santi Asok advocated a return to the fundamentals of Buddhist ethics and openly challenged the authority of the institutional Sangha by ordaining monks and nuns – and, in so doing, broke state laws. Phra Phothirak's refusal to register Santi Asok as a sect within the official Sangha and his pronouncements strongly critical of the religious establishment led to his legal prosecution, but also won him considerable support from progressive and disenfranchised strata. While monks ordained within Santi Asok eventually agreed to comply with the Sangha's code, the sect's wider social concerns led to the creation in 1988 of a political party of Buddhist inspiration, Phalang Tham ('Force of Dharma'). Another 'protestant' sect, Thammakai ('Dharma-Body'), formed in the early 1970s in response to middle-class demands for a spiritual reformation of the institutional Sangha. Similar to Santi Asok, Thammakai imposed a strict moral code on both monks and lay practitioners, but unlike the social concerns of the former, espoused an individual path to nirvana based on meditation (practised according to a technique of mental visualizations developed earlier in the century by the monk *Luang* Phosot). Also, as a sect registered under the Mahanikai, Thammakai operated within rather than outside the institutional Sangha. Its monastery, located in Bangkok's northern outskirts, attracted largely urban upper and middle strata devotees. As a reflection of the social composition of its followers, the Thammakai teachings started increasingly to focus on material achievements.[27]

The spread of consumerism and political corruption that characterized Thailand in the 1980s and '90s was reflected in the commercialization of Buddhist practices (known in Thai as *phutta panit*) and sexual and financial scandals involving prominent monks. An enquiry by the Religious Affairs Department found in 2000 that the abbot of the Thammakai monastery, known for driving around in a Rolls-Royce, had embezzled 36 million Baht of donations intended for the construction of a new, gigantic monastery (the fund-raising campaign involved had been the recipient of the National Management Association's prize for best marketing strategy). Within and around the Sangha there emerged also various 'cults of prosperity'. One such cult was centred on *Luang* Phokhun, a North-eastern monk who after years as a hermit in the forest started producing amulets with his effigy that acquired national reputation for being miraculous after individuals who wore them survived the collapse of a hotel in 1993; by the following year, *Luang* Phokhun's monastery was raking in 100,000 Baht on weekdays and one million at weekends from the sale of his amulets. The commercialization of Buddhism was countered by sects of committed monks such as Sekhiya Tham ('Training in the Dharma', founded in 1989), which were involved in social work and the protection of the environment both through symbolic action – the ordination of trees, wrapped in saffron cloth – and civic mobilization – an example of which was the 'March of the Dharma', staged in 1996 to protest against ecological degradation in the southern province of Songkhla.[28]

The state's design to impose discipline and uniformity over the Sangha was thus far from fulfilment a century after its institutionalization; on the contrary, ecclesiastic, doctrinal and ethical differences were rife. After the amendment to the Sangha Act of 1962, passed in the politically momentous year of 1992, frustrated hopes for a renewal of the Sangha's bureaucratized structure, progressive monks continued to press for reform; conservative ones, on their part, reacted against the non-confessional stand of the constitution of 1997 by campaigning in favour of an amendment that would designate Buddhism as Thailand's national religion. Despite such divisions, the Sangha retained its traditional role as a vehicle of male upward social mobility; it was no accident that, at the millennium's end, North-easterners, the most disadvantaged segment of the Thai population, constituted more than half of the monastic community. Still, the Sangha could not avoid facing the consequences of modernity. In this sense, materialistic degeneration and social commitment within the Sangha reflected sensibilities present in the bourgeois ethos, placing both equally distant from the ascetic ideal of Theravada. This is probably why, for all the involvement of Thai monks in secular affairs, only forest monks living in meditation retreats commanded true respect and veneration as Buddhist saints who had extinguished the chain of rebirth by renouncing worldly desires.

four | Ideologies

A distinctive aspect of the political and intellectual history of the twentieth century was the internationalization of ideologies that had originated in Europe since the Enlightenment. Modern ideologies already possessed a global vocation: liberal democracy, with its free-market corollary, articulated purportedly universal values of liberty and entrepreneurship; nationalism boosted a group of people's common origins and distinct identity vis-à-vis other ones; and socialism and communism were by definition internationalist. But in their adaptation to contexts that differed historically, socially and culturally from their place of origination, ideologies were transformed. In the British colonies of India and Burma as well as in the Dutch East Indies, nationalism emerged in the 1920s as an anti-colonial ideology; in China and Vietnam communism was in the 1930s and '40s a vehicle of nationalism; and in the Philippines under US patronage democracy served in the post-war period as a cover for authoritarianism.

Despite the purported uniqueness of Thailand's political history, modern ideologies had as significant an impact there as in the rest of Asia. This political significance was underscored by the politics of translation. Prince Wan Waithayakorn, who from the 1930s coined a great many words in the Thai lexicon of politics and social sciences, expressed cogently the political import of translation: 'It is the Thai language that will guarantee the security of the Thai nation. This is because if we favour the use of Thai transliterations of Western words about ideas, we may walk too fast ... But if we use Thai words, and hence coin new ones, we will walk in an unhurried way.'[1] Prince Wan's belief raises an intriguing parallel to the role of translation in the colonial project of the West and stands in contrast to the assimilation of political terms to the vocabulary of other South-east Asian languages by means of transliteration.[2] Lexical translation entailed conceptual adaptation. Thai nationalism, communism and, especially, democracy were distinctive ideologies even as they emanated from global intellectual trends – a process that had a parallel in the domain of social and cultural practice examined in the next chapter.

Nationalism

Orthodox historiography attributes a father and a date of birth to Thai nationalism: King Wachirawuth and the Sixth Reign (1910–25). The conventional view of Thai nationalism frames it as an exception in the region, where nationalism was anti-colonial in nature, and rather more similar to that of Europe, where states forged unitary identities by harnessing linguistic, religious and historical commonalities – and inventing them when necessary. In doing so, argues Eric Hobsbawm, nationalism was used as the ideological tool for favouring capitalism, opposing socialism and mobilizing society against 'criminal', 'subversive' and 'alien' elements within it.[3] Hobsbawm's critical characterization of European nationalism suits perfectly Thailand's experience down to Wachirawuth's appropriation of the tropes of anti-Semitism to demonize Chinese immigrants as unassimilable outsiders and parasites who drained away the kingdom's wealth. Following Benedict Anderson's more benign, if somewhat overstated, reading of nationalism as the product of social imagination fostered by 'print capitalism', revisionist historians have reframed Thai nationalism as a contested ideological terrain in which a 'royal' or 'official' nationalism was challenged by a 'popular' nationalism over the two decades leading to the overthrow of the absolute monarchy in 1932.[4]

The notion of opposing nationalisms begs the question of whether the two shared a common matrix or had separate intellectual genealogies. To answer this question one must start by examining the language of politics. Different from the colonies, where nationalism was forged linguistically in the native tongue and in opposition to the language of the colonial elites that claimed the monopoly of civilization, in Thailand official and popular nationalism employed the same language. The lexical material employed to forge a nationalist discourse originated in the laws and treaties drawn up at the turn of the century, for which foreign terms had to be translated into Thai. Some of these terms, such as *ratthaban* (government) and *banmuang* (homeland), were coined by compounding existing words; other terms were already in use but underwent a resignification, such as *issaraphap* (independence; originally, royal authority) and *chat* (nation), a Sanskritic word whose original meaning of 'stock, family' was the cognate of *natio*, the Latin etymon of 'nation'. *Chat*, used also to form compounds (e.g., *chonchat*, national; *sanchat*, nationality), invoked an idea of national community as being identified by common ethnic lineage, an idea that was at odds with the pre-modern notion of Siam as a racially diverse kingdom.

The term *chat* was employed in writing as early as 1889 to refer to the ancestral community of the Thais and again after the Franco-Thai crisis of 1893 in terms of a *chat thai* distinct from other *chat*.[5] David Streckfuss has explained the conflation of nationality with ethnicity as the result of French attempts to demarcate Siam's territorial boundaries along ethnic lines, to which 'the Thai royalty responded by appropriating and "creatively adapting" the concept of race and extending Thai racial boundaries to the existent territorial limits'. The Thai authorities spelt out that, of all the various branches of the Tai race, the 'Siamese alone have assimilated Western civilization and maintained an independent position among the nations of the world'.[6] Still, nationality under the absolute monarchy was defined largely in cultural rather than racial terms. The national community invoked by *chat* transcended ethnic as well as social differences for it was unified by the Buddhist religion and loyalty to the monarch acting according to the dharma (Thai: *tham*), or moral law – a formulation that marginalized the kingdom's Malays more than other ethnic groups such as the Lao and the Chinese because they were non-Buddhist rather than because they were non-Thai.

The model of Thai proto-nationalism would appear to be the United Kingdom, where in the early nineteenth century a 'British' identity was created in order to unify politically the linguistically, culturally and historically distinct English, Scottish and Welsh peoples (though not – in a country where the sovereign was also the head of the Church – the Catholic Irish). Like other inventors of tradition, King Wachirawuth promoted his vision of the Thai nation through the creation of national holidays (Rama v Memorial Day and Chakri Day); the motto 'nation, religion and monarchy' (*chat sasana phramahakasat*), moulded on the British 'God, king and country'; the paramilitary corps of the Wild Tigers (*Sua pa*) and a youth organization modelled on the Boy Scouts; and the tricolour flag (with the white standing for Buddhism, red for the blood of the nation and blue for the throne), which officially replaced the flag with the white elephant on red ground on the same day (1 October 1917) when volunteers' selections were opened for the expeditionary force to be dispatched to the European theatre of war. Also concerned with nationality were two laws promulgated in 1913: the Nationality Act, which decreed everybody born in the kingdom to be a Siamese subject regardless of the father's nationality; and the Family Names Act, which required individuals to adopt family names to conform to civilized norm and promote awareness of patrilineal lineage (Wachirawuth himself coined names for families in the nobility that indicated their place of origins).[7]

Because nationalism notoriously defined itself against an enemy, conflict was critical to the emergence of European nationalisms after the Napoleonic Wars. The colonial pacification of South-east Asia precluded the exploitation of conflict as a source of national unification in Siam. Thus (as discussed at length in Chapter 7), two symbolic enemies were evoked to support nation building in the first decades of the twentieth century: a historic, external enemy represented by the Burmese; and a present, internal enemy embodied by the Chinese, who despite their presence in the kingdom were now demonized as a threat to the nation's economic and cultural well-being. The idea of race assumed increasing importance in the formulation of Thai nationalism in the 1920s as a result of ethnographic and historical investigations about the origins of the Thais. Ironically, it was an American missionary,

W. C. Dodd, who proposed in his *The Tai Race* (1923), published
posthumously, that the Tais were one of the world's most ancient
civilizations and that, in their southern migration from their place
of origin in China, had founded in the sixth century AD the kingdom
of Nanchao before dispersing across a vast region from Yunnan to
east Bengal; it was in Siam, however, that one found 'the only Tai
known in the history and civilization of the present-day world'.
Dodd's theories were popularized domestically by *Khun* Wichitmat's
Lak thai ('The origins of the Thais', 1928) and *Luang* Wichit
Watthakan's *Prawatisat sakorn* ('Universal history', 1930), which exerted great influence on the development of a pan-Thai ideology.
Nationalist sentiments were also behind public calls to learn from
Japan's successful example of self-styled modernity based on the
samurai's martial code, or bushido.[8]

It remains difficult, however, to assess the role that ideological
currents at the turn of the 1920s and '30s played in bringing down
the absolute monarchy. For some historians this event represents
but a transition of power from the royal elite to a coterie of 'new
men' who, despite their chosen name as the People's Party, lacked a
popular base and soon revealed their true colours by turning to
authoritarianism.[9] As already mentioned, the old regime's social
inequalities were much debated by the press in the 1920s and the
government's hesitant response to the impact of the global recession at the end of the decade further weakened the legitimacy of the
absolute monarchy. In this light, the coup of June 1932 can be considered the equivalent of the Russian revolution of 1905 or the
Young Turks revolution of 1908: the rebellion of a vanguard of
'patriots' against autocratic regimes that were perceived to be an
obstacle to the nation's social advancement. The constitutional
government saw the key to national progress in a radical change of
economic policy, especially since the recession had exposed the
dominant role of foreigners in commerce and industry. After the
rejection of the economic plan proposed by Pridi Phanomyong in
1932 as 'communistic', the government headed by *Phraya* Phahon
Phonphayuhasena (1933–38) took nationalizing measures such as
the creation of state industries, the introduction of a Thai quota for
workers in rice mills (owned almost entirely by Chinese) and
restrictions on Western and Chinese enterprises. This economic

nationalism was, in fact, but an instance of a common trend in Europe and America, whereby governments attempted to counteract the consequences of the Great Depression.

Different from economic policy, the cultural nationalism of the 1930s was marked by substantial continuity with the nationalist imagining of Rama VI. The critical figure in this respect was *Luang* Wichit Watthakan (1898–1962). Diplomat, state minister, polymath and ideologue, Wichit was the protagonist of four decades of Thailand's intellectual history, from the twilight of absolutism to the dictatorship of Sarit Thanarat (they both died in the same year). After working for six years in the Siamese legation in Paris, where he participated in the founding of the People's Party, Wichit returned in 1927 to Bangkok. There he made his literary debut with *Maha burut* ('Great men', 1928), a collection of biographies of political leaders such as Napoleon, Bismarck, Mussolini and the Meiji reformer, Okubo. This was followed by the already mentioned *Universal History*, whose argument about racial competition as the driving force behind progress echoed Social Darwinism. After his appointment as director of the Fine Arts Department in 1934, Wichit started composing historical plays that lionized the Thais as a martial and freedom-loving nation and were staged to great acclaim in the department's theatre. Wichit's hugely popular plays and musically Westernized songs, such as *Luat thai* ('Thai blood', 1938), played a fundamental role in the construction of a national identity.

Historians have tended to blame the fascistic degeneration of Thai nationalism, of which the war alliance with Japan is regarded as the natural outcome, on the takeover of government by the military faction of the People's Party in the late 1930s. In fact, as early as 1934 the government had passed a strict Press Control Act and banned the formation of political parties with the declared objective of deflating a possible royalist counter-revolution following the failed Boworadet rebellion in 1933. Likewise, the anti-Chinese measures of the Phibun regime (1938–44) had been anticipated by the economic policies of the Phahon government and enjoyed the support of Pridi, Finance Minister until 1942. And while it is true that nationalist rhetoric achieved an unprecedented intensity in the Phibun era, thanks also to the new Ministry of Information, many

Marshal Phibun
Songkhram.

of its leitmotifs had been outlined over the previous three decades.
Specific to Phibun's nationalist project was the attempt to dislodge
the monarchy from the centre of the Thai symbolic universe and
replace it with the nation, as exemplified by the abolition of Chakri
Day and the institution of National Day on 24 June (the date of the
overthrow of the absolute monarchy in 1932).

The means for fulfilling the Thais' national destiny were the
twelve state edicts issued between 1939 and 1942, starting with that
which changed the country's international name to Thailand. In
this case, translation occurred exceptionally from Thai to English.
Siam's new name evoked – arguably more for the foreign than the
domestic public – an ancestral land for the Thais living both within and outside its borders. The third state edict prescribed *thai* as

the official name for the kingdom's inhabitants regardless of ethnic background, employing a spelling that exploited the graphic homology with the word for 'free'.[10] Nominalistic policy raised the spectre of irredentism by suggesting that Tai people subject to colonial authorities in Burma and Indochina should become Thai citizens – and thus, implicitly, 'free'. The patent inspiration behind the vision of a 'greater Thai empire' (*maha anachak thai*) that should ideally incorporate the Shan territories, Laos and western Cambodia was *Deutschland* as the homeland of peoples of Germanic stock living in Germany as well as Austria and Poland. To promote irredentism, the Ministry of Defence and the Royal Survey Department printed and distributed to schools and barracks historical maps that highlighted the territorial losses suffered at the hands of the British and the French, while the pseudo-scientific racial categories were manipulated to demonstrate the ethnic commonality of the Thais with the Lao and the Shans.

This pan-Thai ideology had a territorial as much as racial configuration. A clause on the redrawing of the border stipulated by the Franco-Siamese treaty of 1907 was included in the pact of non-aggression signed by Thailand and the colonial government of Indochina in 1940, shortly before the Nazi invasion of France. Because of the Vichy government's refusal to acknowledge the validity of the clause, negotiations broke down and large demonstrations were staged in Thailand's major cities to demand the restitution of the 'lost territories'. *Luang* Wichit, acting as the government's spokesman, asserted: 'This territory really belongs to us. It is not a colony, it is not a foreign territory; it is a living place for Thai people of Thai blood.'[11] In January 1941 rhetoric was turned into action when the Thai army seized the western Cambodian provinces; in fact, Japanese pressure on the French authorities was determinant for the transaction of the territory. In May 1942, after declaring war on the Allies, Thailand also annexed allegedly lost territories in the Shan States across the border with British Burma. All territories were returned at the end of the war.

The subsequent state edicts stressed national security, loyalty to the state and autarchy; but even those concerned with sartorial and behavioural norms assumed a direct linkage between civilized manners and national prestige. As in other authoritarian states, the radio, which in Thailand started broadcasting in 1930, was critical to the promotion of nationalist propaganda. The popular programme *Dialogues of Mr Man and Mr Khong* (names that combined together mean 'stability'), broadcast in 1941–2, explained to the listeners the rationale of the state mandates and other government policies. After Thailand joined the war on the Axis side in January 1942, national defence was further emphasized: 'The words Thai and sovereignty always coexist. Without sovereignty Thailand would rather choose not to exist', proclaimed Mr Man.[12] But when, in July 1944, Phibun proposed the construction of a new national capital in Petchaburi and a city dedicated to the Buddha in Saraburi (plans seemingly designed to divorce the symbols of nationhood from the royal capital), the government was defeated in parliament. By then, Phibun was trying to disengage himself from the alliance with Japan while his old ally and now rival, Pridi, who in 1942 had been appointed royal regent and thus removed from the cabinet, coordinated the local end of the overseas resistance, the Free Thai (*seri thai*), and acted as the *éminence grise* behind the post-war government that negotiated with Britain the demands for war reparations (the USA had decided for reasons of *Realpolitik* not to recognize Thailand's war declaration). Pridi himself was prime minister from March to August 1946, when he was forced to resign following King Anantha's mysterious death.

At the end of 1947 a coup d'état restored the military to power. A few months later Phibun again took over the helm of government and revived economic nationalism and anti-Chinese policies in the name of anticommunism. Having shelved the wartime pan-Thai ambitions, Phibun and his cultural adviser Wichit continued to pursue through the new Ministry of Culture a nationalist vision of Thailand grounded in cultural traditions and Buddhism, but in which the monarchy had a marginal position. Under the military dictatorship of Sarit Thanarat, nationalism, like Buddhism, was assimilated to the royalist revival with a return to the formula of 'nation, religion, and monarchy'. In fact, Sarit downplayed nationalism in favour of the concept of 'development' (*patthana*), elevated to legitimating ideology of his regime. The prominence of royal and religious symbols in the official definition of nationality constrained it within conservative ideological boundaries. This limita-

Marshal Sarit
Thanarat.

Opposed nationalists:
armed forces sur-
round a demonstrator,
October 1973.

tion became untenable with the rise of radicalism in the early 1970s. According to the authors of an insightful analysis of the politics of that period, the liberals too 'considered themselves true nationalists who loved their king and respected the Buddhist religion, [but] they were unwilling to "wrap themselves in the flag"'.[13] However, the exclusiveness of such symbols, proved by the use of the motto 'nation, religion, and monarchy' as incitement for the assassination of leftist militants, should suffice to explain the hesitancy of liberals (not to say radicals) to embrace them.

The lack of electoral legitimacy of the governments in power from October 1976 to April 1979 necessitated a more sophisticated ideological operation than the mere restoration of the status quo ante. In the aftermath of the reaction, when thousands of students and political activists fled to the jungle to join the clandestine Communist Party, a pervasive campaign was launched to reaffirm the normative values encapsulated in the notion of a Thai essence or identity (*ekkalak thai*) promoted by the National Identity Board, the brainchild of the National Security Council (a body within the Prime Minister's Office composed of senior military officers and public servants). Within the National Identity Board, a Commission on National Ideology was later set up with the following objectives:

> Preserve the nation, defend independence and democracy, protect religion, treasure and preserve the monarchy, eliminate socio-economic disparities, eliminate suffering and nourish well-being, assimilate interests, maintain rights and freedom, create unity and integrity, uphold the identity of and promote the decent culture of the Thai people.[14]

Thereafter, the commission listed the components of the Thai nation as including territory, people, independence and sovereignty, government and administration, religion, monarchy, culture and pride. At another time of national crisis, the aftermath of the economy's meltdown of 1997, the National Identity Board issued a list of twelve undesirable yet allegedly common values, which included the lack of nationalist sentiment, and five desirable ones, the last of which was abiding by the motto 'nation, religion and monarchy'.[15]

The financial crisis determined a chauvinist resentment against international organizations such as the World Bank and the IMF, which found an outlet in various political parties, but especially the appositely named Thai Rak Thai ('Thais love Thai'). After his appointment as prime minister, Thaksin Chinawat rejected inflammatory nationalism in favour of a pragmatic attitude; in 2002 he clarified his thoughts on the subject: 'I am not calling for people to become nationalistic but to have a sense of nationhood'. Still, chauvinistic antagonism became the cornerstone of Thaksin's first term in office; when Thailand made its final repayment of the IMF loan in August 2003, two years ahead of schedule, he celebrated the event in a televised 'independence speech'.[16] Thaksin also strongly encouraged the extra-institutional display of the flag, routinely invoked national unity against internal threats and alleged foreign interferences in Thailand's domestic affairs. But the commentators who likened Thaksin to Phibun should have been mindful of Marx's dictum that history recurs the first time as tragedy and the second as farce.[17] Phibun's vision of Thailand as a culturally and ethnically homogenous nation, while obviously influenced by European fascism, aimed to abolish class privilege and stamp out the royalty's cultural hegemony; as such, it represented a project of political modernization even if not in the direction of a liberal democracy. Thaksin's mix of neo-liberalism and populism, on the other hand, aimed to support domestic capital in its competition against foreign capital in the global economy. It is in this light that Thaksin's nationalist exhortations disclose their full meaning: 'You can fly the flag on every house. It's legal. You can even put it on products'.[18]

Communism

Throughout the 'short' twentieth century encompassed by the outbreak of the First World War and the collapse of the USSR,[19] communism represented for tens of millions of people across the globe a vision of progress alternative to that of capitalist liberalism. Communism's promise of a society of equals fuelled, among other political endeavours, anti-colonialism in many parts of Asia. In Thailand, however, communism was rejected as an alien ideology avowedly incompatible with Thai civilization. The purported alienness of communism was buttressed by its identification with an ethnic Other. Unlike other intellectual imports that were mediated by Western missionaries and government advisers, communism was introduced in Siam by Vietnamese and especially Chinese immigrants. Communist agents thus faced, in their attempts at proselytizing, a linguistic barrier as arduous as the cultural one. Prince Wan's translation of the key terms of the Marxist lexicon (including 'revolution', 'socialism', 'bourgeoisie' and 'proletariat') determined the paradoxical situation in which 'Thai radicals and communists simply could not open their mouths without echoing some of the Prince's neologisms!'[20] Ironically, the one neologism of Prince Wan that never acquired currency was the word for 'communism' (*sapsatharananiyom*); instead, the choice fell on the transliteration *khomunit*, which had the further advantage of acting as a signifier of communism's ideological alienness by denoting its foreign origins.

The shockwaves of the Bolshevik revolution of 1917 were felt as far as Bangkok, whose royals had close ties with Tsar Nicholas II. The first communist cell in Siam was formed in 1924 as a result of a rift in the local branch of the Chinese nationalist party (Guomindang), which deepened after the breakdown of the alliance between the nationalists and the communists in China in 1927. Members of the Vietnamese Revolutionary League had also been active among Vietnamese immigrants in north-eastern Siam since the mid-1920s; Ho Chi Minh was based there between 1928 and 1930 planning anti-colonial actions. In 1929 the South Seas Communist Party, set up in Singapore one year earlier by the order of the Communist International (Comintern) to make proselytes among overseas Chinese, had established a committee in Siam; however, it limited its propaganda to Chinese workers and petty traders. After its disbandment in 1930, the Communist Party of Siam was formed under the authority of the Communist Party of Malaya; its members were all Chinese. Their lack of circumspection led to mass arrests in the early 1930s; King Prachathipok found one of the documents seized by the police, 'very well written, and not the work of someone foolish . . . among the agriculture classes in Siam, many might find it quite convincing'. In jail, the Chinese communists made the acquaintance of the royalist officers arrested after the failed rebellion of 1933 and tutored them in politics in exchange for training in the Thai language.[21]

The Thai government's criminalization of communism was modelled after French and British colonial legislation in the 1930s and '40s and US legislation in the post-war period. In April 1933, the provisional constitutional government promulgated under pressure from the throne an act that outlawed communism and 'any doctrine which implies the advocation of nationalization of land or industry or capital or labour'.[22] The act was the direct outcome of the accusation made against Pridi Phanomyong's proposed economic plan as 'communistic' that forced him into temporary exile. The commission set up to determine whether Pridi himself was a communist relied on the advice of two European 'experts' (a Briton and a Frenchman) for 'defining the peculiar features of communism by taking into account the programs of various communist parties.'[23] After Pridi was cleared of the accusation and reinstated as a minister in the new cabinet, the Anti-Communist Act was revised so as to exclude social reform from its purview. The 'united people's front' stance adopted by the Comintern's seventh congress in 1935 to oppose fascism and the consequent demise of communist organizations among overseas Chinese, together with the government's anti-Chinese measures, caused the disappearance of communist cells in Thailand in the second half of the 1930s.

In December 1942, a year after the landing of the Japanese troops and the Phibun regime's decision to join the Axis in war, the remaining communist militants reorganized themselves in the clandestine Communist Party of Thailand (CPT) under the leadership of two Chinese cadres, Li Qixin and Qiu Ji. At the top of the party's ten-point programme were the expulsion of the Japanese and the restoration of Thailand's sovereignty; the third point was the overthrow of Phibun.[24] Phibun's collaborationism presented the CPT with a golden opportunity to assert its nationalist – as distinct from revolutionary – credentials; but the CPT failed to take advantage of the opportunity. The communist underground resistance carried out only few and unimportant actions. Most of the credit for opposing the Japanese went to the Free Thai movement, led from the USA by the Thai ambassador, Seni Pramot, and co-ordinated locally by Pridi. After the end of the war, the USSR made its support to Thailand's entry to the UN conditional to the abrogation of the Anti-Communist Act. The legalization of the CPT in 1946 was followed by a surge in the local demand for Marxist texts that was satisfied by local writers, translators and publishers. This demand continued to grow even after the return to power of the military in November 1947 by a coup that promised to 'rid the country once and for all of vestiges of communism' and forced the CPT to operate under the cover of legal associations such as the Bangkok Labour Union and the local committee of the Peace Movement, an international anti-nuclear organization supported by the USSR.[25]

This narrowing of political liberty reflected the enlistment of Thailand in the US international strategy of containment of communism outlined by President Truman in 1947. But good diplomatic relations with the USSR, which in 1948 established in Bangkok its first South-east Asian legation, provided some leeway for communist militants. Thus, during the late 1940s and early '50s, English-language editions of the works of Marx and Engels, Lenin and Stalin, printed in Moscow, were available in the capital's bookshops while Marxism was espoused in Thai periodicals such as *Kanmuang* ('Politics', 1944–51), *Aksornsan* ('The Adviser', 1949–52) and the CPT weekly *Mahachon* ('The Masses', 1942–52). The proclamation of the People's Republic of China in October 1949 meant further backing for Thai communists along with the enlargement of the communist œcumene that opposed politically and culturally the 'Free World' œcumene, within which Thailand was located. In 1950 a key text in the intellectual genealogy of Thai Marxism was also published: 'Thailand, a semi-colony', by Udom Sisuwan, a CPT cadre who in the early 1930s had spent time in Mao Zedong's headquarters in Yenan. Udom, who rose to become a member of the CPT Central Committee, was the first to advocate the Maoist strategy of the countryside encircling towns in contrast to the urban-based, worker-orientated strategy of the CPT at that time.[26]

At the end of 1952 the government cracked down on the local committee of the Peace Movement and promulgated the Anti-communist Activities Act, modelled on the US Control of Subversive Activities Act, 'to ensure the safety and stability of the nation and the people'.[27] Communism was banned as an un-Thai ideology in the same way that it was said to be un-American; yet, Phibun's anticommunism never approximated the fanatical tones of McCarthyism. Thai national interests in foreign policy were always paramount, especially when, following the Bandung conference in 1955, the PRC and Thailand explored the possibility of a diplomatic rapprochement. Political repression intensified considerably in the late 1950s under the Sarit dictatorship, whose beginning saw wholescale arrests of communist activists and sympathizers in Bangkok, with the result that the CPT was forced to reorientate its strategy from the city to the countryside. Among those apprehended in the raids of 1958 was Chit Phumisak (1930–66), a university student and a polymath (poet, linguist, literary critic and historian), who became posthumously an iconic figure of communist martyr, the Thai Che Guevara.

Chit's Marxist education was marked by two circumstances that were symptomatic of the idiosyncratic – if not comedic – nature of anticommunism under the Phibun regime. In the late 1940s Chit helped an American linguist translate *The Communist Manifesto* on behalf of the US embassy in Bangkok, which intended to use the translation to goad the Phibun government into action against supposed communist propaganda. In 1957 Chit published under a pseudonym the seminal text of Thai Marxism, *Chomna sakdina thai* ('The Real Face of Thai Feudalism'), in a special issue of Thammasat University's Law Faculty journal, which had been subsidized by Phibun and his ally, Police General Phao, to artfully evoke the spectre of communism at a juncture when their diarchy was under threat from rival army and police factions. The six years Chit spent in jail between 1958 and 1964 were extremely prolific: he translated works of politics and literature from Chinese, Russian and English; wrote essays on history and anthropology; and composed poems and songs. A year after his release, Chit joined the clandestine CPT; he was killed six months later, in May 1966, by north-eastern villagers he had approached for some food.[28]

The rupture of diplomatic relations between the USSR and the PRC in 1960 and the consequent split of the communist œcumene into two antagonistic blocs resulted in the strengthening of the Maoist influence on the communist movements in South-east Asia, except for Vietnam. The CPT embraced armed insurgency in its third congress in 1961 and the following year started broadcasting from its radio station, the Voice of the People of Thailand. The first armed skirmish between the CPT guerrillas and the army occurred only in August 1965. The base of communist insurgency was the north-eastern province of Sakhorn Nakhorn, where resistance to the state dated back to the early 1900s, had been invigorated by Ho Chi Minh's presence in the 1930s and was rekindled by Sarit's harsh repression of Isan regionalism. In the second half of the 1960s the CPT forged tactical alliances with ethnic minorities that opposed the central government. In the South the CPT had a natural ally in the Malayan Communist Party, composed of ethnic Chinese, which after fighting the British colonialists and the Japanese army had embraced a revolutionary path; but the CPT struck also an alliance with the Muslim separatists of the United Pattani Freedom Movement and later set up the Liberation Army of the Muslim People. Most recruits along the north-western border were from the Meo and Yao minorities, whose settlements were threatened by agricultural colonization and the resettlement policies of the Forestry Department. By 1969, when the CPT officially launched the People's Liberation Army of Thailand, half of the kingdom's provinces had been declared 'communist-infested sensitive areas'.

Counter-insurgency was initially unsuccessful due to poor understanding of the CPT's strategic objectives as well as divisions within the military. Economic and social underdevelopment in peripheral provinces, especially in Isan, coupled with the repression and intimidation of local communities by the armed forces, had the result of increasing support for the CPT: in the mid-1970s it had some 8,000 members. The political activism of university students alerted the CPT leadership to the need for re-establishing a rapport with the urban intelligentsia. From the early 1970s radical literature again circulated freely after two decades of censorship; and between 1974 and 1976 the Socialist Party of Thailand elected deputies to the parliament. After the fall of Saigon, Phnom Penh and Vientiane, which made a communist takeover in Thailand seem more likely, there was a re-compacting of conservative and reactionary forces, including a large sector of the Sangha and paramilitary associations (the Red Gaurs and Village Scouts) established over the previous years. The ferocious acts of violence perpetrated by the police forces and the armed mob that stormed Thammasat University on 6 October 1976, including the lynching and burning alive of students, can only be explained as a result of the dehumanization of leftist militants by military propaganda and the sermons of monks such as *Phra* Kittiwuttho, which were aired on the army-controlled radio stations.

In the aftermath of the reaction, between two and three thousand students, unionists and intellectuals on the run joined the communist insurgency. From 1978, however, the CPT began losing external support and cohesion. In the end, the defeat of the communist insurgency was due less to government actions than to ideological divisions within the CPT as well as feuds between communist countries. The strict Maoism of the CPT cadres, together with their puritanical morals and obtuse anti-Western stance, frustrated the newcomers, who were marginalized on the grounds of age, class background and even gender.[29] More decisively, the pro-West shift in Chinese foreign policy after Mao's death in 1976, the PRC's intention to normalize relations with Thailand, and the communist wars that pitted Vietnam against Cambodia and China against Vietnam in 1978–79 disrupted the logistical basis of the CPT and split it into pro-PRC and pro-Vietnam factions; its radio station, located in Yunnan, ceased broadcasting in July 1979 while Vietnam stopped the supply of provisions.

The government exploited the crisis in the CPT by offering in 1979 a general amnesty for political crimes engineered by defence minister (and later prime minister), General Prem Tinsulanon. Prem's experience in counter-insurgency in the North-east led him to pursue a political rather than military solution to defeat communism. The amnesty led to the defection from the CPT ranks of students as well as of many rural supporters who, after laying down their weapons in ceremonies of reconciliation, were embraced as 'fellow developers of the Thai nation'. Communist insurgency along the southern border was also dwelt a mortal blow by the concerted action of the Thai and Malaysian armies. Mass defection, the takeover of forest sanctuaries and factional struggle threw the CPT into disarray; its fourth clandestine congress in 1982 acknowledged tactical and ideological errors but also reaffirmed the party's Maoist line. Alleged communist activists were sporadically apprehended through the rest of the decade but by 1989, when the fall of the Berlin Wall marked the end of communism in the West and the PRC intensified economic modernization after crushing the opposition in Tiananmen Square, Thai communism was already history.

Democracy

Thailand's imagined place in the civilized œcumene of the second quarter of the twentieth century and the Free World of the second half rested, to a considerable degree, on the adoption of democracy as the official ideology of the post-absolutist state. As the country's second prime minister, *Phraya* Phahon, put it, 'there arose the need to change the form of our government to that of the civilized countries. . . . This is the rule of democracy where the people are the master'[30] – and this despite the fact that the Phahon government disallowed the formation of political parties as early as 1934. The lexical history of 'democracy' in the Thai language is an apt illustration of its vexed career as a political idea. The term that came to signify 'democracy' (*prachathipatai*, literally 'people's sovereignty') was originally coined by King Wachirawuth as a translation of 'republic' – a form of government that was deemed unsuitable for Siam because of its rejection of monarchical rule. Those who were bent on changing the political status quo faced too the dilemma of translation in defining their objectives. Pridi Phanomyong's reminiscences of the founding meeting of the People's Party are revealing: 'At that time, there were no such new terms as *patiwat* or *aphiwat* to translate the term "revolution" . . . We therefore opted for . . . "to change the system in which the king is above the law to one in which the king is under the law".'[31]

Pridi and his comrades may have entertained the idea of abolishing the monarchy and establishing in its place a republic; but when Thailand did become a *prachathipatai* in June 1932, it did so in the sense of a constitutional monarchy. The People's Party's decision not to abolish the monarchical institution and even have King Prachathipok officially promulgate the constitution ran contrary to the discontinuity in the forms and symbols of power typical of revolutions, and laid the basis for the historical myth of the monarchy as a promoter of democratic reform. Legislative power was vested

Pridi Phanomyong.

in a half-appointed and half-elected national assembly of 156 members, which was slated to become fully elected as soon as more than half of the population had completed four years of primary education. Meanwhile, the new government drew its legitimacy from the constitution (*ratthammanun*), which was the iconic focus of the nascent democratic ideology. Initiatives to spread awareness of the constitution included its deification (with an intriguing parallel to 1790s France), its inscription in the nationalist motto and its reproduction in miniature copies distributed to provincial halls, along with the creation of Constitution Day (10 December), which quickly became one of the most important public holidays in the calendar. A bronze cast of the book of the constitution constituted also the iconographic centrepiece of the Democracy Monument, erected in 1939 to commemorate the end of the absolutist regime.[32]

All these initiatives had, however, only a relative success. If the constitution was made tangible to the eyes of the predominantly rural population, the charter itself never acquired the status of the founding text of the post-absolutist state as its frequent rewrit-ings demonstrate. The constitution officially promulgated on 10 December 1932 to replace the provisional constitution issued in June was already the product of negotiations between the government and the throne. In 1946, during his brief term as prime minister, Pridi oversaw the approval of a new constitution that instituted a bicam-eral system with an upper house appointed not by the government but by the elected lower house (until then the national assembly had retained a hybrid composition whereby deputies were half elected and half appointed); besides, serving civil and military officials were excluded from appointment to either house and also to the cabinet. Between 1949 and 1997 fourteen more constitutions were promulgat-ed, generally in the aftermath of coups d'état, in the apparent attempt to 'reconcile democratic forms with bureaucratic substance'.[33]

The immediate post-war years saw the emergence of the tumultuous pattern of late twentieth-century Thai politics, with the constitutional interlude of 1945–47, when political parties were allowed, ended by the military coup that eventually drove Pridi into permanent exile after his failed counter-coup in 1949. The post-war Phibun regime (1948–57) opened with the abrogation of the consti-tution of 1946 and continued with the promulgation of a new con-stitution in 1949, which was abrogated in 1951 (when Phibun staged an internal coup to strengthen his position within the ruling junta); finally, in 1952 the original constitution of 1932 was reinstated. Despite his authoritarian tendencies, Phibun never formally dis-avowed parliamentary democracy and revived it briefly between 1955 and 1957, when political parties were sanctioned again and general elections held. Ironically, it was the blatant rigging of the elections that justified the overthrow of Phibun by his rivals in the army. It was in the late 1950s, in the context of military dictatorship and the resuscitation of the monarchy, that the concept of 'Thai-style democracy' (prachathipatai baep thai) was first formulated as an alternative to 'Western democracy', which was rejected as an alien institution. Upon assuming direct control of the government in 1958, Marshal Sarit Thanarat announced: 'The Revolutionary Council wishes to make the country a democracy ... appropriate to the special characteristics and realities of the Thais ... a Thai way of democracy'.[34]

In a situation in which the parliament was dissolved, the constitution suspended and the country ruled by martial law, 'Thai-style democracy' amounted to nothing more than paternalism as expressed by the traditional principle of 'father of the family, father of the country' (*pho ban pho muang*). Sarit, in antithesis to any model of 'democratic' leader, fashioned his public persona as a peculiar mix of paternal figure and street tough (*nakleng*) who did not shy away from personally performing executions, womanizing and heavy drinking (the cause of his premature death). During the 1960s, Thai-style democracy became closely associated with the doctrine of political development elaborated by the Local Administration Department, a counter-insurgency agency. According to Michael Connors, Thai-style democracy was not simply a propagandistic cover for military rule but a distinctive ideology that served 'the project of creating a particular kind of democratic citizen who would act as border police for the fixity of Thainess (the three pillars) and the common good, so defined as to suit the state's authoritarianism and its security imperatives'.[35]

In 1968, ten years after Sarit's abolition of the constitution, his political heirs, Thanom Kittikhachorn (prime minister and defence minister) and Praphat Charusathian (deputy prime minister and interior minister), promulgated a new constitution and scheduled general elections for the following year; but the elected assembly proved hard to control and thus, in 1971, parliament and constitution were dissolved and martial law reimposed. The move propelled a wave of popular protests that eventually led to the regime's downfall on 14 October 1973. After dispatching Thanom and Praphat into temporary exile, King Phumiphon appointed a caretaker prime minister, Sanya Thammsak (rector of Thammasat University), and a national convention, whose 2,436 members chose in turn the 299 representatives of the legislative assembly that submitted the draft of a new constitution. Its approval, twelve months later, was followed by elections in January 1975 and, again, in April 1976, in which an unprecedented number of political parties competed. The centre-right coalitions headed in succession by brothers Khukrit and Seni Pramot managed to govern despite a fractious parliament and increasing political polarization outside it, but could not forestall the military reaction.

Students gathering around the Democracy Monument, October 1973.

According to political scientist John Girling, by 1975, when communist movements triumphed in Indochina, the Thai establishment (the throne, the Sangha, the bureaucracy and its business clients), even when not in agreement with the extreme right, had come to regard democratic government incapable of resisting leftist manipulation.[36] Democracy, however, continued to figure in official discourse even in the aftermath of the reaction. The vehemently anticommunist Supreme Court judge, Thanin Kraiwichian, appointed prime minister by the king in October 1976, ruled by decree under a draconian provisional constitution; yet he also espoused plans for a British-style system of 'democratic socialism' with two opposing parties. Thanin also revived the formula 'democracy with the king as head of state'.[37] After Thanin's removal in October 1977, his successor, General Kriangsak Chomanan, initiated a political transition (easing of censorship, political amnesty) which culminated in the promulgation of yet another constitution at the end of 1978 and general elections the next April. In 1980 Kriangsak was succeeded by Prem Tinsulanon, the then army commander. Prem enjoyed the support of two factions of middle-rank officers – the 'Democratic Soldiers' and the 'Young Turks' – who, in fighting against the communist insurgency, had developed the belief that political subversion could be eliminated only through social and political reforms.

Between 1980 and 1988 Prem led, as unelected prime minister, a series of coalition governments that started a cautious liberalization of the political process; he also survived two attempted coups by the Young Turks who, disenchanted, had turned against him. Popular participation in politics was encouraged within the boundary of national security distinguishing between 'democratic movements and communist movements which hide behind the banner of democracy'. Farmers, workers, students and intellectuals – in the official view the social groups most likely to fall prey to communist propaganda – were to be closely monitored and at the same time won over with the help of the state-controlled broadcast media.[38] Political analysts characterized the Thai political landscape of the 1980s as a 'semi-democracy' or 'Premocracy'. When Prem finally stepped down in 1988, political continuity was ensured by Chatichai Chunhawan, also a retired general, who became the first elected prime minister since 1976. While technocrats, professionals and the intelligentsia agreed that democracy was the political system better suited to take advantage of economic globalization and boost Thailand's international profile, the Chatichai government showed increasing signs of corruption. By the early 1990s, 'money politics' had considerably eroded the middle class's faith in democracy as an avenue for the modernization of the country.

The coup that ousted Chatichai in February 1991 was both a reaction against rampant political corruption, stigmatized by the coup promoters as 'parliamentary dictatorship', and an attempt to return the military (or, more precisely, a faction within it) to the role of arbiters of the political process. The junta, known as the National Peace-Keeping Council (NPKC), appointed an interim cabinet as well as a committee of lawyers and academics for drafting a new constitution. The committee attempted (with the king's blessing) to draft a constitution palatable to both the military and political parties – among which Phalang Tham, led by the popular ex-Bangkok governor (and ex-Young Turk officer) Chamlong Simuang, had become the major opponent of the NPKC. In the elections of March 1992 the ad hoc party formed by the NPKC (Samakkhi Tham) won a relative majority and proceeded to form a new cabinet. But when in April General Suchinda Kraprayun announced that he would head the government as non-elected prime minister, reneging on his previous pledge, public protests erupted demanding his resignation and amendments to the draft constitution to rule out such a possibility.

The ensuing political confrontation was portrayed in news-paper reports (the state-controlled broadcast media avoided reporting on it) as a struggle between the 'angels' of democracy and the 'demons' of dictatorship. Chamlong, with the support of civil society organizations grouped in the Confederation for Democracy, marshalled in the first half of May an open challenge to Suchinda. On the evening of the 17th, a crowd of some 200,000 demonstrators gathered in central Bangkok to stage a march to the prime minister's residence. Late that night troops charged the protestors in the streets and arrested Chamlong. Clashes between armed forces and pro-testors continued throughout the following day. On the 19th tens of thousands of protestors regrouped in the campus of Ramkham-haeng University, on the capital's outskirts, while clashes between army units pro and against Suchinda were also reported. On the evening of the 20th, King Phumiphon summoned Suchinda and Chamlong and demanded they stop the street violence; four days later Suchinda resigned and the king appointed an interim prime minister to amend the constitution and organize general elections in September.

While the military's retreat from politics invited the celebra-tion of 'Black May' as a new start for Thai democracy, governments over the following five years saw a return to the 'money politics' of the late 1980s in the context of a continuing economic boom.[39] The drafting of a new constitution thus became the focus of hopes for democratic reform among civil society groups, which lobbied the government through extra-institutional initiatives, such as the Committee for Developing Democracy led by the highly respected social activist, Dr Prawat Wasi. The government responded to the pressure by setting up the Constitutional Drafting Assembly, formed by 76 provincial representatives (one for every province) and 23 legal and political experts with the aim of drafting, in the words of the Assembly's president, Anantha Panyarachun (who had been interim prime minister after the coup of 1991 and again after May 1992), a constitution 'of the people, by the people and for the people and not a power constitution'. A draft constitution was submitted to parliament in August 1997 calling for a number of radical changes, including the election of the senate (which, as an appointed body, had been the preserve of the bureaucracy); the separation of legislative and executive powers; the institution of an administrative and a constitutional court as well as several commissions of control; and the extension of the prime minister's prerogatives. In order to contrast the election of provincial 'godfathers' to the lower house, the draft also stipulated that electoral candidates must hold at least a Bachelor's degree – a disposition that effectively excluded almost all the rural population from running for a parliamentary seat.[40]

The government's ambivalence towards the draft was swept away by the financial crisis that erupted in July and dramatically highlighted the inadequacy of the political system. Under pressure from the middle class, big business and the press, the two houses of parliament somewhat reluctantly approved on 27 September 1997 the 'People's Constitution' – a momentous event that was overshadowed by the onset of the 'IMF era' (yuk ai em ep). Article 1 of the new constitution proclaimed Thailand to be a 'one and indivisible kingdom'; Article 2 defined it as 'a democratic regime of government with the King as head of the state'; Article 3 stated: 'The sovereign power belongs to the Thai people. The King as the head of the state shall exercise such power through the National Assembly, the Council of Ministers and the Courts in accordance with the constitution'; and Article 4 specified: 'The human dignity, right and liberty of the people shall be protected'.[41] In the first general elections held under the new constitution, in January 2001, the Thai Rak Thai party won a landslide victory. A month earlier the National Counter-Corruption Commission (one of the new bodies set up under the constitution) had charged its leader, Thaksin Chinawat, with concealing assets worth 4.5 billion Baht. In August 2001 the Constitutional Court (another newly established body) acquitted Thaksin by a split verdict 8–7. Two days later he commented: 'It's strange that the leader who was voted by 11 million people had to bow to . . . two organizations composed of only appointed commissioners and judges, whom people do not have a chance to choose'.[42]

During his term as prime minister, Thaksin contrasted an understanding of democracy as the will of the majority to that of democracy as the public accountability of political actors and

Defenders of democracy? An army tank presides over the Royal Plaza, Bangkok, in front of the Ananta Samakhom Throne Hall and the Rama V equestrian monument, following the coup of 19 September 2006.

institutions. The clash between these two conceptions surfaced prominently when Thaksin was reappointed for a second term after the massive victory in the 2005 general elections. In March 2006 street demonstrations led by the People's Alliance for Democracy asked Thaksin to resign after the sale of his telecommunication group to a Singaporean state company; Thaksin responded by calling snap elections in April. Although the snap elections (later invalidated by the Supreme Court) confirmed Thai Rak Thai's parliamentary majority, political divisions deepened and Thaksin withdrew temporarily from office before his comeback in June as caretaker prime minister, while new general elections were scheduled for October. The confrontation, watched with increasing apprehension by the military as well as the throne, eventually ensued in the ousting of Thaksin by a bloodless coup d'état staged on 19 September 2006 while he was attending a meeting of the UN General Assembly in New York.

The coup promoters, under the leadership of Army General Sonthi Bunyaratkalin, ironically presented themselves to the world as the Council for Democratic Reform under Constitutional Monarchy (the designation's latter half was quickly dropped) even as they proceeded – in the tradition of previous military coups – to dissolve parliament, abolish the constitution, declare martial law and nominate an interim prime minister, the retired general Surayuth Chulalont, with the promise of holding general elections within a year. The coup received a prompt royal imprimatur and appeared to enjoy widespread consensus, at least in Bangkok, but also attracted the censure of a few public intellectuals, who were less than happy to see a controversial but democratically elected government replaced by a military junta for the first time since the landmark events of May 1992. The junta, for its part, promulgated an interim constitution to legitimate its control of the future executive, appointed a committee to investigate the activities of the deposed Thaksin and attempted unsuccessfully to co-opt some respected academics by appointment to an advisory committee. An especially malleable ideology, democracy – in Thailand as elsewhere at the beginning of the twenty-first century – continues to be defined by the power holders as much as by those who seek power.

five | Modernities

The formation of the Thai nation-state as a result of the high imperial age's globalization of bureaucratic governance, religious modernism and ethnic nationalism was followed by the emergence of Thai modern cultural expressions resulting from the localization of modernity's universalistic pursuits of knowledge, progress and individual freedom. Historically this process unfolded in two stages: in the earlier stage, selected features of colonial modernity were localized under the monarchy's aegis to bring Siam on the same level as 'civilized' nations; in the later stage, starting in the 1920s, the new urban stratum of educated commoners articulated through the printed media social values and political aspirations distinct from the royal project of civilization. Bridging these two stages was Bangkok's role as the social space where Thai modernities unfolded. Besides being the seat of the monarchy and government, Bangkok became the locus of nation building with academic institutions, literary and artistic circles and a flourishing publishing industry.

The constellation of intellectual, scientific and cultural phenomena characteristic of modernity entered the orbit of the Thai universe in the 1830s, when newly invented technologies such as print and photography were introduced by American and European missionaries. While indifferent to evangelizing, the Bangkok court was extremely receptive to the West's material and intellectual modernity. The royal brand of civilization fashioned accordingly was, not unlike the colonial modernity embraced by Asian elites from Bengal to the Philippines, the hybrid product of the concurrent trends of cultural standardization and reconstitution of social hierarchies generated by the global diffusion of the state, industry and empire. In the early decades of the twentieth century, Westernized taste spread outside the court among the urban middle strata, who now defined what was in fashion or up-to-date (*samaimai*). Even during the 1930s and '40s, when the ruling elite looked at Japan's self-fashioned modernity as a model, Western civilizational norms continued to be held as the yardstick for measuring Thailand's level of social and cultural advancement. In the post-war period Thailand underwent, like the other countries that were part of the 'Free World' œcumene, considerable cultural Americanization. While the intellectual elite reacted against it by embracing socialism's ideals or advocating the nativist idea of Thainess, the expanding urban population strove for the material modernity imported from the West and Japan – an attitude satirized in the 1984 hit song, *Made in Thailand*, by rock band Carabao: 'Afraid to lose face, worried that their taste isn't modern enough'. Unsurprisingly, the divergent threads of the Thai way to modernity resurfaced in the political, economic and cultural crises of the 1990s.

Bodily Practice

Bodily practice – encompassing dress, deportment, personal hygiene and sexual practices – was one dimension of social life that underwent considerable standardization in the nineteenth century due to the diffusion of the Western bourgeois regime of corporeal propriety by the agents of imperialism in Africa, the Pacific and parts of Asia. Colonial officials and missionaries sought to mould the mind and souls of 'savages' by disciplining their body. Discipline was imposed by covering the more or less naked body of indigenous people; using dress to emphasize gender distinctions; and stamping out 'barbaric' habits, from ritual interventions on the body such as tattooing and scarring to 'unnatural' forms of sexual intercourse. In Siam, where Christian missionaries made only marginal inroads, it was the court that, as in early modern Europe, led the way to civility by adopting selectively Victorian norms of decorum and self-presentation. In the post-absolutist period, policing of bodily practice fell under the

145

Documenting 'tradition':
studio portrait of a female
commoner.

purview of the bureaucratic state, which upheld Western dress as a
symbol of progress, and was eventually open to the transient fashions
of the clothing and cosmetic industry.

Bodily practice at the courts of Ayutthaya and early Bangkok was,
as in the other culturally Indianized courts of the region, highly
refined, requiring a special vocabulary and formalized body movements; climatic conditions, however, discouraged elaborate dress.
Temple murals and engravings in early European travel books provide ample visual documentation on habiliment and bodily adorn-
ment in pre-modern Siam. Both men and women cropped their hair,

146

keeping only a tuft on the crown. Due to the chewing of betel (areca leaves, a natural stimulant), a habit which was widespread across social groups, teeth were stained black. Dress was wrapped, not stitched. Up until the middle of the nineteenth century, people generally wore only a cotton loincloth; women, especially in the countryside, were commonly bare breasted. Walking barefoot was the norm except for the royalty, who wore Persian slippers. Court fashion prescribed the folding of silk loincloths in such a way as to resemble pantaloons (*chongkrabaen*); female courtiers also covered the torso with a loose wrap and adorned themselves with jewels, while noblemen, though only on formal occasions, don jackets and vests of Indian or Persian provenance. The silk and cotton cloths worn by the royalty and the nobility were manufactured in India with designs denoting rank, and sumptuary laws regulated their use until the middle of the nineteenth century. The king and court Brahmans wore ceremonial garb woven in gold brocade and matched by elaborate headdresses.

Because of the social taboo on the vision and representation of the body of royalty, the Thai court did not possess a tradition of royal portraiture. The introduction of photographic technology by Catholic missionaries in the 1840s provided both a mirror and a witness to the reform of royalty's bodily self, which eventually became a living (and, even more, travelling) advertisement of the modernizing mission by which the Thai court asserted its place in the Victorian œcumene. King Mongkut, who at the start of his reign had introduced the requirement of wearing shirts at royal audiences, harnessed photography as an instrument of diplomatic relations. Extant daguerreotypes of Mongkut in fancy uniforms prove his awareness that the sitter must project an image conforming to Western notions of civility and the interaction between photo-portraiture and dress reform in Siam. European envoys to Bangkok publicized military uniform as the official dress of European rulers in the middle of the nineteenth century. Numerous photographs illustrate the successive phases in the restyling of royal dress along Western lines during King Chulalongkorn's reign. In the initial phase (1870s and '80s), hybrid court attire and ceremonial uniforms were fashioned by matching a lace blouse (for females) or Western-style jacket (for males) with the unisex lower silk wrap;

The uniformed monarch: King Mongkut, c. 1865.

shoes and stockings complemented the outfit. Both sexes sported longer hair and men moustaches as well, according to contemporary European fashion. In the 1890s male royalty took to wearing Western suits on overseas trips ('It can be seen at a glance that his clothes were made by an English tailor', remarked a British trade journal at the time of Chulalongkorn's visit in 1897); at home, full military uniform replaced traditional royal garb in the performance of state ceremonies.

The court's emulation of European tastes and self-representational styles was arguably concerned with the gaze of the West as much as with self-regard. Western-style uniform in particular was a prominent signifier of the Thai elite's modernizing attitudes, even though some contemporary foreign observers opined that it de-mystified the royal body's purported sacredness: 'There is very lim-ited religious aura the moment the king appears in a European military uniform and a helmet adorned with feathers', remarked a Belgian adviser to the ministry of justice. As for the dressing standard of Bangkok's inhabitants, a decree issued in 1899 for the forthcom-ing visit of Prince Heinrich of Prussia prescribing women to cover their breasts and men to wear the loincloth at knee length suggests widespread indifference to 'civilized' bodily practice among com-moner strata.[1]

The momentous decade of the 1920s, during which the emerg-ing urban middle class pushed for the redefinition of social and gender boundaries, witnessed also the beginnings of modern Thai visual culture in magazines, advertising and the cinema.[2] Upper-

Hybrid modernity:
Queen Saowapha in
the reformed court
costume, c. 1900.

class women adopted a more conservative version of jazz-age fashion by wearing the tubular sarong of northern Thais (*phasin*) as an ankle-length skirt or undergarment and growing their hair to neck length. Modern fashion was tied to the appearance of new democratic social spaces, such as dancing and cinema halls, and the representation of women in advertisements as sophisticated consumers of cosmetics and cigarettes. This trend mirrored that in other Asian metropolises, such as Bombay and Shanghai, where the encounter between the capitalist cloth industry and local sartorial traditions brought about distinct dressing styles. The comparison with colonial Bengal is especially instructive for what it reveals of the interaction between dress, social status and nationalism. Upper-middle-class Bengalis who took up Western-style dress were criticized from two parties: the colonial elite, who sought to preserve social distinction in the face of imitation by enforcing more stringent sartorial rules; and the nationalists, who rejected Western dress as a symbol of foreign domination in favour of a newly invented 'national' Indian dress.[3]

The Thai elite's hybrid costume shared an aesthetic affinity with the neo-traditional dress fashioned by Asian nationalists, but carried none of its political significance, because in Siam there was no need to signify – sartorially or otherwise – autonomy from the West. Lack of colonial domination prevented Western dress from being rejected as antithetical to Thainess or shelved as a dispensable appendage of modernity. Still, the editorial in the 1929 inaugural issue of the literary magazine *Suphaburut* ('The Gentleman') questioned the assumption that the so-called 'universal suit' (*suit sakorn*) was evidence of the civility of his wearer: 'Dress is only an outward symbol. Indeed, one finds gentlemen who are not interested in such symbols, symbols that can be easily copied or imitated . . . On the surface a man might appear to be a gentleman when in fact he is not'.[4]

The Phibun regime's policies sought to standardize bodily practice as a way of disciplining the body politic in the name of national progress: the chewing of betel, for example, was declared illegal in 1940. The tenth state edict, issued in January 1941, prescribed a dress code 'in accordance with civilization', which stressed the use of shoes and hats. It was followed, a few months later, by a royal decree that prohibited the use of loose garments as damaging to the nation's prestige. 'The Thais are a well dressed nation' and 'Hats will lead Thailand to greatness' were prominent slogans of the period. Their message was reiterated with a racist slant borrowed from imperialist propaganda in a popular radio programme: 'To wear proper dress would show that we do not have barbaric minds as the wild people in Central Africa ... Whether the mind is civilized or not is expressed through dress.'[5] The head of government himself proclaimed: 'proper dress and correct manner [in Thailand] are no different from other civilized countries ... now men remark ... "I met a lady who wore a skirt and hat ... and gorgeous shoes. She was as beautiful as any lady from any other country"'.[6] The Miss Thailand beauty pageant promoted the government's sartorial goals by making Western dress mandatory for the participants; a fashion-design competition was also launched to support the state edict on autarchy.[7] But while well-to-do women in the capital were able to don the latest styles in headgear, those in the countryside had to resort to bamboo and palm leaves to fashion hats for themselves. In general, district officials found it impossible to enforce the state rules on hats and shoes among the rural population, who resisted dress policing and mocked overdressed women as 'smelly madams'.[8]

In the post-war period the popularity of Western dress increased further among urbanites as the influence of the 'American way of life' became predominant. An acerbic comment on the diffusion of Western fashion from Bangkok to the provinces is contained in a short story of 1967, in which a teacher living in the capital is confronted, on a visit back to his home village, by his old girlfriend: 'The girls in Bangkok wear such gorgeous stretch pants! ... Didn't you bring any clothes from Bangkok, Thian? Why are you wearing your father's old things? Aren't you afraid the villagers will say how out of it you are, even though you've come from Bangkok?'[9] In fact, despite the popularity of stretch pants and bell-bottomed blue jeans among the Bangkok youth in the late 1960s and early '70s, contemporary Western youth fashion was by and large rejected as a manifestation of moral decadence that befitted only social outcasts. The rejection of dress counterculture was mirrored by the fashioning of neo-traditional dress, considerably later in Thailand than in the countries that had undergone decolonization.

With her marriage to Rama IX in the 1950s, Sirikit became the country's first resident queen since the mid-1930s and an august model for many Thai women. In the world tour of 1960, she wore Western dresses as a match to King Phumiphon's bespoke suits. Thailand's young royal couple thus projected onto the international stage a modern, cosmopolitan image following in King Chulalongkorn's footsteps. At home, however, Queen Sirikit gave sartorial expression to the ongoing monarchical revival by wearing costumes patterned after pre-1850s royal dress, which left the arms and right shoulder fully exposed. In the early 1970s, taking the lead from Jim Thompson, a US ex-intelligence officer who had revived local silk

Inventing sartorial traditions: King Phumiphon and Queen Sirikit inpurportedly traditional dress, late 1950s.

manufacturing in the 1950s, the queen's charity began promoting the textile cottage industry. Hand-woven cottons and silks were made fashionable by neo-traditional outfits for day and evening wear adopted by Queen Sirikit and the royal princesses, which consisted of an ankle-length sarong and a blouse. The fashion spread among middle-class women, who wore 'Thai' dress both at work and on formal occasions as an alternative to Western dress, but complemented it with accessories such as leather bags and shoes.

The economic boom from the mid-1980s to the mid-1990s saw the diffusion of the 'executive look' among the urban professionals and the bureaucracy's upper echelons. In Bangkok, next to the older local and Japanese department stores, there appeared new upmarket malls housing the boutiques of major international fashion labels – while near-perfect fakes manufactured locally were sold at a fraction of the price on the pavements outside their air-conditioned spaces. Concurrently, TV advertisements and magazines propagated fashion and aesthetic ideals that had their physical embodiment in widely admired Eurasian models. However, the internationalization of dress was a phenomenon limited to Bangkok's upper strata that highlighted persistent cultural as well as socio-economic disparities between the capital and the provinces. In their frequent mass protests staged in the streets of Bangkok, villagers would proudly don the countryside's traditional indigo cotton tunic (mor hom) as a mark of their social identity.

Knowledge

A critical moment in the emergence of Thai modernity was the displacement of indigenous knowledge by Western knowledge. The start of this epistemological shift can be dated to the publication of *Nangsu sadaeng kitchanukit* ('A Book of Miscellanea', 1867), which attempted to reconcile Buddhist doctrine with scientific theories. The next phase, at the turn of the century, saw the localization in the Thai intellectual landscape of Western disciplines by means of neologisms rooted in Pali and suffixed with the word *-sat* ('science'; Sanskrit: *sastra*); a short-lived Etymological Commission was even set up in 1907 to oversee the translation of foreign scientific and technical terms. The third phase was marked by the establishment of modern academic institutions: Chulalongkorn University in 1916 and Thammasat (Jurisprudence) University in 1934. The domains of knowledge that most directly participated in the project of nation building were geography (rendered as *phumisat* or 'earth-science'), which constituted the physical space of the Thai state; and history (*prawatisat*, 'story-science'), which validated Siam's civilizational lineage according to the parameters of 'civilized' nations. On the contrary, domains of knowledge not organic to the reproduction of absolute power were rejected. One such case was economics (*setthasat*). An economic treatise penned by an ex-minister of finance in 1911 was banned for its critique of free trade and economics was excluded from the subjects taught at Chulalongkorn University; ten years later the teaching of economics was prohibited by law.[10]

The topographical mapping of Thailand discussed in Chapter 2 had its epistemological premise in the shift from Indo-Buddhist cosmology to the concept of the earth's space as finite and measurable. The main text in the Thai cosmological tradition, and a masterwork that inspired religiosity, folklore and art through the centuries, is *Trai phum phra ruang* ('The Three Worlds of Lord Ruang'), originally composed in the reign of King Lithai of Sukhothai (1347–68) and revised several times as late as the 1820s.[11] In a startling parallel to Dante's almost contemporary versified cosmology of the Christian universe, the treatise illustrates the three worlds of the Buddhist cosmos: the lower world, inhabited by humans as well as spirits, demons and deities; the world of desire, centred on Mount Meru, beyond which lay seven rings of mountains and oceans and the four continents; and the world of form, Brahma's realm, capped by the formless world or realm of perfection. While the *Three Worlds* cosmology was illustrated pictorially by cosmographs orientated by a vertical axis, impressionistic maps (similar to European portolan charts) were also drawn for military and sailing purposes. It is thus arguable whether the indigenous Thai cartography reflected poor geographical knowledge or, rather, the subordination of cognizance of the physical world to a religious worldview.

Buddhist cosmology became in the 1830s the target of the attacks of missionaries, who deployed maps, globes and models of the solar systems to prove the superiority of the West's Christian civilization; a manual on astronomy was composed in 1843 specifically to challenge the *Three Worlds*. In his *Book of Miscellanea* (1867), one of the first books published by the palace's press, *Chaophraya* Thiphakora-wong, a prominent court official, dismissed indigenous cosmology in the name of religious modernism. Elsewhere he commented scathingly on reports of supernatural phenomena occurring at the stupa in Nakhorn Pathom: 'Whether such marvels were caused by the power of the Buddha, or the magic of the Buddha's relics, or the power of the deities, or whether electricity from the sky and from the earth clashed, was left to each individual to decide according to his own intelligence.'[12] A year after the publication of *Chaophraya* Thiphakorawong's treatise, King Mongkut (then aged 64) travelled with a court retinue and some British and French officers to the peninsula in order to observe a solar eclipse whose timing he had calculated. After ascending the throne Mongkut had shown his concern at the inability of court astrologers to calculate time accurately, compromising both the auspicious timing of state ceremonies and the precise recording of events; he thus had a clock tower built in the Grand Palace's grounds. Mongkut's calculations of the phases of the eclipse proved correct, but during the expedition he contracted malaria and died shortly after his return to Bangkok; fifteen-year-old Prince Chulalongkorn, who had taken part in the expedition as well, also fell gravely ill.

To Chulalongkorn was dedicated, with best wishes for the future of the kingdom, the first atlas printed in Siam (1874) for use in missionary schools. Geography was one of the subjects of study in the first school curriculum (1892), and later on elementary cartographic techniques were also included. Textbooks such as *Phumisat sayam* ('Geography of Siam', c. 1900) and *Phumisat* ('Geography', 1902–4) popularized the notion that the earth was divided into continents divided in turn into countries (*prathet*, a word which originally defined an area or region) under the authority of a king, emperor or president; the kingdom of Siam, whose name was rendered alternatively as *prathet sayam* or *sayam prathet*, was one such country. Geographical knowledge was imparted visually through maps and lexically through a specialized terminology that, as noted in Chapter 4, was eventually subsumed under the vocabulary of nationalism.[13]

An epistemological shift parallel to that from Buddhist cosmology to geography underlay the localization of history as the 'science of the past'. Knowledge of the past in pre-modern Thailand took two forms: tales about the Buddha and related places and people (*tamnan*); and dynastic chronicles (*phong sawadan*). The concept of the past underlying *tamnan* was universalistic; the history of individual cities or kingdoms had a place in it insofar as it dealt with the diffusion of Buddhism and was framed temporally by the cosmic time of religion and spatially by the pre-modern notion of the Theravada œcumene. On the contrary, dynastic chronicles were geographically and chronologically specific, being concerned with the events of singular reigns.[14] The dynastic chronicles of Ayutthaya were compiled anew in the early Bangkok period (the only contemporary version was discovered in 1907); the last complete chronicles, those of Mongkut's reign, were written in the early 1870s. By then, a historical consciousness informed by modern conceptions of time, space and human action, had made its appearance among the elite in the form of a novel interest in ancient monuments. This antiquarianism signalled a departure from the worldview orientated by the Buddhist doctrine of impermanence, which postulates the inexorable decay of all physical entities.

Antiquarian pursuits began with Prince Mongkut's alleged discovery of the stone inscription of King Ramkhamhaeng and his legendary stone throne in 1833. As a result, the kingdom of Sukhothai, whose traces had been almost entirely erased from public memory, was put back on the map of the Thai past. The accidental discovery of the ruins of Angkor by the naturalist Henri Mouhot in 1860 was followed by a series of French explorations in the frontier region between Siam and Cambodia after this had been made into a protectorate in 1863. After entertaining the idea of removing to Bangkok one of Angkor's temples, King Mongkut settled on having a miniature model of Angkor Wat installed inside the royal monastery's compound, an initiative that can be read as a symbolic move counteracting French expansionist moves. Mongkut showed his appreciation of history as a means to validate territorial claims when he showed the French that the suzerain status of the province of Siemreap, in which Angkor lies, was acknowledged in the Khmer court chronicles. But the French, who were to develop a cult of Angkor as one of the world's monumental wonders on a par with the Parthenon and the Pyramids of Giza, pressured Bangkok to return Siemreap under the authority of the puppet king of Cambodia until the province's retrocession was agreed in the Franco-Siamese treaty of 1907.

The establishment of colonial archaeological services at the start of the twentieth century transformed the antiquarian pursuits of European explorers and military officers into a professional endeavour undertaken by Orientalists trained in metropolitan academic institutions. The brief of the École Française d'Extrême-Orient (EFEO), officially established in Hanoi in 1901 though active under a different name since 1898, was the production of know-ledge on the culture and history of Asia from India to Japan. This objective was directly linked to the colonial project of governing the three countries (Laos, Cambodia and Vietnam) France had merged into the colonial entity of Indochina. The EFEO was also involved in the study of Siam; as late as 1921, its bulletin boosted: 'the scientific knowledge of Siam is for the most part a French accomplishment'.[15] In this climate of blooming Orientalist scholar-ship, 37 individuals, mostly expatriates in the employ of the Thai government, founded in February 1904 a society for 'the investiga-tion and encouragement of art, sciences and literature in relation to Siam and neighbouring countries'. A club of gentlemen-scholars, the Siam Society, was modelled on eighteenth-century learned societies, such as the Asiatic Society of Bengal, rather than modern colonial archaeological services. Among its founding members, an especially important role was played by its second president, Dr Oscar Frankfurter, the German secretary of the Royal Library; and Colonel G. E. Gerini, an Italian instructor at the Cadet Academy, who wrote essays on archaeology, historical geography, rituals and ancient laws. The Siam Society's initiatives, most notably the pub-lication of a scholarly journal which started in 1904 and still contin-ues, were entirely financed through membership subscriptions.[16]

Soon after the foundation of the Siam Society, the Thai author-ities took two initiatives for the study and preservation of historical documents and monuments. The first was the establishment in 1905 of the Royal City Library (the National Library after 1932) by the amalgamation of the Grand Palace's library and two collections of ancient Buddhist texts. Along with palm-leaf manuscripts and Thai printed books (200,000 volumes by 1932), initially the library

housed also stone inscriptions and archaeological finds, which
were later transferred to the National Museum. In 1908 the library
started the publication of court chronicles under the editorship of
Prince Damrong Ratchanuphap. After his resignation from the
post of Minister of the Interior in 1915, he devoted his energies to
the library, where he started the tradition of printing commemora-
tive volumes for distribution at royal cremations. In 1917, Damrong
called the young French orientalist, George Cœdès (1886–1969), to
replace the departing Dr Frankfurter. Between 1917 and 1921, Cœdès
established on the basis of epigraphic evidence the dynastic chronology of the Sukhothai kingdom, and in 1924 published a complete
edition of its inscriptions (dating, in the process, the Ramkhamhaeng
Stele to AD 1292).[17]

The second initiative was the creation in 1907 of the Archaeological Society, whose mission was to delineate a civilizational
lineage for Siam. King Chulalongkorn's inaugural speech to the
society, delivered on the last day of celebrations for his reign's
anniversary in Ayutthaya, sketched a picture of Siam's past and
incited noblemen and officials in the audience to participate in the
project of compiling a history based on newly collected documents
and material remains. The next day the royal exhortation was put
into practice with a tour of the local ruins.[18] An amateurish association for civil service officials, the Archaeological Society did not
accomplish much. It was another seventeen years before the
Archaeological Service was instituted by royal decree (in January
1924), 'in consideration of the many vestiges of monuments and
artefacts created by past kings and artists, and of the fact that such
archaeological remains have an important historical value and can
contribute to increase knowledge of the past for the country's
benefit and glory'.[19] From 1924 until his departure for Hanoi five
years later, Cœdès was the driving force behind the Archaeological
Service, whose tasks included the inventory of historic sites and the
training of conservators.

The combination of Cœdès' epigraphic expertise and Prince
Damrong's first-hand knowledge of the antiquities scattered in the
national territory coalesced into the history of Thailand's art.
Damrong outlined the stylistic chronology that was employed for
ordering antiquities in the National Museum in a volume published

Cultural tourists in Ayutthaya, c. 1900.

in 1926, the same year as the museum's inauguration.[20] Religious
architecture and plastic arts were classified into eight chronologically sequential (though partly overlapping) stylistic periods that
were named after historic polities: Dvaravati, Srivijaya, Lopburi,
Chiangsaen, Sukhothai, Uthong, Ayutthaya and Rattanakosin
(Bangkok). The designation of the Dvaravati and Srivijaya art periods rested on speculative grounds. The Lopburi period designated
Khmer sculpture and architecture from central Siam, leaving open
the question (still debated today) of whether its creators were
'provincial' Khmer artisans or Thai imitators of the metropolitan
style of Angkor. The Chiangsean period identified the Burmese-
influenced sculpture and architecture of the northern kingdom
of Lanna. The Sukhothai period was taken to mark the appearance
of the 'national', and indeed 'classic', Thai style of Buddhist imagery,
thus placing the emergence of the Thai artistic genius within the
broader narrative of the political ascendancy of the Thai race.
This intent was well served by the distinctive iconography of the
Sukhothai icons: supple bronze images of the Buddha in seated,
standing and characteristically walking postures, with oval faces,
hooked noses, arched eyebrows and lowered eyelids, which re-

159

elaborated foreign motifs into an original indigenous style. The Ayutthaya period was dismissed as a protracted period of artistic decline, characterized by the sterile replication of a fixed formula that reached its nadir by the start of the Bangkok period. By assimilating art styles to historical periods, Damrong and Cœdès conflated, however, the history of art with political history, relying on the former to fill the lacunae of the latter and on the latter to provide a temporal framework for the former.[21]

During his term as head of the library from 1915 to 1933 (when he went on self-imposed exile to Penang), Prince Damrong outlined Thailand's master historical narrative by sequencing the kingdoms of Sukhothai, Ayutthaya and Bangkok as the successive incarnations of the Thai nation. Taking up Leopold von Ranke's call to approach historical documents philologically in order to reveal the past 'as it really was', Damrong compared and collated extant versions of court chronicles, which he then published with lengthy introductions. In so doing, Damrong literally 'edited' Thailand's past to evoke an image of the Thais as being distinguished, as he put it, by 'love of national independence, toleration and power of assimilation'.[22] Damrong also emphasized the Thais' vocation to syncretism: 'The Siamese do not reject the good and the beautiful just because it is of foreign origin. They borrowed the good and the beautiful features of various different styles and merged them together.'[23]

During the absolutist era knowledge was subjected to the royal monopoly of power, and those who produced and circulated it outside of this monopoly incurred the state's wrath. Such was the fate of K.S.R. Kulap (1834–1921), a commoner who, after working for foreign commercial firms, established a printing press and a journal in which he published historical and biographical essays based on texts he was able to borrow from the palace library. Kulap's publishing activity led to his prosecution on charges of forgery; convicted in 1902, he was granted royal pardon because of his age. With the fall of the absolute monarchy, the royal elite's monopoly over the writing of history also came to an end and national history was rewritten, as Craig Reynolds puts it, by braiding together the old plot of dynasty and the new plot of nation-state.[24]

The rewriting of the national past took place in the domain of popular rather than academic history; its main architect was the chief nationalist ideologue, *Luang* Wichit Watthakan, who in his many historical plays interwove the themes of heroic kingly deeds and commoners' bravery. Wichit subscribed to the view established since Wachirawuth's reign that Thai civilization had originated with the kingdom of Sukhothai but gave it a new spin. In a public lecture delivered in 1940, Wichit contended that the Indic customs adopted from the Khmer court had a corrupting effect on the Thais: 'Thailand was a strong and vibrant nation in the Sukhothai period . . . since then we should have made great progress . . . but it was not possible because we cast off our fundamental culture'.[25] Paralleling the Fascist invocation of *Romanitas* as the model for modern Italy, Wichit mythologized Sukhothai as an age of robust moral and cultural values that should form the basis of the Thai nation. The spread of public education in the post-absolutist period was crucial to making hegemonic the nationalist historical narrative of the continuity of the Thai kingdom from Sukhothai to Bangkok, as school textbooks provided the main vehicle for its diffusion.

The first challenge to this came in the 1950s from Thai Marxist historiography. Udom Sisuwan's *Thailand, a Semi-colony* (1950) and Chit Phumisak's *The Real Face of Thai Feudalism* (1957; see Chapter 4), recast Thai history in class terms as the royal-noble exploitation of commoners. Chit made a major contribution to the political and historical debate by resignifying the term *sakdina* as the equivalent of feudalism in his Marxian scheme of Thailand's historical development from primitive communism (among the Tais before their migration) to slave society (Sukhothai), feudalism (Ayutthaya and early Bangkok) and capitalism (from the middle of the nineteenth century).[26] Proscribed by the dictatorial regime of Sarit and his heirs, Marxist historiography attracted a great deal of interest when it re-emerged in the early 1970s. Through a more rigorous reading of Marx than Chit's, Chatthip Natsupha and his associates in the Political Economy Group at Chulalongkorn University grounded the study of Thailand's history into an analysis of economic structures and social formations centred on the Marxian concept of the Asiatic mode of production; the critique of the royal elite's 'neo-colonial' role revealed also the influence of contemporary dependency theory. Chatthip's interest later shifted to the study of the Central Thai village, seen as a primordial communistic society based on subsistence economy eventually displaced by the joint intrusion of foreign capitalism and an equally foreign central state – an idyllic representation that has been critiqued for overlooking both social differentiation within rural communities and the role of the central government in shaping villagers' identity.[27]

Another historiographic trend that emerged in the late 1970s was 'Local History' (*Prawatisat thongthin*). Local History's agenda was not as overtly political as the Political Economy Group's; its objective was to de-centralize historical knowledge of Thailand both socially, from the court to the village, and spatially, from Sukhothai–Ayutthaya–Bangkok to provincial centres. However, Local History soon became a mirror image of the dominant historiography by focusing on the history of provincial dynasties, such as those of Chiang Mai in the North and Nakhorn Sithammarat in the South.[28] The more sustained attack on the official historical narrative came from two scholars, Nithi Iaosiwong and Sisak Walipodom, who were not purveyors of radical ideologies. Nithi's work, influenced by French Annalist historians more than Marxism, is concerned with economy, politics, culture as well as historiography, especially the manipulations and concealments of history by Prince Damrong and his followers. Sisak, an archaeologist by training, challenged the racialized definition of 'Thai-land' as a nation whose history started with the Thai settlement in the Central Plain. According to Sisak, Thailand's primordial basin of civilization was in the Khorat Plateau, and its indigenous inhabitants must be considered as the 'first Thais' regardless of the ethnic and territorial boundaries imposed in the region by Western colonialism. Significantly, both Nithi and Sisak have consistently endeavoured to address a wider audience than academia by publishing short essays and commentaries in periodicals and newspapers; at the same time, their choice of communicating exclusively in Thai has limited the impact of their scholarship among the wider community of historians of South-east Asia.[29]

News-stand historical and cultural magazines, such as *Muang boran* ('Ancient Cities', founded in 1974) and the popular *Sinlapa watthanatham* ('Art and Culture', founded in 1979), have played a major role in undermining the tenets of the official historical narrative – from questioning the authenticity of the Ramkhamhaeng Stele to redefining Thainess and rehabilitating Chineseness. The emergence of a public history domain as a reflection of the cultural values of the educated middle class was mirrored by the increasingly influential role of cinema and television in the representation (and re-invention) of national history in the context of the partial liberalization of the media in the 1990s.[30] The pluralization of history stopped short, however, of the monarchy, which remained a taboo subject for historical enquiry as for any other kind of public scrutiny.

Literature

In Thailand, as in the rest of South-east Asia, literature and journalism have played a critical role in spurring, sustaining but also critiquing the nation-building project. The concomitant growth of an urban readership and a local publishing industry in the early 1900s laid the foundations for the formation of a Thai public sphere animated by the modern professional figures of the writer and journalist, within which issues of national interests were raised and debated. Such development, while admittedly circumscribed to Bangkok, is central to the revisionist historiographic thesis of a popular nationalism in whose milieu matured the overthrow of the absolute monarchy. Afterwards, literature continued to be an outlet of political dissent despite the strict press censorship that, except for short periods of relaxation, persisted until the early 1990s.

Dissenting political views were circulated in the printed media as early as the Fifth Reign. Besides K.S.R. Kulap, mentioned above, another pioneering figure of public discussion was Thianwan Wannapho (1842–1915), a merchant and practising attorney popular as an advocate of the lower classes, who promoted an agenda of reforms to render Siam as 'civilized' as the nations of Europe. Thianwan, who gave bodily expression to his modern views by sporting a Western hairstyle and clothes, was jailed for contempt of court from 1882 to 1898, yet this experience did not silence him. Thianwan spent the rest of his life publishing a periodical in which he pressed the government on a range of issues, from the prohibition of gambling, opium and betel to the abolition of slavery and polygamy, and from the creation of industrial enterprises to the institution of a parliamentary system.[31]

The court retained throughout the Sixth Reign its traditional role as a centre of literary production. In the mid-1880s the palace's library started publishing a monthly literary review, and in 1901 a group of princes founded a literary magazine with the revealing title *Lak withaya* ('Stealing knowledge'). King Chulalongkorn was a prolific writer whose major works include a treatise on Brahmanic rituals, the itinerary of his visit to Java in 1896 and the letters written from Europe to Queen Saowapha in 1897 and to his daughter, Princess Nipha, in 1907 (published under the title *Klai ban*, 'Away from Home'). The king recorded what he saw during his travels with a keen eye for detail. In Europe not everything impressed him as being more civilized than in Siam, for example, the sight of working-class quarters in London's East End. Chulalongkorn also projected himself as a connoisseur of European culture and society. It is a measure of his international profile that the New York publisher Scribner offered to publish an English translation of *Klai ban*. One of his lesser known works is the play *Ngo pa* ('The Savages of the Forest', 1907), a tale of jealousy and revenge set among the aborigines of Peninsular Siam, which reveals an affinity with Orientalist literature in the almost ethnographic description of the Semang as a barbaric tribe – dark skinned, curly haired and skimpy clothed – living at the margins of the civilizing Thai state.

If Chulalongkorn followed in the tradition whereby Thai kings exercised both power and letters, for his successor literature took precedence over royal duties. Beside the political commentaries he published in papers owned by the crown, King Wachirawuth wrote short stories, plays, poems, and translated and adapted into Thai both classic and modern English authors such as Shakespeare and Conan Doyle. Although historians have tended to exaggerate the significance of his belletrism in engendering a sense of nationhood, the historical mythology he evoked in plays such as *Huachai nakrop* ('Soul of a Warrior') and *Phra Ruang* ('King Ruang') helped promote values such as love of the leader, spirit of independence and martial prowess that were central to the nationalistic rhetoric of the post-absolutist era. Other writings were driven by a polemical urge that targeted the increasing Westernization of the middle class – for example, in this poem that stigmatized the corruption of the Thai language:

The more I read, the more I grow annoyed
At modern writings in an incomprehensible style
That is not Thai. This modern language
Makes me dizzy. They excel at destruction.
This modish language, presumably Western,
Is unbearably dull to read and nauseating to hear.[32]

The Literary Society was instituted in 1914 to ensure compliance
with literary etiquette, compile a canon and award prizes. In fact,
what made Wachirawuth dizzy was not just the style of modern writings but their content as well. In 1923 the Books, Documents and
Newspapers Act was passed to curb increasing criticism of the government by the press; as a result, many papers were closed, printing
presses confiscated and editors imprisoned in the name of public
order.[33] Still, some three hundred dailies and periodicals (in Thai,
Chinese and English) circulated in Bangkok in the late 1920s. It was at
that time that the writers who ran the literary magazine *The Gentleman*
proposed that 'freedom of journalists is freedom of the people'. They
also coined the neologism for 'novel' (*nawaniyai*), a recently localized
foreign literary form. During the first two decades of the century
translations of European novels in serialized form had been a feature
of many Thai magazines. From the 1920s the emerging middle class's
aspirations to egalitarianism and romanticism found representation
in 'bourgeois novels' written by local authors and centred on new
social figures (civil servants, students and journalists) struggling to
overcome the social boundaries of the old regime.

The impending demise of the old regime was the implicit subtext in three novels published in the late 1920s and early '30s, which
are considered to mark the beginning of modern Thai literature.
The first, *Lakhorn haeng chiwit* ('The Circus of Life', 1929), was written
by Prince Akat Damkoeng (1905–32), a lower-rank grandson of
Rama V who killed himself at twenty-six because of gambling debts.
The novel, which was dedicated to 'the Thai nation and her people',
revolves around the themes of class and gender inequality and the
destabilizing yet irresistible allure of the West. Its central character
is a young commoner who, lacking support to pursue his studies
overseas, finds his own way to Britain, becomes a journalist and
travels widely in Europe and America while falling in love with

different Western women until his return to Bangkok with little
financial gain but confidence in the future. The novel's concluding
lines were highly prophetic: 'The past is past, and I must forget the
circus of life. Something new is about to start, and I hope it is not
as grievously sad as what has just ended.'[34] The second novel,
Khwamphit khrangraek ('The First Mistake', 1930), marked the debut of
Dokmai Sot (pseudonym of Buppha Kunchara, 1905–63), a female
author of noble origins who ranks among Thailand's major twentieth-century writers. The novel's central theme is the clash between
the hierarchical nature of the old regime and the liberating but
socially disruptive individualism imported from the West.

Even more representative of the spirit of the times was
Songkhram chiwit ('The War of Life', 1932), published weeks before
the overthrow of the absolute monarchy. The novel established the
literary reputation of Kulap Saipradit (pen name Siburapha, 1903–74),
the son of a Railways Department clerk who started his career as
publicist of the short-lived literary magazine *The Gentleman*. Kulap's
epistolary novel, modelled on Dostoevsky's novella 'Poor Folk',
narrates the relationship between a junior government official with
literary aspirations and a young woman from an impoverished
upper-class family who, despite being in love with him, ends up
marrying a well-off film director. The novel popularized the concept of 'humanitarianism' (*manutsayatham*) as a belief in the moral
superiority of the lower classes: 'Thailand is still sadly lacking when
it comes to arousing sympathy and compassion among its people.'[35]
Kulap's most successful novella, *Khang langphap* ('Behind the
Painting', 1937), adapted more than once for the screen, recounts
the infatuation of a middle-class student for an older and unhappily
married noblewoman he meets in Japan, where he is completing
his education and she lives with her Thai husband. An epistolary
relationship develops between the two after she returns to Bangkok,
but eventually the student's passion subsides. A heart-breaking re-
encounter takes place at the end of the novel between the recently
wed young man and the dying woman, who on her deathbed admits
to having reciprocated his love.

In Kulap's *Behind the Painting*, as in Prince Akat's *The Circus of Life*,
a romantic plot set in a reputedly more civilized country (Japan,
where the author had lived for a year) provides the excuse for the

espousal of Thailand's social backwardness – from the persistence of arranged marriage to the lack of recreational provisions for the working class. After being incarcerated for two years in the early 1940s, Kulap turned towards social realism and even wrote essays on Marxism. His short stories of that period focus on social injustice and the plight of peasants and workers. After leading a relief mission by the socially committed Writers' Club to the flood-stricken population of Isan, Kulap was imprisoned from 1952 to 1957 under the Anticommunist Act. After his release he returned to writing and travelled to the USSR and the PRC. While in Beijing, Kulap received news of Sarit Thanarat's coup; he decided not to go back and spent the remaining sixteen years of his life in China as a university lecturer and translator.

The principles of the socially committed writers of the 1950s were outlined in an essay on art and literary criticism by Chit Phumisak, 'Art for life, art for the people' (1957).[36] Chit's conception of literature was rooted in the humanism of nineteenth-century Russian writers like Tolstoy and Gorky (whose novel *The Mother* Chit translated in prison), but reflected also the ideological dictates of Socialist Realism. The openly didactic objectives of the committed literature of the 1950s must not overshadow that its representation of rural poverty and workers' exploitation was an open challenge to the Sarit era's rhetoric of 'development'. The government issued periodical statements to deny the social and economic problems denounced by journalists and writers, who were harassed and prosecuted as subversives and communists. Arguably the most accomplished of the committed writers that emerged in the 1950s was Khamsing Sinaok (b. 1930), whose north-eastern origins are evident in his short stories, in which farmers are cast in opposition to Bangkok people, whose aim to bring 'development' to Isan is merely a cover for self-interest. Khamsing's best-known short story, *The Politician*, is a satirical portrayal of the campaign rallies of MP candidates in the countryside.[37]

The most popular novel of the 1950s was the product of a very different milieu from the 'art for life, art for people' movement, even though it too cast a rather critical – if distinctively elitist – view on the modernization of Thai society: *Si phaendin* ('Four Reigns', 1953),[38] by Khukrit Pramot (1911–85), an eclectic personality who was variously a banker, journalist, litterateur and politician (prime minister in the critical years 1973–75). *Four Reigns* is the saga of a family from the lower Bangkok nobility from the 1890s to 1945. The epochal changes of the period that encompassed the Fifth to the Eighth Reigns (hence the title) are presented in the novel through the eyes of a female character, Ploi, who is the embodiment of traditional upper-class values and habits replaced, after the revolution of 1932, by the materialistic ethos of the Sino-Thai bourgeoisie. The novel's autobiographical and deeply nostalgic tone reflected Khukrit's palace upbringing as a great-grandson of Rama II: 'In the pages of *Four Reigns*, it is made clear that everything admirable, lovely, and worthy of praise in Siamese culture was present on the eve of the overthrow of the absolute monarchy in 1932; and that most of what has transpired since has been tainted with vulgarity and sadness.'[39]

The huge success of *Four Reigns* was repeated, some fifteen years later, by another family saga, which picked up chronologically where Khukrit's narration stops but adopted the opposite social viewpoint – that of a Chinese family. The novel *Chotmai chak muang thai* ('Letters from Thailand', 1969), written by a female student, Supha Sirising (who signed it with the pen name Botan), tells the story of an immigrant from Shantou over a timespan of 22 years – from his arrival destitute in Bangkok in 1945 to his second marriage to his dead wife's sister in 1967 – through the letters he writes to his mother in China. *Letters from Thailand*, writes its American translator, 'was a controversial novel because Botan had made no attempt to soften or leave out aspects of Chinese-Thai culture, opinions, or family matters that another author might well have decided were better left unexamined or unexposed'.[40]

The growth of tertiary education in the 1960s resulted by the end of the decade in a new wave of writers, many of whom had a provincial background even if they had later moved to Bangkok to pursue education and writing careers. Their experience of village life constituted a prime source of inspiration; the other main motif in their work was the looming American presence in Thailand, both in terms of direct military presence and the spread of consumerism. Suchit Wongthet (b. 1945) perhaps the most representative writer among the literary new wave of the turn of the 1970s, espoused as a journalist, essayist, novelist and poet (as well as founding editor of the monthly *Art and Culture*) an unorthodox notion of Thai culture together with a biting critique of Westernization. Suchit's mentor was Sulak Siwarak (b. 1932), possibly Thailand's best-known public intellectual and the founder of *Sangkhomsat parithat* ('Social Science Review'), which between 1963 and 1976 provided a forum for writers, artists and intellectuals. In the early 1970s the forums available to writers and literary critics expanded considerably while international organizations, government agencies and private foundations became variously involved in supporting literature. The abolition of press censorship after October 1973 gave new impetus to the 1950s slogan 'art for life, art for the people'; proscribed works by Chit, Kulap and other radical writers were republished while the literary canon was rejected by a new generation of committed writers and critics.

The authoritarian backlash of October 1976 affected negatively writers and intellectuals, and it was only at the end of the decade that literary activity resumed fully in parallel to national reconciliation. Literature received the support of the increasingly numerous literary prizes sponsored by private organizations (such as the much-coveted South-east Asian Write Award) and the National Culture Commission, which in 1985 instituted the National Artists Project to honour writers as well as visual and performing artists. Such institutional recognition acknowledged the role of novelists and poets as social critics by celebrating as National Artist Khamsing Sinaok, who as vice-chairman of the Socialist Party of Thailand had been forced in 1976 to flee to the jungle and later to seek refuge in Sweden. A recipient of several literary prizes was controversial poet Angkhan Kalayanaphong (b. 1926), whose innovative style is married to the denunciation of the ethical, social and environmental consequences of modernization:

> That is why Thailand is so beautiful
> Evil is done, the open forest is killed
> The dense jungle is thoroughly destroyed
> Until all streams have dried out.[41]

Social criticism was, however, hardly in line with public sentiment in the 'boom time' of the 1980s. In works of literature as in other cultural expressions the new middle class looked for models after which to fashion their social identity as well as means to validate culturally their pretensions to status. Most novels and short stories in the 1980s and '90s pandered to middlebrow taste for sentimental melodrama, while biographies of businessmen and 'how to' (*hao thu*) manuals based on Chinese classics of military strategy satisfied the public's craving for success stories and ways to achieve it.

Of major significance in a media landscape in which the state exerted close control on radio networks and TV channels was the continuous growth of the readership of newspapers and news magazines, all of which (with the exception of one Chiang Mai daily) were published in Bangkok. Established conservative papers such as the elitist *Siam rath* (founded in 1950 by Khukrit Pramot) and the mass-circulation *Thai rath* were challenged in the 1970s by quality dailies with a progressive editorial line, such as *Matichon, Thai Post* and the English-language *The Nation*. The press's role as the 'fourth estate' capable of influencing public opinion became fully evident when newspapers first challenged the attempt by the generals behind the coup of February 1991 to impose censorship and then gave ample coverage to the street protests of May 1992, which were ignored by the state-controlled broadcast media. Newspapers gained considerable credibility as a result and entered a phase of expansion, interrupted by the financial crisis of 1997. Continuing suspicion of the press explains why the Press Act of 1941, which subjected all printed material to the controlling authority of the Police Director-General, was not repealed even after the promulgation of the constitution in 1997, in which the enshrinement of freedom of speech is in obvious conflict with the act. The numerous libel suits filed against journalists and publishers by the ex-prime minister, Thaksin Chinawat, led the Thai Journalists Association to denounce the situation in 2006 as 'an era of fear and hatred . . . due to systematic, relentless state efforts to discredit their work'.[42] Such a cry was itself testimony of Thai journalists' commitment to free information in a region where most governments are notoriously inimical of press scrutiny and the press is notoriously complacent.

six | Mnemonic Sites

Historians have in recent years devoted considerable attention to the symbols and physical sites whereby the nation's biography is collectively memorialized. While ancient and pre-modern societies were no less expedient than modern ones in perpetuating social memory through myths, memorials and rituals, public commemorations and national celebrations became a prominent aspect of nation- and empire-building projects worldwide in the later nineteenth century. Thai monarchs too, like their European counterparts, manipulated the past to sanction change via the authority of historical custom as well as continuity via newly invented traditions. The post-absolutist period saw the use of monuments and commemorations as tools to instil in the population loyalty to the nation and the constitution. Registration and restoration of Thailand's historic sites were also initiated in the 1930s and carried out randomly through the 1960s. However, it was only in the 1970s that the notion of heritage (*moradok*) acquired a space in public discourse both in connection to the bureaucratic promotion of national identity and the globalization of the conservation ethos by the UNESCO Convention on the Protection of the World Natural and Cultural Heritage adopted in 1972. Princess Sirinthorn's birthday was made into Thai Cultural Heritage Conservation Day (2 April), while Rama IX declared: 'Historical sites are our nation's prestige. Even a single block of old bricks is valuable to preserve. With no Sukhothai, Ayutthaya and Bangkok, Thailand is meaningless.'[1]

The turning point in the rise of a social awareness of the nation's heritage was arguably the campaign in 1988 for the restitution of a carved lintel spirited from the Khmer mountain temple of Prasat Phanom Rung and on display in the Art Institute of Chicago. There was of course some irony in a Khmer artefact becoming the focus of public furore over the dissipation of Thailand's heritage while antique dealers in Bangkok enjoyed international notoriety for selling stolen Cambodian antiquities. This irony was redoubled in January 2003, when comments by a Thai soap-opera actress about Thailand's entitlement to the ownership of Angkor Wat sparked a series of vicious attacks on the Thai embassy and businesses in Phnom Penh. As important as domestic ideological motivations for the valorization of Thailand's cultural and monumental heritage were international factors: tourism and the cultural policy of UNESCO, on whose coveted World Heritage list Sukhothai and Ayutthaya were inscribed in 1991. But the restoration and commercial exploitation of historic monuments by government agencies was not without critics; some charged that historic sites were being turned into fictional landscapes and used as stage sets for touristic spectacles. Another notable aspect of the politics of public memory was the commemoration at last of the victims of state violence. Accordingly, Thailand's globally marketed heritage of venerable temples and imposing ruins is now compounded by dissonant mnemonic sites that are reminders of the contested, and at times violent, nature of the nation-building project.

Sacred Sites

In a context where the linkage between Buddhism and political legitimacy continues to pervade public discourse, religious monuments represent not simply a large part of the Thai national heritage but also 'mnemonic environments' where the unity of faith and nationality is ritually performed.[2] Before the coinage in the early twentieth century of a neologism for monuments of a secular nature (*anusaori*), the word in use (*chedi*, from the Pali *cetiya*) denoted Buddhist materials such as relics and reliquaries, images and aniconic representations (e.g., the footprint and the Bodhi tree), inscriptions and the canon of the scriptures itself. All were 'monuments' (that is, 'reminders') of the Buddha and his teachings. Devotional practice linked to specific sites, such as the cult of relics and images, bonded Buddhist communities across the Theravada œcumene, which included Ceylon, Burma, Laos and Cambodia as well as Siam. Following the exemplum of Indian emperor Asoka, who in the third century BC disseminated Buddhist reliquaries and inscriptions throughout his kingdom, Thai rulers had *wat* and *chedi* built and images cast to acquire merit. The makers of religious monuments and images, rather than pursuing stylistic innovation, tended to reproduce existing ones that commanded special reverence within the Theravada œcumene.

Royalty and the nobility also bore the responsibility for the upkeep of temples and images; yet the purpose of conservation was to preserve their intrinsic potency (*saksit*) rather than any historic value. This approach to restoration as reconstitution, typical of religious worldviews, is documented in a mid-fourteenth century inscription from Sukhothai. In the 1850s King Mongkut followed the same principle when he had a ruined *chedi* in Nakhorn Pathom preserved by incorporation into a new structure (the gigantic *chedi* visible today dates, however, to the 1870s). The construction of new monasteries was still an important aspect of royalty's patronage of religion throughout Mongkut's reign, but it declined sharply in the next. Only two royal *wat* were built in Bangkok during the 42 years of Chulalongkorn's reign. As a result of the decline in the construction of temples and the concomitant trend of renting out plots of monastery land for commercial use, by the beginning of the twentieth century Bangkok had lost most of its original character as sacred cityscape. But its historic core, the canal-encircled Rattankosin Island, still retains a high concentration of buildings (the Grand Palace and adjoining Wat Phrakaeo, Wat Mahathat, Wat Po and the city's pillar or Lak Muang) that evoke the pre-modern urban topography shaped by the Indic cosmological principle of the correspondence between earthly realm, centred on the palace-temple complex, and the universe, which has its pivot in Mount Meru.

Along with its symbolic function, the Grand Palace naturally served as the court's place of residence. When the court moved to

Sacred grounds: Wat Phrakaeo, Bangkok, c. 1895.

the new Dusit Park suburban palace at the start of the twentieth century, the Grand Palace lost its immediate function and was eventually turned into something resembling a museum; within its compound, Wat Phrakaeo retained, for Thais at least, its place as the prime site in the kingdom's sacred landscape, even if under the guise of a tourist attraction. A difference can be noted in the way foreigners and Thai nationals approach Wat Phrakaeo: the former, who are required to pay an entry fee, go for tourist sightseeing; the latter, who enjoy free admittance, to gain merit. The religious pre-eminence of Wat Phrakaeo, which is exceptional in not having resident monks, is redoubled by the fact that it enshrines the Emerald Buddha (*phrakaeo morakot*), a small image of jadeite which is the kingdom's palladium – the protector of its security and the guardian of its prosperity.

According to the legend which enshrouds its social life, the Emerald Buddha was discovered, still covered by stucco, when lightning struck a *chedi* in Chiang Rai in 1434. When the stucco cracked and revealed the image's glowing green aspect underneath, the Emerald Buddha was taken to have miraculous powers and became coveted by the rival rulers of neighbouring chiefdoms. Removed first from Chiang Rai to Chiang Mai and from there to Vientiane in the sixteenth century, the Emerald Buddha was finally taken to Bangkok as war booty by Rama I and installed in the palace's monastery as a palladium of Bangkok and the dynasty.[3] The solemn ritual of the changing of the Emerald Buddha's seasonal robe, concluded with the sprinkling of lustral water on the worshippers gathered outside the temple, is still performed by the sovereign or his representative.

The devotional attitude of those seeking merit must not overshadow the recreational dimension of pilgrimages, especially among the lower and middle social strata. The famed temples of Chiang Mai, such as Wat Phrathat, perched on the hilltop of Doi Suthep overlooking the city, are favourite domestic destinations. The mountain monastery, accessed by a high stone staircase (and now a lift as well), dates to the sixteenth century and is built in the style of Burmese temples. In the 1930s a local monk started the construction of the sealed road between Chiang Mai and Doi Suthep, allowing for the expansion in the number of visitors. Another aspect of merit-making pilgrimage, which became popular among

The past improved: Sukhothai Historical Park.

urban middle-class devotees in the 1970s, is the visit to forest monasteries, especially those in Isan. In the case of Phra Phuttabat Buabok, a natural site in the north-eastern province of Udon Thani whose rock formations are associated with folk tales of the Buddha's previous lives (*jataka*), ongoing devotional practice eventually led to its monumentalization, when the site was included in the select group of 'historical parks' (see below), despite possessing neither historical nor artistic significance. Such inclusion by the Fine Arts Department, as well as its controversial restoration of the ruins of Sukhothai and more recently of the sixteenth-century Wat Chedi Luang in Chiang Mai, is an acknowledgement of the fact that the historically minded approach to ancient monuments championed by the modernizing elite never fully displaced the religious and devotional one amongst the broader population, who still wrap monks' robes around the Buddha images located amidst ruins and make offerings to them. Thus, religious sites in Thailand, particularly Buddhist ones, continue to represent foci of local worship as much as physical manifestations of the nation's historical unfolding and catalysts for its social recollection.

Museums and Historical Parks

Thailand possesses a patrimony of archaeological sites and historic monuments that is among the richest in South-east Asia. The origins of the assemblage of national heritage may be found in King Mongkut's antiquarian pursuits, which included the discovery of the Ramkhamhaeng Stele and the conservation of the palaces of King Narai in Lopburi and King Naresuan in Ayutthaya. Mongkut also kept a collection of scientific instruments and curios in a hall of the Grand Palace called *phiphithaphan* ('miscellaneous things'), the term later used to translate the word 'museum'. In 1887 the royal collection was moved to the Palace of the Front (opposite the Grand Palace), which eventually was to house the National Museum. However, the most artistically valuable religious images and artefacts, both Buddhist and Hindu, were still displayed in monasteries. In the early 1900s, after the new Wat Benchamabophit (known in English as the Marble Temple from the white Carrara marble that covers it) had been built, King Chulalongkorn entrusted Prince

Damrong to search both in the capital and the provinces for 50 antique Buddha images in different styles for installation in the temple's cloisters. Damrong reported that the images were to be 'displayed in such a way that the public might acquire knowledge of Buddhist iconography'.[4]

As mentioned above, the appreciation of history and archaeology as important for the authentication of Siam's civilizational lineage led to the establishment of the Royal Library (1905) and the Antiquarian Society (1907). However, a more systematic approach to historic conservation began only with the creation of the Archaeological Service in 1924 (later reconstituted as the Archaeological Division of the Fine Arts Department), followed by the reorganization of Bangkok's museum in 1926, both under the direction of George Cœdès. The Museum of the Royal Capital, renamed the National Museum in 1934, provided both the model of and the model for the national history of art outlined by Prince Damrong with Cœdès by mapping out, in the space of its galleries, the archaeological landscape of the kingdom (as defined by boundary demarcation at the turn of the century) according to a sequence of epochs and schools in which the art of Sukhothai stood as the 'classical' period. The art-historical aspects of this chronology were illustrated by religious icons, which, as museum exhibits, acquired a new epistemological status as national antiquities.[5]

From the mid-1930s to the mid-1970s intermittent attention was paid to historical conservation. A preliminary registration of the kingdom's historic sites was carried out in 1935. In his post-war term as prime minister, Phibun was a great sponsor of the restoration of major *wat*, especially on the occasion of the twenty-fifth Buddhist centennial (1956–7). After the death of Sarit, who had identified his leadership with development, the government approved conservation plans for Sukhothai (1964) and Ayutthaya (1969). The National Museum was expanded in 1967 by the addition of two new wings while branches were established in the main provincial capitals. Conservation of antiquities was given unprecedented emphasis under the Fourth National Economic and Social Development Plan (1977–81), at the time of an economic slowdown and when fighting the communist insurgency was a priority. The official call to 'cultivate the love for Thai traditional art and culture' through the preservation of the country's cultural heritage partook of a wider policy designed to reinforce state-endorsed definitions of culture and identity as an ideological barrier against radicalism.[6]

Under the Fourth and Fifth Development Plans nine historic sites (Sukhothai, Ayutthaya, Prasat Phanom Rung, Prasat Muang Sing, Prasat Phimai, Si Satchanalai, Khamphaeng Phet, Si Thep and Phra Nakhon Khiri) were developed into 'historical parks' (*utthayan prawatisat*). Place of pride was however assigned to the ruins of Sukhothai and Ayutthaya, whose restoration was financed by the government, private and foreign donations, and UNESCO sponsorship. A master plan for the Sukhothai Historical Park, covering the area enclosed by the old city walls as well as major monumental sites within a 5km radius, was drawn up by a team comprising archaeologists, anthropologists, historians, architects, economists, engineers and technicians. The park was inaugurated in November 1988 to celebrate King Phumiphon's achievement of the longest reign in Thai history. However, the restoration of monuments and the landscaping in the park's area also attracted considerable criticism. Archaeologist Sisak Walipodom stigmatized the Fine Arts Department's actions as 'the "legally authorized" process of destroying ancient and historic sites'; and historian Thida Saraya spoke of 'newly created environments stemming from historical fictions and myths'. The Fine Arts Department responded to the criticism by citing the authority of the Ramkhamhaeng Stele, whose description of Sukhothai was said to have inspired the landscaping – and this, ironically or opportunely, just at the time when the stele was at the centre of a controversy over its authenticity.[7]

Charges of fabrication were also levelled against the Loi Khrathong festival, held in the Sukhothai Historical Park in November, the highlight of which is a son et lumière show staged on the night of the full moon. Marketed as a genuine custom from the time of Sukhothai, the Loi Khrathong festival became a major attraction for domestic visitors after its first staging in the early 1980s. The popularity of the Loi Khrathong festival led to the staging of other shows at several historic sites. One such son et lumière show on an especially grand scale is the 'Golden Era of Ayutthaya', whose climax is the representation of the razing of the city by the invading Burmese army in 1767. Public memory of this event as a

The new and the reconstructed: Ayutthaya Historical Park.

national cataclysm continues to obscure the fact that the thorough destruction of Ayutthaya was partly the result of the recycling of building materials for new constructions in Bangkok. Resettlement in the Ayutthaya area from the 1830s caused further dissipation of architectural remains.

By 1900, the ruins of Ayutthaya were already a tourist attraction. The province's high commissioner, a keen antiquary who was bestowed the title of 'Lord Conservator of the Old Capital', regularly cleared the vegetation around the ruins and established in 1907 the first provincial museum inside the local Chantrakasem Palace. Hasty monument restorations took place for the 25th Buddhist centenary and, again, in the first half of the 1970s, when concrete Buddha images were installed among the ruins. The Ayutthaya Historical Park project, approved in 1977, was designed to evoke, as in Sukhothai, a monumental and celebratory image of Siam's royal capital. Its realization over an area of three square kilometres required the resettlement of two hundred households and extensive landscaping of the cultivated area to give visitors an impression of the city's system of waterways as represented in seventeenth-century Dutch and French maps. Interpretation of the history of Ayutthaya, not only as a royal capital but also as a port city open to international commerce and the centre of a feudal agrarian state, was left to the privately founded Ayutthaya Historical Study Centre, opened in 1990. What was then its state-of-the-art permanent exhibition aroused considerable (if short-lived) interest as an openly didactic approach to museums not centred on the value of individual artefacts. A short distance from Ayutthaya lies the royal summer palace of Bang Pa In, built in the 1870s by King Chulalongkorn on a seventeenth-century site. The palace, which contains edifices in both Western and Oriental styles, including an Italianate building, a Swiss chalet, a Chinese mansion shipped in sections from China, and a now-demolished Moorish pavilion, adapted the fantastic environments of late nineteenth-century international exhibitions to create a recreational space for his court and foreign guests. On the opposite bank of the river from the palace site stands the small Wat Niwet, whose peculiar ordination hall, built in the shape of a Gothic chapel, complements Bang Pa In's reversed architectural exoticism.

The Thai government had nominated the historic sites of Ayutthaya and Sukhothai (with its two satellite towns, Si Satchanalai and Khamphaeng Phet) for inclusion in the UNESCO World Heritage List as early as 1980. The sites were inscribed on the List in 1991; the next year was the turn of the prehistoric site of Ban Chiang. The

The Thai and the neoclassical: summer palace at Bang Pa In.

inclusion of Sukhothai and Ayutthaya in the World Heritage List amounted to the ultimate validation of their central place in the national historical narrative. The World Heritage committee appraised Sukhothai as 'capital of the first kingdom of Siam' and Ayutthaya as 'the second Siamese capital after Sukhothai . . . destroyed by the Burmese in the eighteenth century'. As for Ban Chiang, it was described as 'the most important prehistoric settlement discovered so far in South-east Asia, . . . centre of a remarkable phenomenon of human, cultural, social and technological evolution'. The Ban Chiang site, however, was not given the emphasis it deserved, arguably because of its incongruous place in the national historical narrative, whose beginning is marked by the settlement of the Thais in the early thirteenth century.

It is instructive to contrast Ban Chiang's 'eccentricity' in Thailand's historical narrative to the assimilation into the national heritage of the North-east's Khmer stone sanctuaries of Prasat Phimai and Prasat Phanom Ruang. Built in the tenth to twelfth centuries along the imperial route that led to Angkor, capital of the Khmer empire, the two sanctuaries were re-erected and improved in the late 1980s by the Fine Arts Department under the 'historical parks' scheme. Their restoration, together with that of several other smaller Khmer shrines, was primarily intended to boost Isan's appeal as a tourist destination at a time when Angkor was still off-limits because of the activity of the Khmer Rouge guerrillas; implicit in the restoration, however, was a claim to Khmer architecture as being part of Thailand's cultural heritage. Concomitant with the restorations was the proposal advanced by some scholars to revise the notion of the twelfth- and thirteenth-century Khorat Plateau polities as vassals of Angkor by considering them as autonomous principalities within an imperial federation led, but not dominated, by the Khmers.[8] The political subtext of this revisionist thesis was obvious, especially given that the restoration of Prasat Phimai and Prasat Phanom Ruang coincided with the Thai government's launch of the slogan 'transforming Indochina's battlefields into market-places', which was to pave the way for the penetration of Thai business into neighbouring countries.

The improved version of the past evoked by the Fine Arts Department was not confined to isolated ruins but also included Bangkok's historic core. After the court's transfer to the palace in Dusit, Rattanakosin Island drew its identity from the presence of cultural institutions (the National Museum and National Theatre, and the universities Thammasat and Silpakorn) as well as a vibrant community of street vendors and petty traders. The Bangkok Bicentenary in 1982 powerfully reasserted the connection between the capital and the dynasty by making urban heritage virtually synonymous with royal and Buddhist architecture. The main project occasioned by the Bicentenary was the renovation of the Grand Palace-Wat Phrakaeo complex. A second nucleus of royal heritage was created away from Rattanakosin Island by transforming King Chulalongkorn's Dusit Park palace into a museum (opened in 1985) where royalist nostalgia and nouveau-riche aspirations came literally under one roof. Its centrepiece, the decaying teakwood Wimanmek Palace, was renovated and refitted with period furniture and fittings (including a bathtub and electric chandeliers); other exhibits include gilded thrones, paintings, *objets d'art* and assorted kitsch – all imported from Europe. On entering the room where a full-length portrait of Rama v in Western uniform hangs, the guides require Thai visitors to crouch on the floor as a sign of respect to his memory.

Urban beautification: restored fort at Phra Athit Road, Bangkok.

More recently the adjacent Anantha Samakhom Throne Hall was open to the public and included in the sightseeing tour of the Dusit Palace. King Chulalongkorn wanted the classicizing Anantha Samakhom – designed and decorated by Italian architects and artists – ready for the celebration of his fortieth year on the throne; but at the time of his death it was still unfinished. To his heir, the throne hall epitomized that 'cult of imitation' of the West that King Wachirawuth ridiculed in his writings. Thus, after its lavish inauguration in January 1917, the Anantha Samakhom remained deserted until 24 June 1932, when it was utilized as temporary place of detention for members of the royalty – an episode that has been erased from public memory. Its subsequent conversion into the seat of the national assembly after 1932 was not particularly successful either, despite a design that resembled many nineteenth-century parliament houses (in 1974 another assembly hall was built on an adjacent plot). Yet, royalist myth-makers have attempted to reinvent the building's social life as evidence of Chulalongkorn's alleged intention, devoid of any historical foundation, to build an assembly hall

183

for the time when the parliamentary institution would be politically suitable in Siam.

In the wake of the Chakri Bicentenary, land use and building height in the Rattanakosin Island area were regulated by decree. A government-level committee produced a master plan for the 'preservation and development' of a 6.2 sq. km area, termed Old Town, at a projected cost of 1.5 billion Baht. Reactions by academics and civic society activists to the release of the plan in 1995 were highly critical as the plan required the demolition of some of the more recent buildings in the area and the resettlement of street vendors in order to benefit the historic architecture and develop green areas in the thick inner city fabric. In 1996 the Bangkok Metropolitan Authority drafted an alternative plan, in which not only historic monuments and architecture but cultural practices too were approached as heritage. The plan's aim to revitalize the social fabric of the capital's historic districts was not limited to Rattanakosin Island. In the face of a traffic and pollution alert, the election of a new metropolitan administration in 1998 produced yet another plan, drawn up with UNESCO assistance and significantly named 'Humanize Bangkok', which aimed to involve local residents in sustainable urban development. However, in May 1997, just weeks before the financial crisis erupted, the government approved the much criticized Old Town conservation plan.[9] Its first outcome was the restoration of a ruined eighteenth-century fort on the river bank and the landscaping of the surrounding area, a project which imposed the state idea of heritage as monumental in character and celebrative in intent onto Bangkok's living urban environment, paying little attention to the social memories of its inhabitants. Concurrent initiatives endeavoured, however, to assert a different idea of heritage as detailed in the next section.

Monuments and Commemorations

The equestrian statue of King Chulalongkorn, unveiled on the opening day of celebrations for his fortieth anniversary on the throne in November 1908, was Thailand's first 'public' monument – in the double sense of being placed in a public place and being paid for by public subscription. The royal jubilee aimed at shaping public memory of the Fifth Reign as an age of progress by commemorating history in the making. In this memorial project, ordinary subjects were largely spectators to the ruling elite's self-celebration, though some were able to purchase a modicum of agency by contributing to the realization of the king's monument (excess donations were utilized to build Chulalongkorn University). The larger-than-life statue had been sculpted by two French artists (one for the king's figure, the other for the horse's) and cast in a Parisian foundry in the late summer of 1908; it was then shipped to Bangkok and erected on a tall marble pedestal in the middle of the Royal Plaza, the wide open expanse where the 'avenue of royal progress', linking the Grand Palace to the Dusit Park palace, terminates. The huge bronze statue must have struck many an onlooker, as a realistic portrayal of a sovereign had never before been shown in a public space; perhaps some also wondered why the king was astride a horse since the animal associated with royal status in Siam, as in all the Indianized polities of the region, was the elephant.[10]

Monumentalizing himself: Rama V unveils his equestrian statue, 11 November 1908.

The equestrian monument became the focal point of Rama V Memorial Day, instituted by his successor on 23 October 1912, when school pupils, teachers and civil servants congregate as representatives of the Thai body politic in the Royal Plaza to lay floral wreaths at the base of the monument in a civic ritual of nationhood. In the early 1990s the monument became the focus of a different kind of commemoration, not initiated by the state but born spontaneously among the new middle social strata. People began gathering around the statue every week, on the evenings of Tuesday and then also Thursday, with traditional offerings of floral wreaths, incense sticks and candles but also, and characteristically, imported luxury consumer items, such as French cognac and Cuban cigars. According to historian Nithi Iaosiwong, the cult of Rama V originated among Sino-Thai entrepreneurs who had grown richer during the boom decade 1987–96 but felt threatened by the corruption of the civil service and the volatility of the global economy, and so took to praying to the king's benign spirit for protection.[11] Later on, the cult spread socially, from the middle class to the lower middle and working classes, and geographically, from the capital to the provinces. Unlike students on Rama V Day, worshippers commemorate the late king as a purveyor of prosperity rather than as 'father of the nation'; they invoke his memory not through his title of 'great king' (*piya maharat*) but the more familiar epithet 'royal father' (*sadaet pho*); and pay homage to him individually, for the sake of personal benefit, rather than collectively on behalf of the national community.

In 1919 King Wachirawuth instituted another national holiday, Chakri Day, on 6 April to commemorate the dynasty's foundation. Celebrations were also held in May and September 1919 on the return of the corps that had participated in the First World War. In 1921, on the fourth anniversary of Siam's declaration of war, a monument enshrining the ashes of the nineteen Thai war casualties (none died in action) was dedicated on a site near the Royal Plaza.[12] But although Wachirawuth patently appropriated the contemporary militarized nationalist rhetoric, Bangkok was immune to the 'statuomania' that swept the cities of Europe and even Japan in the wake of the First World War.[13] While Thai craftsmen's technical limitations may in part account for it, this absence reveals the absolutist regime's disinterest in memorializing figures of state notables as participants in the state-building project. The second specimen of public statuary erected in Bangkok was the larger-than-life statue of the dynasty's founder sitting on the throne. The monument was dedicated in April 1932 at the foot of the new Memorial Bridge, the first traffic bridge to span the Chaophraya River; both were erected to celebrate Bangkok's and the dynasty's sesquicentennial, only two months before the overthrow of the absolute monarchy.

The statue of Rama I, cast in Milan, was the first major commission of Corrado Feroci (1892–1962), the last in a long series of Italian artists active in Thailand. Arriving from Florence in 1923, Feroci joined the Fine Arts Department; in 1933 he was given the task of setting up the curriculum of the school of fine arts, Silpakorn, which was re-founded in 1943 as a university under his deanship. Feroci, who in 1944 was naturalized with the name Sin Phirasi, is memorialized as the 'father of Thai modern art'; his statue inside Silpakorn University is regularly bedecked with flower garlands. However, his role as the official artist of, consecutively, the waning absolute monarchy, the constitutional government and the authoritarian regimes of the 1940s and '50s is still largely unexamined. Feroci's first commission under the constitutional government was the statue of Thao Suranari, the heroine of the North-eastern town of Nakhorn Ratchasima (also known as Khorat), who, as the wife of the province's governor, had allegedly helped defeat an invading Lao army in 1827. The invasion was in fact a revolt by the Lao lord of Vientiane against the Thai suzerain; its suppression, which entailed the razing of Vientiane, was documented by Prince Damrong in a work written in 1926. In it Damrong briefly mentioned the episode involving the governor's wife and explained that the title of Thao Suranari ('Dame Gallant') had been bestowed on her by Rama III. Thao Suranari had died in 1852 and social memory of her deeds was unlikely to be strong in the mid-1930s, when she became the focus of national memorialization.

Prince Damrong, queried by his brother on the historical reasons for a monument to Thao Suranari, opined that it was 'one more example of how present-day thinking is totally at odds with that of the past'. The decision to make her a focus of public commemoration through the erection of a statue at the gate of Khorat's reconstructed city walls, unveiled in January 1935, has been explained with reference to the royalist rebellion led by Prince Boworadet, which erupted in the local provincial garrison in 1933 and cast doubts on the town's loyalty to the constitutional government. The monument to the heroine who had defeated an earlier rebellion against the central authority was thus probably intended as a reminder of patriotic virtues for Khorat's inhabitants. In 1967 a second statue, modelled on Feroci's, was placed in the central square. By the 1990s this statue had become the focus of a cult akin to that of Rama V and centred on the popular incarnation of Thao Suranari as 'Grandmother Mo' (ya mo). The cult was an important source of local income by attracting throngs of domestic tourists; but a local schoolteacher who demystified the figure of Thao Suranari and the politics of her monument in a study published in 1995 was forced to flee Khorat to escape public hostility and mob threats – an episode that underscored how intractable national history, intertwined in this case with public memory, can still be in present-day Thailand.[14]

In the immediate post-absolutist period, the events of June 1932 were considered too controversial for public commemoration. The change in government was memorialized by a bronze plaque installed on the pavement of the Royal Plaza, in front of the Rama V equestrian monument; its inscription reads: 'On this spot, at dawn on 24 June 1932, the People's Party created the constitution for the benefit of the nation'. The plaque was allegedly removed during the Sarit era and reinstalled on an unspecified date; to this day, its existence remains unknown to most Bangkok inhabitants.[15] Phibun Songkhram, upon becoming prime minister, added to Constitution Day (10 December), instituted in the mid-1930s, another national holiday by replacing Chakri Day with National Day (24 June), which commemorated the overthrow of the absolute monarchy. On the inaugural National Day in 1939, construction was initiated of the Democracy Monument, which was inaugurated the following year. Built, with an apt choice of location, in the middle of a traffic roundabout in the inner section of Ratchadamnoen, the avenue of royal progress, the Democracy Monument features four wing-like slabs placed diagonally around a cylindrical shrine, on top of which lies a gilded bronze cast of the book of the constitution resting on two ceremonial bowls; planted around the monument's circular base are 75 cannons. The monument was designed by architect Meo Aphaiwong, brother of an influential member of the government, and furnished with Feroci's large bas-relief panels depicting the People's Party plotters, soldiers and workers. Meo's design was laded with a heavy numerical symbolism that baffled beholders, nor was Feroci's sculptural decoration in the style of socialist realism able to propagate the regime's message; the group of rushing soldiers in particular was reportedly understood as acting in the defence of the monarchy rather than the constitution.[16]

The Victory Monument (1941) was the other piece of visual propaganda built in the capital during the Phibun years. The monument – a fluted cement obelisk allusive of a sword, with bronze statues of a sailor, a pilot, a soldier and a policeman placed on the four sides of the pedestal – was positioned in the middle of a traffic junction in what was then Bangkok's northern outskirts. The monument was realized at great speed to celebrate the military victory over the French colonial army in January 1941, which temporarily returned Cambodia's western provinces under Thai control. Its straightforward iconography allowed for a much easier reading than the Democracy Monument's, even though Feroci allegedly referred to it as 'the victory of embarrassment'.[17] Also conceived in those years, but realized by Feroci only during Phibun's post-war term, was the equestrian monument of King Taksin (1953). The monument, situated in Thonburi (on the opposite bank of the Chaophrya), where Taksin had established his headquarters in the 1770s, represents the mounted sovereign with his sabre raised to the sky before leading a charge. Its belligerent pose and its origins in the nationalist climate of the late 1930s invites an interpretation of it as an antagonistic statement towards the Chakri dynasty, whose founder had Taksin dethroned and executed on charges of impiety.

Unlike the Victory Monument and the equestrian statue of King Taksin, whose original meaning is almost irrelevant to today's passers-by caught in the flow of car traffic, the Democracy Monument underwent a symbolic resignification as the focal site of the popular uprising that on 14 October 1973 ousted the military from power – an event etched in Thai collective memory by the iconic image of an ocean of demonstrators engulfing the roundabout

Memorial to democracy: the Democracy Monument engulfed by
demonstrators, 14 October 1973.

with the Democracy Monument at its centre. Its new social function
as the mnemonic site for the 'October generation' resurfaced in
May 1992, when people again took to the streets and engaged in
an equally dramatic and eventually victorious confrontation with
the generals in power. On the thirtieth anniversary of the October
1973 events, Bangkok's most recent monument, officially named
'Memorial to the Martyrs of October 14', was unveiled a short distance from the Democracy Monument. The memorial is formed by
a sunken area for temporary exhibitions, from which rises into the
open air a *chedi*-like conical shaft capped by a 'torch of democracy';
at street level a roofed gallery is delimited by a curved wall on which
are pasted giant photographs of the October demonstrations and
placards narrating the events.

The memorial had a long and difficult gestation. After the fall
of military rule in 1973, the National Student Council of Thailand
collected 4 million Baht to erect a memorial to the casualties of the
armed repression of the previous days. The new civilian government put aside a plot of land formerly occupied by the State Lottery
Bureau, which had been set on fire. Following the coup of 6 October
1976, the money collected was confiscated from the student organizations and the project cancelled. In 1989 a provisional memorial

– a cement cast of five figures intertwined around a flag – was installed on the site originally set aside for it (which, in the meantime, had been reoccupied by lottery sellers) and an annual commemoration began to be held there in October. After several false starts, and despite the military's continuing opposition, in 1998 the then Prime Minister, Chuan Likpai, announced the government's intention to build the memorial in order to commemorate also the victims of 'Black May'.

The memorial is, however, fundamentally ambivalent. On the one hand, it acknowledges political struggle as part of national history; on the other, it sets the limits of the public representation of those events by emphasizing the 'triumph' of October 1973, when the throne stood on the students' side, over the military reaction of 1976, which enjoyed the throne's support. In other words, public commemoration was allowed on condition that the uncomfortable implications of the Thammasat University massacre would not be raised. The task of perpetuating public memory of what in Thai is colloquially known as *hok tula* (6 October) was taken up in recent years by some of those who experienced that event, even though others have chosen to forgive – and forget. On the twentieth anniversary of the student massacre, a symbolic cremation for the forty-three official victims was staged on Thammasat University's central lawn. A prominent historian who had been one of the student leaders in 1976 and was now an organizer of the 1996 commemoration reflected thus on the interplay of amnesia and amnesty in the event's aftermath: 'It remains to be seen if, and in what ways, the memories of the massacre in the broader context of recent Thai history have really changed, and in what ways ambivalence remains among the culprits and the victims . . .'[18]

Despite unresolved ambivalences, the commemoration of the student massacre exemplified the pluralization of histories and memories in Thailand at the turn of the millennium. In 2000 several initiatives commemorated the centenary of the birth of Pridi Phanomyong, the statesman of the early constitutional era considered by many the father of Thai democracy. An installation by artist Suti Kunawichayanont, *History Class*, consisting of fourteen wooden school desks carved with captioned images of controversial episodes in the nation's history, was set up along the Democracy Monument roundabout; guided tours of the historic district's mnemonic sites associated with the struggle for democracy were also organized to offer an interpretation of the Rattanakosin Island cityscape alternative to the official one, which subsumes urban history under the rubric of dynastic achievements. Ironically, a few months later a plan to relocate to a suburban campus the undergraduate population of Thammasat University, which had been founded by Pridi, was made public. The new government also proposed to refashion the inner section of Ratchadamnoen Avenue, where stands the Democracy Monument, into a shopping street providing a showcase for the Thaksin government's slogan, 'One district, one product'. While the relocation plan eventually prevailed, the vociferous opposition to it and the unveiling of the 14 October Memorial in 2003 underscored public commitment to keeping alive the dissonant memories embedded in Bangkok's Rattanakosin district.

seven | Others

The promotion of a national identity since the beginning of the twentieth century necessitated the textual and visual configuration of Others in relation to or against which the Thai self could be fashioned, defended and measured. Siam was traditionally characterized as a Buddhist kingdom with an ethnically diverse population; but when the notion of ethnic lineage (*chat*) was assumed as the template for the imagination of the modern Thai nation, such inclusiveness was rejected and figures of alterity were engendered through jurisprudence, historiography, literature, dramaturgy and cinematography to serve the different rhetorical needs of the nation-building project. The Burmese, whose historical enmity with Thai rulers stemmed from competition for power and merit, were reconfigured as the number one national enemy; the Chinese, despite their secular history of settlement, were represented in the face of mass immigration and emerging nationalist loyalties as profiteering and unassimilable aliens and later as communist agents; and Westerners (*farang*), active in Thailand since the seventeenth century as traders and missionaries, were assigned the ambivalent role of civilizational paradigms and irreconcilable opposites, the Other Thais love to hate.

The Burmese Enemy

For generations of Thais nationhood was grounded in the received memory of the Burmese destruction of Ayutthaya in 1767 – an event memorialized even in the Thai language by the idiomatic expression *sia krung* ('laying the capital to waste'). Countless novels, plays, films, history books and, more recently, a son et lumière show staged amidst the ruins of Ayutthaya propagated the image of the Burmese as aggressors of the peace-loving Thais. In reality, conflict with Burma was prominent only in three periods during Ayutthaya's four hundred years of history: the so-called 'elephant wars' of 1548–69, which ended with the first fall of Ayutthaya; the military campaigns of King Naresuan from 1584 to 1605, which drove the Burmese out of Siam; and the protracted wars that began in 1759 and culminated in Ayutthaya's second and definitive fall.[1]

One of the consequences of the sack of Ayutthaya was the loss of its dynastic records; when the chronicles were recompiled in the first Bangkok reign, the description of the destruction of the city was added as a postscript. By insisting on the iconoclastic violence against the temples and sacred images of Ayutthaya, the chronicles represented the Burmese as impious destroyers of Buddhism as much as enemies of the Thais. Rama I himself composed a poem in which he celebrated his victory as a Buddhist triumph:

> The Burmese ran and fled for their lives
> A great many were killed
> With this transcendent virtue I have accumulated
> I vow to give all my support
> To the upholding of the Buddhist religion.[2]

A son of Rama I, Prince Paramanuchit, commemorated in another poem, *Lilit talaeng phai* ('The Defeat of the Talengs', 1832), the victory of King Naresuan over the crown prince of the Burmese kingdom of Pegu in a mounted elephant duel in 1592. As a high-ranking monk, Prince Paramanuchit was certainly aware of the religious and cultural connections between Ceylon, Burma and Siam; and, indeed, in those same years Prince Mongkut, then also a monk, designed an ordination rite for its Thammayut sect following the advice of a monk from Burma (probably of Mon ethnicity). Indeed, the Burmese community of Bangkok was still noticeable in the early 1900s.[3]

In 1854 King Mongkut sent an army to capture Chiangtung, a Shan vassal to Pegu, taking advantage of the recent British occupation of lower Burma, but the Burmese routed the Thai army. Sixty years later, in 1914, Rama VI officially commemorated Naresuan's 'glorious victory' around the ruins of a stupa in Suphanburi province, which Prince Damrong had identified as the memorial erected on the battle site. Naresuan's victory had, in King Wachirawuth's words, 'secured our national freedom and made our nation respected by the Burmese and the Talengs [Mons]'.[4] In 1917 Damrong published the first version of a history of the wars between the Thais and the Burmese, which was to have a profound effect on the emerging national consciousness. Between the first and the second, expanded edition of the book in 1920, the title changed from *Thai rop phama* ('Thai wars with Burma') to *Rao rop phama* ('Our wars with Burma'), although the definitive 1928 edition (reprinted several times since) reverted to the original title.[5] The book chronicled a total of forty-four wars: twenty-four fought during the Ayutthaya period and twenty from 1767 to 1854.

Projecting back in time the racial boundaries of colonial states, Prince Damrong reframed the wars between rival Buddhist kingdoms as a conflict between nations. But although his nationalist bias surfaced openly at times ('the Burmese were not able to hold the Siamese in their sway like the people of other countries'), his analysis was not totally obfuscated by chauvinism. Damrong acknowledged that 'sometimes the Burmese invaded Siam and sometimes the Siamese invaded Burma' and that the Thai incursions were not always reprisals. Nor was the fall of Ayutthaya blamed solely on the magnitude of the attack; rather, it was because of the lack of valiant political leadership and court factionalism that the Thais were unable to preserve the 'independence' of their 'homeland' in 1767.[6] The book also validated the legendary episodes involving Queen Suriyothai and the villagers of Ban Rachan, which would become the stuff of the nationalist mythology. In the 1950s the book's section on the Ayutthaya period was translated into English by a Burmese employee of the Thai Forestry Department who was a member of the Siam Society and had advised Prince Damrong on Burmese sources.

During the publishing boom of the 1920s and '30s, a genre of fiction emerged known as 'stories of war and love' (*ruang roprop rakrak*), which competed with the translations of Chinese historical novels for the favour of the middle-class readership. The authors of these historical novels drew their inspiration from both Chinese literary classics and, ironically, the Thai version of a Burmese historical romance. Several 'stories of war and love' drew on episodes in Ayutthayan history, such as *Bang rachan*, which fictionalized the episode of villagers' resistance to the Burmese invaders found in the chronicles and in Damrong's book.[7] Even Wichit Watthakan turned to the Thai-Burmese wars as a source of inspiration for his first historical play, *Phra naresuan prakat issaraphap* ('King Naresuan Declares Independence', 1934), and his much more popular first musical drama, *Luat suphan* ('Blood of Suphanburi', 1936), which played to full houses for months, was serialized for the radio and made into a film the following year. The play, set in the town of Suphanburi at the time of the Burmese occupation in the late sixteenth century, tells the story of the good soldier Mangrai and the brave Duangchan, the villager with whom Mangrai is in love and whom he helps to flee captivity with her family. After Mangrai's execution for treachery, and Duangchan's unsuccessful attempt to save his life by returning to Suphanburi, she plots with the villagers to overthrow the Burmese. They are overcome and killed but, after the final battle, Mangrai's spirit appears to appeal for an end to war and for peaceful coexistence between the Burmese and the Thais.[8]

In the play Wichit added a twist or two to the cliché of heroic resistance to the Burmese invaders. One was the personification of Thai patriotic virtues in a female character, which accorded with the nationalist celebration of martial heroines (and, incidentally, provided for the depiction of tantalizing scenes of intimacy between the two protagonists). But the play's most significant element was the conciliatory ending that turned old enemies into new potential allies and thus supported the idea of Pan-Asianism, propagated by the Japanese as an ideological cover for their imperialist aims. In the post-war period, the wars with the Burmese continued to provide a reservoir of stories for screenplays: a second version of *Blood of Suphanburi*, notable for its torrid eroticism and gory violence, was filmed in the early 1970s. A quarter of a century later, at the time when the cult of the semi-legendary figure of King Naresuan's sister had spread among the Thai middle class struggling to recover national self-confidence after the crisis of 1997, the historical enmity with Burma was once again represented cinematographically in two major productions, *Bang rachan* (1998) and *Suriyothai* (2002).

Suriyothai was the most expensive Thai film ever made and broke all box-office records: its battle scenes, involving thousands of extras and hundreds of elephants, were publicized as rivalling those of Hollywood blockbusters. Directed by Prince Chatrichalem Yukon (known as a socially committed director) and financed in part by the royal household, *Suriyothai* fell short of its director's goal of winning the Oscar for best foreign film in 2002; but its reconfiguration of the Burmese Other for the era of ASEAN cooperation was unquestionably a success. The film was soon imitated in a television advertisement for an energy drink marketed by the popular rock band Carabao, with the difference that, in this cleverly crafted ad, the past – in which the Thai heroine leads the fight against the Burmese invaders – was juxtaposed to the present and the Thai police's war on methamphetamines, or *ya ba* ('crazy drug'), which had invaded Thailand's cities.

After the notorious drug lord Khun Sa retired from activity in the early 1990s, drug production in the border region with Myanmar shifted from opiates (like heroin) to methamphetamines, the main consumers of which were Thai teenagers. After becoming prime minister in 2001, Thaksin Chinawat launched a 'war on drugs' which was intensified at the beginning of 2003, when the government put pressure on police and border patrol officers, many of whom were believed to participate in drug trafficking. In a briefing session, the Interior Minister harangued them: 'If the knights see the enemies but do not shoot them, they can be beheaded by their commanders'; three weeks later he clarified his statement by adding: 'They should check out history books about what King Naresuan did to his generals who failed to keep up with him on the battleground during his great fight against the Prince of Burma. The king had all of them beheaded'.[9] The minister's message did not fail to register with his audience; in the following three months some 2,600 suspected drug dealers were reportedly killed (a figure the Thai authorities scaled down to about 1,600), mostly as a result of extra-judicial executions.[10] Through the 1990s Myanmar was also the subject of much negative coverage in the Thai national media – not for its government's appalling human rights record, however, since the member countries of ASEAN (which Myanmar joined in 1997) agree not to interfere in each other's domestic policy, but as a source of illegal immigrants.

While the characterization of the Burmese as enemies has hardly changed over time, the target of their destructive fury has: from Buddhism to the homeland to the body social. These shifts underscore the changing anxieties of Thailand's governors, for whom the Burmese enemy is arguably an allegory for more insidious threats. In the 1830s, when King Naresuan's sixteenth-century deeds were celebrated in an epic, these anxieties stemmed from the possibility of a confrontation with a rather more dangerous Other – Europeans. In the second decade of the twentieth century, when the wars with Burma were made into the leitmotif of the national narrative, the royal elite was concerned with the lack of 'unity' – a byword for the political docility of the emerging urban intelligentsia. In the crypto-authoritarian climate of the Thaksin era, the state worried about its ability to impose order within the constraints of the law established by the constitution of 1997. Another difference concerns the means of representation. Once evoked through poems, plays and history books, the legendary past in which the enmity with the Burmese is played out is now evoked by culture industry products, such as films and advertisements. Despite their commercial *raison d'être*, such products are, however, no less capable than older forms of historical representation of mobilizing national loyalty against an enemy, either real or imaginary.

The Chinese Settler

As already mentioned, immigration from southern China shaped to a large extent the ethnic, social and economic landscapes of modern Thailand, especially between the middle of the nineteenth century and the middle of the twentieth. Chinese settlers and their descendants spanned the whole social spectrum – from ennobled merchants to coolies, although their density was highest among the middle strata of entrepreneurs, traders and salaried intellectuals.

Chinese immigrants injected a strain of cosmopolitanism in the Thai social space by linking it with business and revolutionary transnational networks, and importing exotic products, architectural styles, ideologies and, last but not least, cuisine.

Sociologists have stressed the unique degree of integration between locals and Chinese in Thailand in comparison to other South-east Asia countries, which resulted from several factors: local women's propensity to marry immigrants, Buddhism's inclusiveness and, above all, the absence of the racial boundaries imposed by colonial governments in Burma, Indochina and Indonesia to divide and rule. In the second decade of the twentieth century the Chinese were, however, presented as aliens whose assimilation into the Thai body politic was superficial or, worse, illusory. Such a representation took shape as a direct consequence of the emergence and clash of nationalisms: Chinese nationalism, on the one hand, which unified the disparate identities of imperial China's myriad ethnicities and drew economic support principally from overseas communities; and Thai nationalism, on the other hand, which because of the lack of a unifying antagonistic cause (struggle against invaders, anti-colonial resistance) needed to evoke the spectre of enemies. The millions of Chinese immigrants that settled in Siam during the first half the twentieth century (some only temporarily, other permanently) represented a convenient embodiment of such an enemy.

A message directed by King Chulalongkorn to the community in 1907 expresses the official attitude towards Chinese settlers shortly before the proclamation of the Chinese Republic: 'I regard them not as foreigners but as one of the component parts of the kingdom and sharing in its prosperity and advancement'.[11] A few months later, in 1908, the Chinese nationalist leader, Dr Sun Yatsen, visited Bangkok and secured the support of the Sino-Siamese Bank to the nationalist cause. Support to the republican cause also provided overseas Chinese with a novel political consciousness and 'national' identity (as opposed to clan identities), both of which badly accorded with the Thai royalist nationalism promoted by the throne. Another dimension of the politicization of the Chinese community was the nascent class-consciousness: at the start of the Sixth Reign, a three-day strike of Chinese workers brought

Bangkok to a standstill. Accordingly, official rhetoric towards the Chinese took a drastic turn. King Wachirawuth penned a scathing portrayal of the Chinese in a notorious pamphlet entitled *Phuak yew* ('The Jews of the East', 1914):

> One is either a Chinaman or a Siamese; no one could be both at the same time and people who pretend that they are so are apt to be found neither. Such people, like the chameleon, change their colour to suit their surroundings; when they come among us they are Siamese, but when they go among the Chinese they become Chinese, while many of them also owe their allegiance to some European powers.

The manifest inspiration of this attack was the contemporary discourse of anti-Semitism, whose tropes Wachirawuth appropriated when accusing the Chinese of being 'aliens by birth, by nature, by sympathy, by language, and finally by choice', 'utterly without morals, conscience, mercy, pity ... where money is concerned' and 'no more Buddhist than are the Jews Christians'.[12] Significantly, Wachirawuth's pamphlet was published the year after the promulgation of the Nationality Act, whereby every individual born in the kingdom was automatically registered as a Siamese subject in contrast to the disposition of the Qing Code (promulgated in 1909, on the eve of the dynasty's collapse), which regarded as Chinese every male born of a Chinese father regardless of place of birth. Rama VI proclaimed Thai and Chinese to be not only distinct but incompatible 'races', although his real concern was not racial mixing but political sedition.

In practice, identity continued to be defined not by racial but by legal and cultural criteria. New Chinese immigrants were able to become Thai nationals by registering as subjects, acquiring Thai names and pledging loyalty to king and country.[13] Immigrant arrivals increased further in the 1910s with the start of Chinese female emigration and surpassed the one million mark in the 1920s. However, more than the coolies, whose conditions were close to slavery, Wachirawuth was irritated most by 'the "politicians" among the Chinese community, the self-constituted leaders of "modern thought", the demagogues and journalists of Bangkok'.[14] Overseas

Chinese supported en masse republicanism if not communism –
political ideologies that were both antithetical to Thainess because
of their rejection of monarchism. Moreover, the Sino-Thai intelligentsia that animated the capital's burgeoning publishing industry
and whose criticism of the absolute monarchy was becoming
alarmingly open were singled out as enemies of the state and the
object of royal scorn. The support Chinese settlers gave to the illegal
local branch of the Guomindang and the appearance of Chinese
communist cells in the later 1920s, along with record levels of immigration, increased suspicion and distrust and configured a 'Chinese
question' in Siam. King Prachathipok noted in memoranda:

> Now the Chinese bring their wives from China and are deter-
> mined to remain Chinese. They organize schools in which they
> teach practically only the Chinese language. There is a rather
> disturbing state of affairs . . . Can something be done to make
> the Chinese become Siamese as in the old days?

And, on the hypothesis of constitutional reform:

> The parliament would be entirely dominated by the Chinese
> Party. One could exclude all Chinese from every political right;
> yet they will dominate the situation all the same, since they hold
> the *hard cash*.[15]

The attempt by the Society of Chinese of Siam, founded on the
eve of the fall of the absolutist regime, to forge a link with the Thai
middle strata was far from successful. Chinese education became a
bone of contention between state and community after the establishment of the constitutional government: strict regulations were
imposed on Chinese private schools in 1933, requiring that they
take on pupils who had already attended four years of national
education or adopt the same curriculum as government schools,
limiting the teaching in Chinese to afternoon classes. The Chinese
predominance in industry and commerce, especially in the rice
trade, was an even bigger cause of tension. The economic nationalism of the Phahon government was reinforced in the Phibun era by
the state edict on autarchy and the prohibition for the Chinese to

engage in a variety of industrial and commercial activities (including the production of salt, tobacco and pork meat, and the operation of taxis and fishing boats). Even Chinese cuisine was nationalized by making stir-fried noodles into the iconic dish, *pat thai*. To reinforce the image of the Chinese as enemies of the nation, *Luang* Wichit Watthakan hastily wrote a play, *Nanchao* (1938), dramatizing the flight of the Tais from the eponymous kingdom in Yunnan because of Chinese expansionism.[16]

The establishment of diplomatic relations between Thailand and China at the end of the Second World War momentarily eased political pressure on the Chinese community, but the situation was soon reversed by Mao's victory in 1949, which, however, brought an end to migration. In the 1950s and '60s Thailand, like the rest of the 'Free World', considered China's legitimate government to be in Taipei rather than Beijing. At home, the Anticommunist Act (1952) legitimated the repression of the resurgent political activism of the Chinese community, now split between nationalist and communist supporters, who occasionally clashed in the streets of Bangkok. Repression intensified under the Sarit regime, when the Chinese press was censored, Chinese political activists arrested and deported, remittances to China curbed, restrictions reimposed on occupations and schools, a stringent quota imposed on arrivals and the law on nationality modified in order to impede the naturalization of further immigrants.[17] Significantly, admission to the Royal Cadet Academy was long restricted to applicants who could prove that both their grandfathers had been born in Thailand. But while the Thai government's anticommunist rhetoric remained strong until 1973, the relationship between the state and the Chinese community was multifaceted. In Bangkok, the informal partnership instituted between Chinese businessmen and high-ranking officers allowed the former to prosper and the latter to enjoy the payoff of their patronage. In the kingdom's peripheral provinces the largely ethnic Chinese Communist Party of Thailand launched the armed insurgency with Beijing's support.

In 1975, two years after Washington's recognition of the PRC, it was Bangkok's turn to establish diplomatic relations with Beijing during the visit of Prime Minister Khukrit Pramot. In 1978 another head of government, General Kriangsak, paid an official visit to

Beijing, reciprocated later in the year by Deng Xiaoping. As a result, the bogey of Chinese/communist aggression, which the Thai authorities had agitated over the previous thirty years, was put to rest. The acclaim won by the novel *Letters from Thailand* at the time of its publication in 1969 had already signalled a turning away from the cliché representation of the Chinese in pulp fiction and films as opportunistic profiteers and devious communist agents. The novel's bitter-sweet portrayal of a Teochiu settler in Bangkok illuminated the experience of displacement and resettlement in a foreign and not always hospitable land from the Other's point of view. As a character in the novel explains to the protagonist,

> I have lived in this land many tens of years, Suang U, and I have learned much about my own people, seeing them struggle and often prosper among people of another race. What makes us so different and what keeps us that way? . . . Listening to Thais talk about the Chinese, you would think we all came from one village, were born of the same father and mother, and all think and act alike. So many thousand grains of rice thrown into one basket. Still, I can understand why we appear that way to them. We are strangers here and we know that we must share our strength.[18]

The success of *Letters from Thailand* was replicated twenty years later by another rags-to-riches story of a Chinese immigrant (a character allegedly based on two real-life tycoons), *Through the Dragon Design*.[19] The novel became a bestseller and in 1992 was transposed into a phenomenally popular TV drama.

By the early 1990s, the local-born Chinese (*luk chin*) were the object of a re-evaluation, prompted by the role of Sino-Thai entrepreneurs at the forefront of globalization. The new-found cultural clout of Thailand's Chinese community was underscored by the popularity of business manuals based on Chinese classics, such as Sun Tzu's *The Art of War* and *The Three Kingdoms* (first translated in Thai as *Sam kok* in the 1790s and printed as early as 1865), and media interest in the cultural heritage of *luk chin*.[20] The commodification of Chinese culture was most obviously a celebration of the business acumen of Sino-Thais – Thailand's only *national* bourgeoisie – but also a covert reminder of their hybrid identity, whose compatibility

China outside China: a Bangkok cinema screening of Hong Kong films, mid-1950s.

with Thainess continued to be defined by the political agenda of the Thai bureaucracy.

The Paradigmatic Farang

Whether European or American, tourist or resident, male or female, every white-skinned foreigner is referred to by Thais as a *farang*, an adaptation of the medieval Arabic *frangi* ('Frank').[21] Ambivalence characterizes the *farang* as a figure of alterity: at once alluring and threatening, admired and ridiculed, imitated and rejected, the *farang* represents nevertheless the paradigmatic Other against which Thailand's progress, civility and fashionability have been measured since the second half of the nineteenth century. Such a situation was underscored even by King Wachirawuth, who pleaded: 'Please understand that others are taking our measure'.[22]

Interaction between Thais and *farang* has a long history. The first Westerners to land in Siam were Portuguese coming from Malacca, which they had founded in 1511. They were followed by Dutch, English, Danes and French, all of whom established trading stations in Ayutthaya. In the second half of the seventeenth century the Greek adventurer Constantine Phaulkon rose to the position of adviser to King Narai while French Jesuits built edifices and an observatory for the king's palace in Lopburi. The Jesuits persuaded Narai to send embassies to Louis XIV and Pope Innocent XI; the first mission, sent in 1680, was lost at the sea but the second mission, dispatched in 1684, reached Versailles and was accompanied back to Ayutthaya by an embassy with the aim of renegotiating the trading terms already secured by the French East Indies Company. Another French embassy reached Siam in 1687; it was led by Simon de la Loubère, who wrote *Du Royaume de Siam* (1689, translated into English in 1693), the first example of the still-flourishing literary genre of *farang* writings about Thailand. Conversely, Thais began to portray Westerners in temple murals and cabinet inlays.[23] But the missionary zeal of the French Jesuits, the presence of French troops and the fracture between pro- and anti-European factions at court precipitated in 1688 a political crisis that resulted in a dynastic overthrow and the expulsion of European traders from Ayutthaya.[24]

Parallel others: inlaid figures of a European and an Arab on the doors of a cabinet, later Ayutthaya period.

The isolationist turn in Siam's foreign policy, the collapse of the kingdom of Ayutthaya in 1767 and the 'world crisis' of 1780–1820 kept Europeans temporarily away from South-east Asia. By the mid-1820s they were back, this time along with Americans. Both sought permission to trade and proselytize in Siam, reinforcing the image of *farang* as religious zealots and pushy traders. Rama III signed reluctantly the first commercial treaty with Great Britain in 1826, following his ministers' advice that 'if we were not flexible, we would make an unwanted enemy'.[25] A similar treaty was concluded with the United States in 1833; but 'things Western' (*khong nok*) still had little interest in the eyes of the royalty and the urban elite while tributary missions to Beijing and the junk trade with ports in southern China were booming. The scarce interest in the West's exports was reflected in the marginal position of Europeans in the geography of *Klong tang phasa* ('Poem on Various Languages', c. 1820), which is mentioned in an inscription in Bangkok's Wat Phra Chetuphon.[26] Guarding the gates of that monastery's compound, as well as those in Wat Suthat, are giant stone figures of Europeans, recognizable by their beards and top hats, which were brought back from China on ships in which they served as ballast. *Farang* appeared also in *Phra Aphaimani*, a picaresque poem by poet laureate Sunthorn Phu (1786–1855), even though their geographical location was still not clearly distinct from the western lands that entertained trading relations with Siam.

Stone figure of a Dutch commodore used as ballast on Chinese ships, Wat Suthat, Bangkok.

The growing Euro-American presence in Bangkok during the 1830s and '40s was, however, a source of tensions at court; Rama III was worried about it, but other princes, such as Issaret and Mongkut, made no secret of their curiosity for *farang* culture. Missionaries rather than traders acted as cultural brokers and middlemen of Western technology. The medical and educational activities Protestant missionaries carried out as part of their activity of evangelization attracted the interest of the Thai elite despite their indifference to Christianity. Two figures in particular stood out: Dr Dan Beach Bradley and Samuel McFarland (both American), who are commemorated for their contribution to the kingdom's progress. Bradley, who lived in Bangkok from 1835 until his death in 1873, was the typical embodiment of the imperialist evangelizer, whose technological versatility was combined with a staunch belief in the superiority of Anglo-Saxon Christian civilization and in its mission to eradicate ignorance and evil from the world. Besides treating patients daily at his dispensary, Bradley was court physician, tutor to Prince Mongkut in English and astronomy, editor of the country's first newspaper, the *Bangkok Recorder* (started in 1844), and contributor of local news to Singapore's colonial press. His wife too taught English to the women in the court, opening the way for the employment of the British governess Anna Leonowens in the next reign.

Historians of Thailand are generally unwilling to take seriously Anna Leonowens (1831–1915). Not only are her memories of the five years she spent in Bangkok (from 1862 to 1867) considered largely fictitious, they also spawned a sub-genre in popular culture that includes a novel, a Broadway musical and three films.[27] While such cultural artefacts belong rightfully to the study of Thailand as an exotic Other of the West, one should not forget that Anna – the historic figure, not the fictionalized character of her memories – played an important role as a cultural broker by engaging King Mongkut over issues central to the Victorian idea of civilization. Rama IV responded to her plea to free two bonded girls based on the moral argument of abolitionism with an informed reply in English, which noted that the condition of slaves in Siam was better than that of the urban proletariat of 'all your civilized cities such as London, Manchester, Glasgow . . .' and that 'all of Christian nations has [sic] made rich profiting by commerce, England even not excepted in holding slaves as well as in trading slave ships, etc. etc.' (Britain had abolished slavery in 1807).[28]

In the early 1850s, after China, Siam's main commercial partner over the previous quarter century, had been humiliated at the hands of the British in the Second Opium War (1842), the Bangkok court repositioned itself from the dissolving Sinic œcumene to the emerging Victorian œcumene. The official reason for the discontinuation of the tributary missions to China was the subordinate status assigned to Siam in diplomatic relations with the Middle Kingdom. King Mongkut in a royal proclamation in 1868 denounced the allegedly distorted translation of diplomatic missives by Chinese intermediaries that presented Siam as a vassal of Beijing.[29] On the contrary, Mongkut addressed Queen Victoria in his missives in English, as 'Our most respected and distinguished Friend, and by race of royalty Our very affectionate sister'.[30] In so doing, he asserted – verbally at least – an equality in status that was unthinkable under the Chinese tributary system. Precisely because Siam was a civilizational equal to Britain, its customs and institutions could not be questioned even when they contrasted with Western values (which, as Mongkut reminded Anna Leonowens, were not historically consistent anyway). Still, the abolition of prostration at court and, more importantly, debt bondage at the start of Chulalongkorn's reign acknowledged the 'barbarism' of such practices, as confirmed also by the international echo of the reforms, especially in America, where the freeing of slaves resonated, however misleadingly, with the still recent memory of the Civil War.

Interest in Western science and technology also gave way to admiration for European culture and the emulation of Western tastes and social norms even as colonialism posed a danger to the dynasty through the early 1890s. The subsequent acceleration in reform of the state and infrastructural modernization relied on the massive employment of European and American advisers and technicians. Belgian lawyers were employed to negotiate international treaties, German engineers to build the railway that connected Siam to Burma and Singapore, Italian architects to render Bangkok suitably grand, American professors to act as state secretaries and British comptrollers to manage the state finances. Still, the absence of colonial domination had a paradoxical effect on the social perception of Europeans in comparison to Thailand's neighbours: on the one hand, the royal elite was able to negotiate modernity on its own terms, free of the normative control exerted by colonial elites on the upper echelons of indigenous societies; on the other hand, even those embryonic Thai middle strata that held a different vision of Siam's progress from the royal elite did not question Europe's civilizational hegemony. The princes who in 1885 unsuccessfully petitioned Rama V for the institution of a constitutional monarchy argued that, in order to deflect the peril of colonization, '. . . Siam must be accepted and respected by the Western powers as a civilized nation'.[31] Likewise, Thianwan Wannapho incited the royal government from the pages of his paper to introduce measures to ensure Siam's progress along the lines of Western nations while he also stigmatized the European domination of the Thai economy.

The availability by the 1920s of overseas education to young commoners reinforced the perception of the West as a benchmark for assessing Siam's progress. Such perception and its implication in the Thai context figure prominently in the literature of the end of the old regime, as expressed by the protagonist, an expatriate journalist, of Prince Akat's novel *The Circus of Life*: 'I wanted to learn the secret of other countries' advanced development. I wanted to learn why those who returned from abroad looked so prosperous, clever and smart, and gained high salaries and prestige quicker than anyone else.'[32] Westerners' perceived freedom from social hierarchies and rules, which so strongly appealed to the emerging Thai middle class, became in turn a trope in the discursive representation of *farang* as people of loose morals and thus ethical inferiors – a trope still current in the 1990s. The schizophrenic perception of *farang* as objects of both admiration and repulsion had been prefigured by none other than the British-educated King Wachirawuth. He had invited European royals and government representatives to his coronation ceremonies in 1912, which lasted two weeks and broke the state finances, yet in an article first published in 1915 he ridiculed the urban middle class's adoption of Westernized tastes as 'the cult of imitation' and blamed 'low-class Europeans' for the 'immoral' behaviour (i.e., heavy drinking) of some Thai youth.[33]

The discursive strategy of deflecting domestic responsibilities on a more powerful, though not necessarily more civilized, Other, with whom Thailand could not avoid dealing, underpinned recurrent censure of the behaviour of American soldiers stationed in Thailand during the Vietnam War, which was admittedly the only practicable avenue for criticizing the massive US military presence in the country (around 50,000 troops in the late 1960s). Despite the much celebrated 'special relationship' that bonded Bangkok and Washington in the fight against communism in Asia, many in Thailand found unpalatable the unprecedented degree of American intromission in domestic affairs – not to mention the flourishing trade in sex and drugs pandering to 'ugly Americans'.[34] But in the 1960s there was also a reverse movement of Thais going to the USA to pursue higher education thanks to the scholarships made available through the US Agency for International Development (USAID) and the Fulbright Program. Upon returning home, Thai postgraduates were able to access, in virtue also of the social connections of alumni associations, the upper ranks of the bureaucracy and the private sector. The craving for an American university degree, satirized in the short story *Michigan Test* (1974),[35] perpetuated the turn-of-the-century conception of the West as the source of cultural and symbolic capital to be appropriated in order to buttress personal status at home.

This ambivalent relationship was compounded by the hegemonic position achieved by the American scholarly discourse on Thailand in the post-war era. One of the consequences of Thailand's escape from imperialism is that, unlike India, Burma or Vietnam, it did not become an object of colonial scholarship. As part of the policy of containment of communism, in the 1950s American universities set up area studies to train specialists to be employed in US government agencies. Consequently by the late 1960s a body of – to all effects – 'neo-colonial' scholarship on Thailand – informed by modernist paradigms such as 'bureaucratic polity', 'loosely structured social system' and 'modernization without development' – had accumulated and helped shaping US aid and counter-insurgency schemes as well as developmental policies by US-trained Thai technocrats.[36] The picture was complicated in the 1980s when the liberal climate of American (and occasionally British and Australian) universities gave Thais studying for postgraduate degrees there the chance of exploring issues that were taboo in the conservative environment of Thai academia.

During the last quarter of the twentieth century *farang* became a common presence in Thailand as tourists. When Thailand's tourism industry was first developed in the 1960s its main targets were the US troops on Rest & Recreation leave as well as a few affluent Westerners. By the 1990s tourists from Europe and North America amounted to around a third of Thailand's annual tourist arrivals, while the largest share comprised tourists from Asia. And yet *farang* continued to catalyse public discontent about problems more or less directly connected to tourism – from prostitution and the spread of HIV/AIDS to environmental degradation and insensitivity towards Thai culture. Many of these accusations echoed those made against American soldiers during the Vietnam War. Such continuity is not surprising, both because the hospitality and sex industries catering to American soldiers were effortlessly converted after the end of the Vietnam War to attract foreign tourists, and because the importance of tourism to the national economy and its intense promotion makes it easier to lay the blame for its ugly side on the consumers rather than the service providers.[37] In Thailand itself very little attention has been paid to the long-term impact of some forty years of tourism development on the society and the environment. However, recurring polemics in the media stigmatize *farang* behaviour by focusing on marginal phenomena such as the backpacker subculture, centred in Bangkok's inner city district of Banglamphu, and its negative influence on youth morality – a topos in the discursive construction of the *farang* as Other whose origins lay in King Wachirawuth's reprobation of 'low-class Europeans'.

Reference to *farang* in public discourse as a trope for focusing blame and resentment reached its apex in the aftermath of the financial crisis of 1997, the domestic causes of which were largely neglected in favour of external factors over which the government claimed to have little or no control – and, hence, little or no responsibility. The critique of 'Western' (i.e., capitalist) models of development from quarters as different as NGOs and the throne has since became commonplace in Thai public discourse. Such critique, articulated by academics and public intellectuals such as Sulak

Siwarak and Thirayut Bunmi, who are themselves often foreign-educated, tends to restate the nineteenth-century dichotomy between a material realm, where *farang* hegemony is unchallenged, and a spiritual realm, in which Thais are superior.[38] Perhaps the most striking aspect of the Thai critical discourse on the West is the fact that it cuts across political and ideological divides, bringing together upper-class conservatives and ex-Marxist revolutionaries. Still, the predominantly antagonistic portrayal of *farang* over the past decade did not erase the figure's significance as a benchmark of Thai modernity. When still prime minister, Thaksin Chinawat said of street fighting among youth gangs: 'The culture and life-style of today's teenagers is frightening. They superficially adopt Western culture about having freedom but don't understand that Western kids have freedom along with responsibility.'[39]

Sociologists and anthropologists have only recently begun to examine the nexus where Thainess is literally fused with the Western Other: mixed marriages between *farang* (mostly male) and Thais (mostly female) and their offspring – *luk krung* ('half-and-half child'). Although still undocumented, the history of *luk krung* is arguably as old as the history of the European presence in Thailand. A well-known *luk krung* was the *littérateur* Prince Chula Chakraphong, son of Prince Chakraphong and his Russian wife, Ekaterina Desnitsky, whom he had married in St Petersburg while studying at the local military academy. As a *luk krung*, Prince Chula Chakraphong was deemed unsuitable for the royal succession even though his late father was the full brother of the sonless kings Wachirawuth and Prachathipok and, reputedly, Chulalongkorn's favourite son.[40] During the Vietnam War, *luk krung* fathered by American soldiers embodied Thailand's political subservience to the USA and were marginalized as social outcasts with the derogative expression of 'red-haired children' (*dek phom daeng*).

From the late 1980s Eurasians became very fashionable in the Thai media as models, actors, singers and TV entertainers. Their popularity was epitomized by the blue-eyed Siriya Winsiri (alias Cindy Burbridge), the Thai-American winner of the 1996 Miss Thailand competition. According to political scientist Chi Giles Ungphakorn, himself a Eurasian (his father, economist Puai Ungphakorn, was forced to flee to Britain, his wife's country, after the military coup of 1976), Thai society's fascination with *luk krung* was but a superficial trend that did not undermine the centrality of ethnicity in the construction of Thainess. However, the *luk krung* fad, along with the parallel rediscovery of Sino-Thai identity, may also be seen as evidence of the attempt to redefine Thainess within the transnational œcumene of corporate capitalism, in which the hegemony of Western culture is challenged by products – from cinema to comics and popular music – that originate from Japan, Hong Kong, Korea, Taiwan and lately Thailand, too, but are hybrid in nature. For the most worldly among Thai urbanites – those who study and travel abroad, read English-language magazines and newspapers, and watch CNN and MTV – *luk krung* may well represent the ultimate expression of cosmopolitanism, the most adequate answer to the unfathomable dilemmas of globalization.

Chronology

The Thai calendar follows the Buddhist Era, beginning in 543 BC (hence AD 2007 corresponds to 2550 BE). The twelve-month Buddhist year, based on the lunar cycle, starts in April; in 1941 it was synchronized with the Gregorian calendar and it now officially runs from January to December.

15000	Hunter-gatherers' settlements begin in north and north-east Thailand
5000 BC	Migration of Austroasiatic-speaking populations
3000 BC	Beginning of rice cultivation; sedentary settlements in the Khorat Plateau
1500 BC	Ban Chiang Bronze Age culture
500 BC	Ban Chiang Iron Age culture
AD 500	Mon principalities in the Central Plain
1000–1250	Khmer empire now extends over Khorat Plateau and the Central Plain
1238	Foundation of the Sukhothai kingdom
1259	Foundation of the Lanna kingdom
1296	Foundation of Chiang Mai, capital of Lanna
1351	Foundation of the Ayutthaya kingdom
1432	Ayutthaya overthrows Angkor
1569	First fall of Ayutthaya to the Burmese
1593	King Naresuan defeats the Burmese in battle at Nong Sarai
1684	King Narai's embassy to Versailles
1688	Xenophobic backlash against European traders; dynastic usurpation
1767	Second fall of Ayutthaya

1767	King Taksin establishes new royal centre in Thonburi
1782	Foundation of Chakri dynasty
1788	Buddhist council in Bangkok revises canon
1826	Commercial treaty with Great Britain
1833	Commercial treaty with USA
1851	Accession of King Mongkut (Rama IV)
1853	Last Thai tributary mission to Beijing
1855	Bowring Treaty signed with Great Britain
1860	H. Mohout discovers ruins of Angkor in Khmer province
1863	French establish protectorate over Cambodia except western provinces
1867	First Thai display at Paris Universal Exposition
1868	Accession of King Chulalongkorn (Rama V)
1874	Bondage abolished by royal edict
1885	Rejection of princes' proposal for constitutional monarchy
1892	Creation of royal cabinet and start of administrative centralization
1893	French blockade of Chaophraya River; Siam's surrender to territorial demands
1897	Rama V's first tour of Europe
1901–2	Anti-centralist rebellions in the North-east and the South
1902	Sangha Act institutionalizes the monastic order
1905	National Library inaugurated
1907	Franco-Siamese treaty on eastern boundaries; Rama V's second visit to Europe
1909	Anglo-Siamese treaty on Siam's northern and western boundaries
1910	Accession of King Wachirawuth (Rama VI)
1913	Nationality Act and Surnames Act
1918	Thai contingent joins the Allied forces in Europe
1921	Primary Education Act
1925	Accession of King Prachathipok (Rama VII)
1926	National Museum opens in Bangkok
1927	People's Party formed in Paris; first Thai film production
1930	Impact of the Great Depression; foundation of Communist Party of Siam; start of radio broadcast
1932	End of the absolute monarchy (24 June); promulgation of constitution (10 December)
1933	Government of *Phraya* Phahon Phonphayuhasena
1934	First edition of *Miss Thailand*
1935	Abdication of Rama VII; Anantha Mahidon proclaimed successor (Rama VIII)
1938	Phibun Songkhram becomes prime minister
1939	Issue of first state edict: Siam is renamed Thailand

1941	Press Act; Japanese army lands in Thailand (8 December)
1942	Thai declaration of war on Allies; re-foundation of CPT
1944	Fall of Phibun government
1945	Settlement of war reparations with Britain; USA considers war declaration invalid
1946	New constitution; Rama VIII shot dead; accession of King Phumiphon (Rama IX)
1947	Military coup ends constitutional period
1948	Phibun becomes prime minister
1951	Rama IX returns permanently to Thailand
1952	Anti-communist Act
1954	SEATO formed with HQ in Bangkok
1955	Television broadcasting begins
1957	Phibun toppled by rival military clique
1958	Sarit Thanarat becomes prime minister (until 1962)
1959	World Bank report; creation of Tourist Organization of Thailand
1961	Implementation of first five-year national plan
1967	ASEAN formed (Thailand, Philippines, Indonesia, Malaysia and Singapore)
1969	First general election since 1957; CPT launches armed struggle
1971	Internal coup abolishes constitution and parliament
1973	Student uprising (14 October); caretaker government
1974–6	Elected governments led by Khukrit and Seni Pramot
1976	Military coup (6 October); rule by martial law
1979	Constitution restored
1980–88	Coalition governments led by Prem Tinsulanon
1988	Chatichai Chunhawan is first elected prime minister since 1976
1991	Military coup (February); technocratic government
1992	General elections followed by political bloodshed (May); caretaker government
1997	Outbreak of financial crisis; promulgation of new constitution
2001	Thai Rak Thai's landslide electoral victory; Thaksin Chinawat becomes prime minister
2003	Thaksin launches 'war on drugs'
2005	General elections: Thaksin re-appointed PM
2006	Thaksin downgraded to caretaker PM diamond jubilee of Rama IX; Thaksin overthrown by military coup (19 September)

References

Introduction: Civilization, Globalization and the Thai Nation

1 Prince Damrong Rachanuphap, *Monuments of the Buddha in Siam*, trans. Sulak Sivaraksa and A. B. Griswold, 2nd edn (Bangkok, 1973) p. 4.
2 Raymond Williams, *Keywords* (New York, 1976), pp. 48–50.
3 Charnvit Kasetsiri, 'Siam/Civilization–Thailand/Globalization: Things to Come', paper presented at the IAHA conference, Bangkok, May 1996; Thongchai Winichakul, 'The Quest for "Siwilai": A Geographical Discourse of Civilizational Thinking in Late Nineteenth and Early Twentieth Century Siam', *Journal of Asian Studies*, LIX/4 (2000), p. 531; Craig J. Reynolds, 'Globalizers vs. Communitarians: Public Intellectuals Debate Thailand's Future', *Singapore Journal of Tropical Geography*, XXII/3 (2001), pp. 257–8.
4 Charles Higham and Rachanie Thorasat, *Prehistoric Thailand: From Early Settlement to Sukhothai* (London, 1998), p. 174.
5 George Cœdès, *The Indianized States of Southeast Asia*, ed. Walter Vella, trans. Susan Brown Cowing (Honolulu, 1968; [Paris, 1964]).
6 O. W. Wolters, *History, Culture and Region in Southeast Asian Perspective*, 2nd edn (Ithaca, NY, 1999).
7 In works on Thailand the word is commonly used in its original Pali form rather than Thai (*samgha*).
8 Cœdès, *The Indianized States*, p. 222.
9 Anthony Reid, *Southeast Asia in the Age of Commerce, 1450–1680*, 2 vols (New Haven, CT, 1988–93).
10 D. R. Howland, *Borders of Chinese Civilization: Geography and History at Empire's End* (Durham, NC, 1996), pp. 13–14.

11 The deva (Thai, *thep*) are the 33 deities that inhabit with Indra the heaven at the top of Mount Meru, pivot of the lower world in the Hindu universe (see Chapter 5). Because of the deva iconography as winged figures, the name Krungthep is often rendered in English as 'City of Angels'. The name of the dynastic era of Rattanakosin ('Jewel of Indra') comes from Krungthep's appellation. The most likely etymology of the name 'Bangkok' is that of 'village (*bang*, also *ban*) of plumes (*kok*)'.

12 C. A. Bayly, *The Birth of the Modern World 1780–1914* (Oxford, 2004), pp. 42–4.

13 C. A. Breckenridge, 'The Aesthetics and Politics of Colonial Collecting', *Comparative Studies in Societies and History*, XXXI/2 (1989), pp. 195–216. See also David Cannadine, *Ornamentalism* (London, 2001).

14 Michael Herzfeld, 'The Absent Presence: Discourse of Crypto-Colonialism', *South Atlantic Quarterly*, CI/4 (2002), p. 900. The definition of semi-colony was first employed by Thai Marxists in the 1950s (see below, Chapter 4).

15 Bayly, *The Modern World*, p. 41.

16 *Luang* Phibunsongkhram ('Lord Master of War') was the title by which Plaek Khittasangkha (1897–1965) was commonly known. In 1941, when prime minister, Phibun granted himself the rank of field marshal, skipping those of lieutenant-general and general.

17 Thak Chaloemtiarana, *Thailand: The Politics of Despotic Paternalism* (Bangkok, 1979).

18 Figures from John Girling, *Thailand: Society and Politics* (Ithaca, NY, 1981), pp. 235–6.

19 US aerial bombing of suspected North Vietnamese installations in Cambodia, which had declared its neutrality in the Indochinese conflict, started in March 1969 without the authorization of Congress. By the time bombing raids ended in 1973, US planes taking off from bases in Thailand had dropped on Cambodia half a million tons of bombs. The American aerial annihilation of Cambodia was a determinant factor in unleashing the fury of the Khmer Rouges, who came to power in 1975. See Ben Kiernan, *How Pol Pot Came to Power*, 2nd edn (New Haven, CT, 2004).

20 Walden Bello, Shea Cunningham and Li Kheng Poh, *A Siamese Tragedy: Development and Disintegration in Modern Thailand* (London, 1998), pp. 1–2.

21 Reynolds, 'Globalizers vs. Communitarians', p. 258.

22 Ibid., pp. 263–5.

23 Sulak Sivaraksa, 'The Crisis of Siamese Identity', in *National Identity and its Defenders: Thailand Today*, ed. Craig J. Reynolds (Chiang Mai, 2002), p. 34.

one | Landscapes

1 Pinkaew Laungaramsri, 'Ethnicity and the Politics of Ethnic Classification in Thailand', in *Ethnicity in Asia*, ed. Colin Mackerras (London and New York, 2003), p. 158.

2 The *rai* is a local acreage unit equivalent to 0.16 hectares/0.4 acres.

3 Norman Owen, 'The Rice Industry of Mainland South-East Asia, 1850–1914', *Journal of the Siam Society*, LIX/2 (1971), pp. 75–143; Pasuk Phongpaichit and Chris Baker, *Thailand: Economy and Politics* (Kuala Lumpur, 1995), Maps 1 & 2, pp. 5–6; Tables 1.1, p. 16 & 1.4, p. 34.

4 Ibid., pp. 20–22.

5 Ibid., pp. 35–40, 51–7.

6 Walden Bello, Shea Cunningham and Li Kheng Poh, *A Siamese Tragedy: Development and Disintegration in Modern Thailand* (London, 1998), chap. 9; *Thailand in Brief 2004* (Bangkok, 2004), p. 54. The resettlement scheme was termed (in English) Land Redistribution Programme for the Poor Living in Forest Reserves (*Khor Chor Kor*, in the Thai acronym); it was devised in 1990 by Army general Suchinda Kraprayun (the leader of the coup that in February 1991 ousted the elected government led by ex-general Chatichai Chunhawan and was in turn brought down by street demonstrations in May 1992) and initiated by the Internal Security Operations Command, created in the 1960s to coordinate the fight against the Communist Party of Thailand.

7 *Atlas of Thailand: Spatial Structures and Development*, under the direction of Doryane Kermel-Torrès (Chiang Mai, 2004), pp. 74–5, 116–17.

8 Bello et al., *A Siamese Tragedy*, chap. 7.

9 *Atlas of Thailand*, p. 36. The percentage of Thailand's urban population was 19 per cent according to the 1990 census and 31 per cent according to the census of 2000.

10 *The Bangkok Recorder*, December 1866, cited in Charnvit Kasetsiri, 'Siam/Civilization–Thailand/ Globalization: Things to Come', paper presented at the IAHA conference, Bangkok, May 1996, p. 22.

11 Marc Augé, *Non-places: An Anthropology of Hyper-modernity*, trans. J. Howe (London, 1998).

12 Linguists and anthropologists make a distinction between the name 'Tai', referring to the group of languages and speakers thereof present across an area spanning Yunnan, the Shan states in north-eastern Myanmar, southern Vietnam, Laos and the western provinces of Cambodia; and 'Thai', referring to the Tai idioms and speakers thereof within modern Thailand.

13 For an overview of Thailand in the first millennium AD, see Charles Higham and Rachanie Thorasat, *Prehistoric Thailand: From Early*

Settlement to Sukhothai (London, 1998).

14 See Georges Condominas, *From Lawa to Mon, from Saa' to Thai:
    Historical and Anthropological Aspects of Southeast Asian Social Spaces*,
    trans. Stephanie Anderson, Maria Magannon and Gehan
    Wijeyewardene (Canberra, 1990).

15 Estimates by Charles Keyes in *Thailand: Buddhist Kingdom as Modern
    Nation-State* (Boulder, CO, 1989), p. 16, table 1.2.

16 The chronology of the establishment of self-support societies
    among Chinese ethnic groups in Bangkok was in reverse order to
    their size and influence, the smallest group being the first to form a
    society and the largest the last: Cantonese, 1877; Hainanese, 1900;
    Hokkien and Hakka, 1909; and Teochiu, 1919.

17 King Chulalongkorn, *Phraratcha phiti sipsong duan* ['Royal ceremonies
    of the twelve months'] (Bangkok, 1908). See also H. G. Quaritch
    Wales, *Siamese State Ceremonies: Their History and Function* (London,
    1931); and Nerida Cook, 'A Tale of Two City Pillars: Mongkut and
    Thai Astrology on the Eve of Modernization', in *Patterns and Illusion:
    Thai History and Thought*, ed. Gehan Wijeywardene and E. C.
    Chapman (Canberra, 1992), pp. 276–309.

18 Nidhi Eoseewong, *Pen and Sail: Literature and History in Early Bangkok*,
    ed. and trans. Chris Baker and Benedict Anderson (Chiang Mai, 2005
    [Bangkok, 1982]), p. 106.

19 Mary Louise Grow, 'Laughter for Spirits, A Vow Fulfilled: The Comic
    Performance of Thailand's *Lakhon Chatri* Dance-Drama', PhD diss.,
    University of Wisconsin-Madison, 1991, pp. 102–3.

20 Maurizio Peleggi, *Lords of Things: The Fashioning of the Siamese
    Monarchy's Modern Image* (Honolulu, 2002), p. 24 (Bock's quote), p. 19
    (Caddy's quote), p. 36. On the *bricoleur*, see Claude Lévi-Strauss,
    The Savage Mind (Chicago, 1966 [Paris, 1962]). I owe this suggestive
    parallel to Craig Reynolds, who suggested it in conversation.

21 The five basic precepts of Buddhism are: do not take life; do not
    steal; do not be unchaste; do not lie; and do not take intoxicants.

22 Figure from the website of the Office of the Prime Minister
    <www.opm.go.th/T2000>.

23 See David K. Wyatt, *Reading Thai Murals* (Chiang Mai, 2004).

24 Dome Sukwong and Suwannapak Sawasdi, *A Century of Thai Cinema*
    (London, 2001), pp. 33–4.

25 Scot Barmé, *Luang Wichit Wathakan and the Creation of a Thai National
    Identity* (Singapore, 1993), pp. 160–62.

26 Thamsok Numnonda, 'When Thailand Followed the Leader', *Social
    Sciences Review*, 4 (1977), pp. 197–223. The text of the state prescrip-
    tions are translated in Thak Chaloemtiarana, ed., *Thai Politics
    1932–1957* (Bangkok, 1978), pp. 244–54.

27 Anthony Diller, 'What Makes Central Thai a National Language?', in *National Identity and Its Defenders: Thailand Today*, ed. Craig J. Reynolds (Chiang Mai, 2002), pp. 88–9.

28 Jiraporn Wilayasakpan, 'Nationalism and the Transformation of Aesthetic Concepts: Theatre in Thailand during the Phibun Period', PhD diss., Cornell University, 1992, pp. 112–23, 151–6.

29 Craig J. Reynolds, 'Introduction', in *National Identity and Its Defenders: Thailand Today*, ed. C. J. Reynolds (Chiang Mai, 2002), pp. 12–15.

30 See Erik Cohen, *The Commercialized Crafts of Thailand: Hill Tribes and Lowland Villages* (Richmond, Surrey, 2000); Patrick Jory, 'Thai Identity, Globalization and Advertising Culture', *Asian Studies Review*, XXIII/4 (1999), pp. 461–87.

two | Boundaries

1 C. A. Bayly, *The Birth of the Modern World 1780–1914* (Oxford, 2004), p. 399.

2 H. G. Quaritch Wales, *Ancient South-East Asian Warfare* (London, 1952).

3 O. W. Wolters, *History, Culture and Region in Southeast Asian Perspective*, 2nd edn (Ithaca, NY, 1999), p. 27.

4 Thongchai Winichakul, *Siam Mapped: A History of the Geo-body of a Nation* (Honolulu, 1994), pp. 117–19.

5 Ibid., p. 94.

6 Ibid., pp. 62–74, 107–8.

7 Ibid., pp. 124–5, 128–9.

8 The eighteen administrative macro-units (*monthon*) created in 1899 were reduced to ten in 1915 before being abolished in 1933; they were headed by royal commissioners (*khaluang*) who oversaw provincial governors. Presently, Thailand's territory is organized into seventy-six provinces (*changwat*), subdivided into the smaller administrative units of district (*amphoe*), commune (*tambon*) and village (*muban*). See Tej Bunnag, *The Provincial Administration of Siam, 1892–1915* (Kuala Lumpur, 1977). This classic study, by a descendant of a prominent family of the nobility, presented the reform as a crucial step in state formation. For a critical assessment of the reform, see Thongchai, *Siam Mapped*, and Chaiyan Rajachagool, *The Rise and Fall of the Thai Absolute Monarchy* (Bangkok, 1994).

9 Michael Vickery, 'Thai Regional Elites and the Reform of King Chulalongkorn', *Journal of Asian Studies*, XXIX/4 (1970), pp. 863–81; see also, Tamara Loos, *Subject Siam: Family, Law, and Colonial Modernity in Thailand* (Ithaca, NY, 2006), chapter 3.

10 See Hong Lysa, '"Stranger within the Gates": Knowing Semi-Colonial Siam as Extraterritorials', *Modern Asian Studies*, XXXVIII/2 (2004),

especially pp. 249–51.

11 Alfred McCoy, *The Politics of Heroin in Southeast Asia* (New York, 1972), pp. 30–47, 316–17, 330. There is an obvious parallel with Afghanistan in the 1980s, when opium production boomed to finance the CIA-supported mujahideen guerrillas who fought the invading Soviet army in the Cold War's last war by proxy.

12 Barbara Leitch LePoer, ed., *Thailand: A Country Study* (Washington, DC, 1989), pp. 271–4 (quote from p. 273). Note that this work makes no mention of the BPP's role in the student massacre of Thammasat University. Note also the photograph, on p. 277, presumably from the early 1970s, in which King Phumiphon and Crown Prince Wachiralongkorn appear with the then prime minister, Police-General Thanom Kittikhachorn, wearing the BPP uniform on a tour of the border with Laos.

13 Pinkaew Laungramsri, 'Ethnicity and the Politics of Ethnic Classification in Thailand', in *Ethnicity in Asia*, ed. Colin Mackerras, (London, 2003), pp. 165–7.

14 Jonathan Rigg, *Southeast Asia: The Human Landscape of Modernization and Development*, 2nd edn (London, 2003), pp. 167–9.

15 Members of the royalty bore five different ranks, namely (in descending order): *chaofa, phraongchao, momchao, momratchawong* and *momluang*. The titles of nobility conferred by the crown were (in descending order): *somdetchaophraya, chaophraya, phraya, luang, momkhun* and *phan*.

16 Akin Rabibhadana, *The Organization of Thai Society in the Early Bangkok Period 1782–1873* (Ithaca, NY, 1969).

17 In 1874 a royal edict decreed that the children of bonded serfs born after 1868 (the beginning of Chulalongkorn's reign) would on their twentieth-first birthday be granted the status of free people. Thus, during the time span of one generation the number of serfs considerably decreased; further decrees issued at the end of the century provided the legal framework for freeing the remaining serfs.

18 Scot Barmé, *Woman, Man, Bangkok: Love, Sex and Popular Culture in Thailand* (Lanham, MD, 2002), pp. 8–9, 11 (quote). Barmé reproduces (p. 104) a vignette, published in the periodical *Sayam riwiw* in 1926, shortly after the accession of the last absolute monarch, which depicted a Westerner and an official (recognizable by his uniform) banqueting on a table surrounded by crawling women. To the former's question – 'Aren't these people your fellow nationals?' – the latter replies scornfully: 'True, but they are poorer than me.' The dialogue's already obvious meaning was reinforced visually by figures of stray dogs standing next to the crawling women, which hinted at their equally low status in society (in the Thai worldview dogs possess a

much lower status than in the West).

19 See John Girling, 'Thailand in Gramscian Perspective', *Pacific Affairs*, LVII/3 (1984), pp. 385–403.

20 Between 1961 and 1972 the number of universities in Thailand increased from five to seventeen and undergraduate student enrolments from 15,000 to 50,000. Pasuk Phongpaichit and Chris Baker, *Thailand: Economy and Politics* (Oxford, 1995), p. 301. John Girling, in *Thailand: Society and Politics* (Ithaca, NY, 1981, p. 177), gives for the same period an increase from 18,000 to 100,000 students.

21 James S. Ockey, 'Creating the Thai Middle Class', in *Culture and Privilege in Capitalist Asia*, ed. Michael Pinches (London, 1999), pp. 230–50.

22 Akira Suehiro, *Capital Accumulation in Thailand 1855–1985* (Tokyo, 1989), chapters 1–7.

23 Kevin Hewison, *Power and Politics in Thailand* (Manila, 1989), pp. 32–4; Pasuk and Baker, *Thailand*, pp. 103–7. Police General Phao Siyanon sat on 26 boards, including those of banks, sugar mills, trading businesses, hotels and film companies; Sarit Thanarat on 22. Sarit's successors in the decade 1963–73 were even more spread out: Field Marshal Praphat Charusathian sat on 44 boards and Army General Krit Siwara on 50 (ibid., pp. 280–81).

24 Ibid., chapter 4.

25 Ibid., chapter 5 and p. 168.

26 The labour force employed in the industrial, manufacturing and service sectors increased from 2.2 million in 1960 to 3.2 million in 1970 and 6.6 million in 1998. Over the same time period agriculture's contribution to the GDP dropped from around 40 per cent to less than 12 per cent.

27 James C. Ingram, *Economic Change in Thailand, 1850–1970* (Stanford, CA, 1971), pp. 36–44, 76–9.

28 Girling, *Thailand*, pp. 63–72.

29 Pasuk and Baker, *Thailand*, pp. 174–83.

30 Ibid., 184–90.

31 Ibid., 191–204 (strikes figures from Table 6.3., p. 193).

32 By the end of the 1990s, women constituted on average half of the workforce but as much as 80 per cent in seven of the top ten leading export industries.

33 See Paritta Chalermpow Koanantakul and Marc Askew, *Urban Life and Urban People in Transition* (Bangkok, 1993).

34 In May 1993, 188 workers were killed and some 500 injured (most of them women) in the fire at the Kader toy factory in Nakhorn Pathom (near Bangkok) – the worst factory fire in modern history. The factory (owned by a Taiwanese group) had neither a fire alarm system nor fire escapes. John Girling, *Interpreting Development: Capitalism, Democracy*

and the Middle Class in Thailand (Ithaca, NY, 1996), p. 78.

35 Kevin Hewison, 'Crafting a New Social Contract: Domestic Capitalist
    Responses to the Challenge of Neo-Liberalism', in *Radicalizing
    Thailand: New Political Perspectives*, ed. Ji Giles Ungpakorn (Bangkok,
    2003), pp. 120–151.

36 Two common Thai proverbs recite: 'Men are like an elephant's front
    legs and women like the hind legs'; 'Man is human, woman is buffalo'.

37 Simon de la Loubère, *The Kingdom of Siam* (Singapore, 1969 [London,
    1693]), pp. 73–6.

38 Junko Koizumi, 'From a Water Buffalo to a Human Being: Women
    and the Family in Siamese History', in *Other Pasts: Women, Gender and
    History in Early Modern Southeast Asia*, ed. Barbara Watson Andaya
    (Honolulu, 2000), pp. 254–68.

39 Craig J. Reynolds, 'A Nineteenth-Century Thai Buddhist Defense of
    Polygamy and Some Remarks on the Social History of Women in
    Thailand'. Proceedings of the Seventh IAHA Conference (Bangkok,
    1979), pp. 927–70; reprinted in Reynolds, *Seditious Histories: Contesting
    Thai and Southeast Asian Pasts* (Seattle, WA, and Singapore, 2006), chapter
    9. In the appendix, Reynolds provides a translation of the section on
    polygamy from *Chaophraya* Thipakorawong's *Nangsu sadaeng kitchanukit*
    ['A Book on Miscellaneous Subjects'] (1867).

40 Malcolm Smyth, *A Physician at the Court of Siam* (Kuala Lumpur, 1982),
    p. 146.

41 Barmé, *Woman, Man, Bangkok*, pp. 22–3, 39–40, 135.

42 Quoted in Sumalee Bumroongsook, *Love and Marriage: Mate Selection
    in Twentieth-Century Central Thailand* (Bangkok, 1995), p. 46.

43 Barmé, *Woman, Man, Bangkok*, pp. 26–37 (quote p. 34), 159–62.

44 Sumalee, *Love and Marriage*, pp. 46–7, 59–60.

45 Ibid., p. 67. *Chaophraya* Thammasakmontri, a noted reformer, para-
    doxically defended arranged marriage (in an article published in the
    newspaper *Thai khasem* on 8 April 1932) on the grounds that men and
    women still could not mingle freely in society and come to know
    each other intimately, as a result of which modern marriages were
    based on insufficient reciprocal knowledge between the partners
    (ibid., p. 37).

46 Chiranan Phitpricha, *Lok thi si* ('The Fourth World') (Bangkok, 1975);
    cited in Mattani Mojdara Rutnin, *Modern Thai Literature: The Process of
    Modernization and the Transformation of Values* (Bangkok, 1988), p. 117.

47 Sumalee, *Love and Marriage*, pp. 97–8.

48 Esterik, *Materializing Thailand*, pp. 65–91.

49 Barmé, *Woman, Man, Bangkok*, pp. 76–82, 91–3; Kho Surangkhanang,
    The Prostitute, trans. David Smyth (Kuala Lumpur, 1994).

50 For an early study of Thai prostitution, see Pasuk Phongpaichit, *From*

Peasant Girls to Bangkok Masseuses (Geneva, 1982); for a more recent analysis, Wathinee Boonchalaksi and Philip Guest, *Prostitution in Thailand* (Bangkok, 1994). On prostitutes' support of rural families, see Sanitsuda Ekachai, *Behind the Smile: Voices of Thailand* (Bangkok, 1990), pp. 169–73.

51 'Kama pathibat' ('The Practice of Sex'), in *Ratsadorn*, 24 January 1929; quoted in Barmé, *Woman, Man, Bangkok*, pp. 191–2.

52 R. Morris, 'Three Sexes and Four Sexualities: Redressing the Discourse on Gender and Sexuality in Contemporary Thailand', *Positions*, II/1 (1994), pp. 15–43. For a different perspective, see Peter A. Jackson, 'Kathoey < > Gay < > Man: The Historical Emergence of Gay Male Identity in Thailand', in *Sites of Desire/Economies of Pleasure: Sexuality in Asia and the Pacific*, ed. Lenore Manderson and Margaret Jolly (Chicago, 1997), pp. 166–90.

three | Institutions

1 Quoted in Manas Chitakasem, 'Politics and Thai Literature', in *Texts and Contexts: Interactions between Literature and Culture in Southeast Asia*, ed. L. J. Mallari-Hall and L. R. Tope (Quezon City, 1999), p. 54.

2 Benjamin A. Batson, *The End of the Absolute Monarchy in Siam* (Singapore, 1984), chapters 1–2 and p. 205 (quote).

3 Quoted in Vichitvong Na Pombhejara, *Pridi Banomyong and the Making of Thailand's Modern History* (Bangkok, n.d.), p. 9.

4 The theory of the communist conspiracy was instrumentally used by Phibun, never a royal supporter, to damage the political prospects of Pridi, whose position was also weakened by the Queen Mother's reluctance to announce the cause of Anantha's death as an accident because such announcement might have generated speculations of a suicide or involvement of the king's younger brother in a fatal shooting (the two were known to play with pistols). For a narrative of these events based on British and American sources, see Judy Stowe, *Siam Becomes Thailand: A Story of Intrigue* (London, 1991).

5 Thak Chaloemtiarana, *Thailand: The Politics of Despotic Paternalism* (Bangkok, 1979), pp. 309–25; Roger Kershaw, *Monarchy in South-East Asia: The Faces of Tradition in Transition* (London, 2001), p. 68.

6 David Streckfuss, 'Kings in the Age of Nations: The Paradox of Lese-Majeste as Political Crime', *Comparative Studies in Society and History*, XXXVII/3 (1995), pp. 445–75.

7 Prince Dhani Nivat, 'The Old Siamese Conception of the Monarchy', in *Selected Articles from the Journal of the Siam Society 1929–53* (Bangkok, 1954), pp. 160–75.

8 The three were the prime minister, General Thanom Kittikhachorn;

his deputy, General Praphat Charusatian; and Narong Kittikachorn (Thanom's son and Praphat's son-in-law).

9 Quoted in Kershaw, *Monarchy in South-East Asia*, p. 141.

10 Article 8 of the constitution states: 'The King shall be enthroned in a position of revered worship and shall not be violated. No person shall expose the King to any sort of accusation or action.' The full translation of the constitution is available on the King Prajadiphok Institute's website, http://www.kpi.ac.th/en/con_th.asp.

11 *The Nation*, 15 June 2006, Section A, p. 1.

12 H. G. Quaritch Wales, *Ancient Siamese Government and Administration* (London, 1935), p. 70; Walter F. Vella, *The Impact of the West on Government in Thailand* (Berkeley, CA, 1955), p. 322.

13 F. W. Riggs, *Thailand: The Modernization of a Bureaucratic Polity* (Honolulu, 1966), pp. 335–7, 364; W. J. Siffin, *The Thai Bureaucracy: Institutional Change and Development* (Honolulu, 1966), pp. 161–3. See also Norman Jacobs, *Modernization without Development: Thailand as an Asian Case Study* (New York, 1971). For an analysis by a Thai scholar informed by modernization paradigms, see Likhit Dhiravegin, *Political Attitudes of the Bureaucratic Elite and Modernization in Thailand* (Bangkok, 1973).

14 By 1974, a quarter of the 26,000 officials in the four highest grades of the civil service had received training in the USA; at the top level, two-third of the officials had graduate degrees from foreign (mostly US) universities. John Girling, *Thailand: Society and Politics* (Ithaca, NY, 1981), p. 96, 156.

15 Ibid., pp. 147–9, 159–160.

16 Prime Ministerial order no. 66/BE 2523 (1980), quoted by John Girling, *Interpreting Development: Capitalism, Democracy, and the Middle Class in Thailand* (Ithaca, NY, 1996), p. 28.

17 Anek Laothamatas, *Business Associations and the New Political Economy of Thailand: From Bureaucratic Polity to Liberal Corporatism* (Boulder, CO, 1992).

18 The national budget's share for the defence decreased from 18 per cent in the mid-1980s to 12 per cent in the mid-1990s. James S. Ockey, 'Thailand: The Struggle to Redefine Civil-Military Relations', in *Coercion and Governance: The Declining Political Role of the Military in Asia*, ed. Muthiah Alagappa (Stanford, CA, 2001), pp. 187–208.

19 Pasuk Phongpaichit and Chris Baker, *Thaksin: The Business of Politics in Thailand* (Chiang Mai, 2004), pp. 176–87.

20 David K. Wyatt, 'The "Subtle Revolution" of King Rama I of Siam', in *Moral Order and the Question of Change: Essays on Southeast Asian Thought*, ed. D. K. Wyatt and Alexander Woodside (New Haven, CT, 1982), pp. 9–52.

21 See Craig J. Reynolds, ed. and trans., *Autobiography: The Life of Prince-Patriarch Vajirañana of Siam* (Athens, OH, 1979).

22 Peter A. Jackson, *Buddhism, Legitimation, and Conflict: The Political Function of Urban Thai Buddhism* (Singapore, 1989), pp. 66–70.

23 Charles Keyes, 'Buddhism and National Integration in Thailand', *Visakha Puja* (1971), p. 234; cited in Girling, *Thailand*, p. 155.

24 J. L. Taylor, *Forest Monks and the Nation-State: An Anthropological and Historical Study in Northeastern Thailand* (Singapore, 1993), pp. 133–6.

25 Jackson, *Buddhism, Legitimation, and Conflict*, pp. 70–82. In 1960, *Phra* Phimontham (then aged 59) was removed from his office as abbot of Wat Mahathat on the accusation of homosexuality and stripped of his clerical tile by Sarit's order. Cleared of the accusations by a Sangha internal investigation, *Phra* Phimontham was arrested in 1962 and jailed until 1966 on charges of being a communist and a threat to national security. The promulgation of the Sangha Act in 1962 followed his arrest (ibid., pp. 98–100).

26 Keyes, Thailand: *Buddhist Kingdom as Modern Nation-State* (Boulder, CO, 1989), pp. 140–41, 205–6. See also Peter A. Jackson, *Buddhadasa: A Buddhist Thinker for the Modern World* (Bangkok, 1988).

27 Jackson, *Buddhism, Legitimation, and Conflict*, chapters 7 and 8.

28 Peter A. Jackson, 'The Enchanting Spirit of Thai Capitalism: The Cult of Luang Phor Khoon and the Post-Modernization of Thai Buddhism', *Southeast Asia Research*, VII/1 (1999), pp. 5–60; Chatsurman Kabilsingh, *Buddhism and Nature Conservation* (Bangkok, 1998).

four | Ideologies

1 Adapted from the quotation in Kasian Tejapira, *Commodifying Marxism: The Formation of Modern Thai Radical Culture, 1927–1958* (Kyoto and Melbourne, 2001), p. 197. Prince Wan's coinages included, among many others, the Thai words for society, policy, regime, revolution, reform, proletariat, masses, bourgeoisie, socialism and communism, as well as culture and development.

2 See Eric Cheyfitz, *The Poetics of Imperialism: Translation and Colonization from The Tempest to Tarzan* (New York, 1991); and Vicente Rafael, *Contracting Colonialism: Translation and Christian Conversion in Tagalog Society under Early Spanish Rule* (Durham, NC, 1992).

3 Eric Hobsbawm, *Nations and Nationalism since 1780: Programme, Myth, Reality* (Cambridge, 1980).

4 Benedict Anderson, *Imagined Communities: Reflections on the Origin and Spread of Nationalism*, 2nd edn (London 1991). The classic study on the origins of Thai nationalism, now considerably outdated both conceptually and in term of sources, is Walter F. Vella, *Chaiyo! King Vajiravudh and the Development of Thai Nationalism* (Honolulu, 1978). For revisionist works in English see: Eiji Murashima, 'The Origins of Modern Official

State Ideology in Thailand', *Journal of South-East Asian Studies*, XIX/1 (1988), pp. 80–96; Scot Barmé, *Luang Wichit Wathakan and the Creation of a Thai National Identity* (Singapore, 1993); and Matthew P. Copeland, 'Contested Nationalism and the 1932 Overthrow of the Absolute Monarchy in Siam', PhD diss., Australian National University, 1993.

5 Murashima, 'Origins of State Ideology', pp. 86–8.

6 David Streckfuss, 'The Mixed Colonial Legacy in Siam: Origins of Thai Racialist Thought, 1890–1910', in *Autonomous Histories, Particular Truths: Essays in Honor of John R. W. Smail*, ed. Laurie J. Sears, Center for Southeast Asian Studies, Monograph no. 11 (Madison, WI, 1993), p. 141. The second citation from Streckfuss is from a volume produced for the St Louis World Fair of 1904, *The Kingdom of Siam*, ed. C. A. Carter, reprint edn (Bangkok, 1988). See also Tamara Loos, *Subject Siam: Family, Law, and Colonial Modernity in Thailand* (Ithaca, NY, 2006), pp. 68–71.

7 It is worth noting that people in Thailand still refer to each other by their first name even in official situations.

8 William Clifton Dodd, *The Tai Race: Elder Brother of the Chinese*, reprint edn (Bangkok, 1996), p. 275; B. J. Terwiel, 'Thai Nationalism and Identity: Popular Themes of the 1930s', in *National Identity and its Defenders: Thailand Today*, ed. C. J. Reynolds (Chiang Mai, 2002), pp. 110–11.

9 John Girling, *Thailand: Society and Politics* (Ithaca, NY, 1981), p. 60. This position underpins also Benjamin A. Batson's *The End of the Absolute Monarchy in Siam* (Singapore, 1984).

10 Thailand's preferred spelling was publicized in the following terms: 'Thai with an H is like a sophisticated girl with her hair set, her lips touched with lipstick and her brow arched with eyebrow pencil, while Tai without the H is like a girl who is naturally attractive but without any added beautification.' Thamsook Nunmonda, 'When Thailand Followed the Leader', *Social Sciences Review*, IV (1977), p. 202.

11 Sören Ivarsson, 'Making Laos "Our" Space: Thai Discourse on History and Race, 1900–1941", in *Contesting Visions of the Lao Past: Lao Historiography at the Crossroads*, ed. C. E. Goscha and S. Ivarsson (Copenhagen, 2003), pp. 256–7.

12 Cited in Thak Chaloemtiarana, ed., *Thai Politics: Extracts and Documents 1932–1957* (Bangkok, 1978), p. 264.

13 David Morell and Chai-anan Samutvanija, *Political Conflict in Thailand: Reform, Reaction, Revolution* (Cambridge, MA, 1981), p. 175

14 Quoted in Michael K. Connors, *Democracy and National Identity in Thailand* (London, 2003), p. 139.

15 Craig J. Reynolds, 'Introduction', in *National Identity and its Defenders*, ed. C. J. Reynolds, p. 15; Penny van Esterick, *Materializing Thailand*

(Oxford, 2001), p. 107. The twelve undesirable values were: immorality, materialism, weak work ethic, lack of will to sacrifice, lack of nationalist sentiment, individualism, overspending, consumerism, bully attitude, pursuit of lifestyle above one's status, fatalism and belief in magic, and abandonment of rural lifestyle; the five desirable values were self-reliance and responsibility, frugality, discipline and respect for the law, religious ethic, and abiding by the royal motto.

16 Quoted in Duncan McCargo and Ukrist Pathmanand, *The Thaksinization of Thailand* (Copenhagen, 2005), pp. 181–2.

17 Karl Marx, 'The Eighteen Brumaire of Louis Bonaparte', in *The Marx-Engels Reader*, ed. Robert C. Tucker (New York, 1972), p. 436.

18 Quoted in Pasuk Phongpaichit and Chris Baker, *Thaksin: The Business of Politics in Thailand* (Chiang Mai, 2004), p. 142.

19 The expression is from E. J. Hobsbawm, *Age of Extremes: The Short Twentieth Century, 1914–1991* (London, 1994).

20 Kasian, *Commodifying Marxism*, p. 197.

21 Ibid., pp. 11–13, 19–21. Prachathipok's comment quoted by Batson, *End of Absolute Monarchy*, p. 171.

22 Text of the act translated in Thak, ed., *Thai Politics*, pp. 236–7.

23 Ibid., pp. 186–90.

24 Kasian, *Commodifying Marxism*, p. 52–3. Between 1942 and 1952 the party's official name was Phak Khommunit Thai (Thai Communist Party), officially rendered in English as Communist Party of Siam. The name change to Communist Party of Thailand attempted to emphasize its national, as opposed to ethnic Chinese, character.

25 Ibid., chapters 4–5. Quote from Thak, ed., *Thai Politics*, p. 31.

26 Craig J. Reynolds and Hong Lysa, 'Marxism in Thai Historical Studies', *Journal of Asian Studies*, XLIII/1 (1983), pp. 80–81.

27 Act translated in Thak, ed., *Thai Politics*, pp. 819–21.

28 Craig J. Reynolds, *Thai Radical Discourse: The Real Face of Thai Feudalism Today* (Ithaca, NY, 1987), pp. 18–38. On Chit's historical work, see below, Chapter 5.

29 On the marginalization of runaway students within the CPT, see Yuangrat Wedel, *The Thai Radicals and the Communist Party* (Singapore, 1983), pp. 32–3, 38–9, 55–6.

30 Quoted in Connors, *Democracy and National Identity*, p. 32.

31 Thak, ed., *Thai Politics*, pp. 51–2.

32 Barmé, *Wichit Wathakan*, pp. 110–13, 139–44. See also Chapter 7.

33 Girling, *Thailand*, p. 151.

34 Connors, *Democracy and National Identity*, pp. 48–9.

35 Ibid., p. 82.

36 Girling, *Thailand*, pp. 206–9.

37 Connors, *Democracy and National Identity*, pp. 92–3.

38 John Girling, *Interpreting Development: Capitalism, Democracy, and the Middle Class in Thailand* (Ithaca, NY, 1996), p. 28–9, citing the Prime Ministerial orders 66/BE 2523 (1980) and 65/BE 2525 (1982).

39 The three governments in power from September 1992 to November 1997 were headed by Chuan Likpai (1992–5), Baharn Silpa-archa (1995–6) and Chawalit Yongchaiyut (1996–7).

40 See Connors, *Democracy and National Identity*, chapter 7.

41 Official English translation by the Office of the Council of State, available at http://www.kpi.ac.th/en/con_th.asp.

42 Pasuk and Baker, *Thaksin*, pp. 1–5.

five | Modernities

 1 Émile Jottrand, *In Siam*, trans. E. J. Tips (Bangkok, 1996 [Paris, 1905]), p. 226 (quote), 96.

 2 See *A Century of Thai Graphic Design*, comp. Anake Nawigamune, trans. David Smyth (Bangkok, 2000).

 3 Emma Tarlo, *Clothing Matters: Dress and Identity in Modern India* (Chicago, 1996), chapter 3.

 4 Quoted in Scot Barmé, *Woman, Man, Bangkok: Love, Sex, and Popular Culture in Thailand* (Lanham, MD, 2002), p. 182.

 5 Translation of the state edict, royal decree and radio programme in Thak Chaloemtiarana, ed., *Thai Politics: Extracts and Documents, 1932–1957* (Bangkok, 1978), pp. 252–3, 257–8, 272.

 6 Quoted in Thak Chaloemtiarana, *Thailand: The Politics of Despotic Paternalism* (Bangkok, 1979), p. 143.

 7 Barmé, *Woman, Man, Bangkok*, p. 235.

 8 Mattani Rutnin, *Modern Thai Literature: The Process of Modernization and the Transformation of Values* (Bangkok, 1988), p. 6.

 9 Sujit Wongthet, 'Second Nature' ('Kamonlasandan', 1967), in *In the Mirror: Literature and Politics in Siam in the American Era*, ed. and trans. Benedict R. Anderson and Ruchira Mendiones (Bangkok, 1985), pp. 91–108 (quote from pp. 98–9).

10 Ian Brown, 'Economic Thought in Early Twentieth-Century Siam', in *Thai Constructions of Knowledge*, ed. Manas Chitakasem and Andrew Turton (London, 1991), pp 84–98. Scot Barmé in *Luang Wichit Wathakan and the Creation of a Thai Identity* (Singapore, 1993), p. 47, writes that Suriya Nuwat's work was an unacknowledged translation of a European socialist treatise.

11 *Three Worlds According to King Ruang: A Thai Buddhist Cosmology*, trans. Frank E. Reynolds and Mani Reynolds (Berkeley, 1982).

12 *Chaophraya* Thipakorawong, *The Dynastic Chronicles, Bangkok Era: The Fourth Reign*, trans. Chadin Flood, vol. 2 (Tokyo, 1966), p. 515.

13 Thongchai Winichakul, *Siam Mapped: A History of the Geo-body of a Nation* (Honolulu, 1994), pp. 47–51, 132–7.

14 Charnvit Kasetsiri, 'Thai Historiography from Ancient Times to the Modern Period', in *Perceptions of the Past in Southeast Asia*, ed. Anthony Reid and David Marr (Singapore, 1979), pp. 156–9.

15 *Bulletin de L'Ecole Française d'Extrême-Orient*, XXI/2 (1921), p. 313 ('La connaissance scientifique du Siam est pour la plus grand part une œuvre française').

16 See Bonnie Davis, *The Siam Society under Five Reigns* (Bangkok, 1989).

17 George Cœdès, *Recueil des inscriptions du Siam. Première partie: inscriptions de Sukhodaya* (Bangkok, 1924).

18 'The Antiquarian Society of Siam Speech of King Chulalongkorn', trans. Chris Baker, *Journal of the Siam Society*, LXXXIX/1–2 (2001), pp. 95–9

19 Walter F. Vella, in *Chaiyo! King Vajiravudh and the Development of Thai Nationalism* (Honolulu, 1978, pp. 312–13), writes that the creation of the Archaeological Service was stimulated by the comment made in 1922 by an unidentified 'French minister', for whom 'Siam's failure to establish an archeological department . . . betokened "a lack of progress, moral as well as material, in this fine country".'

20 Prince Damrong Rachanuphap, *A History of Buddhist Monuments in Siam*, trans. Sulak Siravaksa (Bangkok, 1962); republished in a revised translation as *Monuments of the Buddha in Siam* (Bangkok, 1973); George Cœdès, 'Les collections archéologiques du Musée National de Bangkok', *Ars Asiatica*, 12 (1928).

21 Maurizio Peleggi, 'Royal Antiquarianism, European Orientalism and the Production of Archaeological Knowledge in Modern Siam', in *Asia in Europe, Europe in Asia*, ed. Srilata Ravi, Mario Rutten and Beng-Lan Goh (Leiden and Singapore, 2004), pp. 133–62.

22 Prince Damrong Rachanuphap, *Laksana kanpokkhrong prathet sayam tae boran* ['The Nature of Government in Siam since Antiquity'] (Bangkok, 1927), pp. 6–7.

23 Damrong, *Monuments of the Buddha*, p. 19.

24 Craig J. Reynolds, 'The Case of K.S.R. Kulap: A Challenge to Royal Historical Writing in Late Nineteenth-Century Siam', *Journal of the Siam Society*, LXI/2 (1973), pp. 63–90; idem., 'The Plot of Thai History: Theory and Practice' in *Patterns and Illusions: Thai History and Thought*, ed. Gehan Wijeyawardene and E. C. Chapman (Canberra, 1991), pp. 313–32.

25 Barmé, *Luang Wichit Wathakan*, p. 162.

26 Craig J. Reynolds and Hong Lysa, 'Marxism in Thai Historical Studies', *Journal of Asian Studies*, XLIII/1 (1983), pp. 81–5.

27 Chatthip Nartsupha, *The Thai Village Economy in the Past*, trans. Chris Baker and Pasuk Phongpaichit (Chiang Mai, 1999 [Bangkok, 1984]). For a critique, see Katherine Bowie, 'Unraveling the Myth

of the Subsistence Economy: Textile Production in Nineteenth Century Northern Thailand', *Journal of Asian Studies*, LI/4 (1992), pp. 797–823; Jeremy Kemp, 'The Dialectic of Village and State in Modern Thailand', *Journal of Southeast Asian Studies*, XXII/2 (1991), pp. 312–26.

28 See Dhida Saraya, *Tamnan and Tamnan History: A Study of Local History* (Bangkok, 1982).

29 Thongchai Winichakul, 'The Changing Landscape of the Past: New Histories in Thailand since 1973', *Journal of Southeast Asian Studies*, XXVI/1 (1995), pp. 99–120.

30 Hong Lysa, 'Twenty Years of *Sinlapa watthanatham*: Cultural Politics in Thailand in the 1980s and 1990s', *Journal of Southeast Asian Studies*, XXXI/1 (2000), pp. 26–47; Patrick Jory, 'Problems in Contemporary Thai Nationalist Historiography', *Kyoto Review of Southeast Asia*, 3 (2003), web publication.

31 Walter Vella, 'Thianwan of Siam: A Man who Fought Giants', in R. D. Renard, ed., *Anuson Walter Vella* (Chiang Mai and Honolulu, 1986), pp. 78–91; Barmé, *Woman, Man, Bangkok*, pp. 23–6.

32 King Wachirawuth, *He khruan thung nangsu* ('Song on Book Nostalgia', 1915), adapted from the translation in Vella, *Chaiyo!*, p. 240.

33 Ibid., pp. 239, 253.

34 Akartdamkeung Rapheephat, *The Circus of Life*, trans. Phongdeit Jiangphattanarkit (Bangkok, 1995), p. 255.

35 Quoted in David Smyth, 'Introduction', Siburapha, *Behind the Painting and Other Stories*, trans. D. Smyth (Singapore, 1990), p. 10.

36 Chit Phumisak, *Sinlapa phua chiwit sinlapa phua prachachon* (Bangkok, 1978). The essay was first published in the 1957 edition of Silpakorn University's *Welcome to Freshmen* handbook.

37 Khamsing Srinawk, *The Politician and Other Stories*, trans. Domnern Garden, 3rd edn (Chiang Mai, 2000). This volume is the translation of the short-stories collection *Fa bo kan* ('The Sky is no Barrier'), first published in Thailand in 1958.

38 Khukrit Pramot, *Four Reigns*, trans. Thulachandra (Bangkok, 1987).

39 Susan Fulop Kepner, *Lioness in Bloom: Modern Thai Fiction about Women* (Berkeley, CA, 1996), p. 20.

40 Ibid., p. 161; Botan, *Letters from Thailand*, trans. Susan Fulop Kepner (Bangkok, 1986; reprint edn, Chiang Mai, 2002).

41 Stanza translated in Klaus Wenk, *Thai Literature: An Introduction* (Bangkok, 1995), p. 93.

42 Statement issued on World Press Freedom Day (3 May 2006) and posted on the Thai Journalist Association's website, www.tja.or.th/modules.php?name=News&file=article&sid=398.

six | Mnemonic Sites

1 Quoted in Thongchai Winichakul, *Siam Mapped: A History of the Geo-body of a Nation* (Honolulu, 1994), p. 140.

2 On the distinction between 'sites of memory' and 'environments of memory', see Pierre Nora, 'General Introduction: Between Memory and History', in *Realms of Memory*, ed. Pierra Nora, trans. Arthur Goldhammer (New York, 1996), I, pp. 1–23.

3 See Karen Schur Narula, *Voyage of the Emerald Buddha* (Kuala Lumpur, 1994).

4 Prince Damrong, 'Wat Benchamabophit and its Collection of Images of the Buddha', *Journal of the Siam Society*, XXII/1 (1928), pp. 19–28 (quotation from pp. 20–21).

5 See Maurizio Peleggi, 'From Buddhist Icons to National Antiquities: Civilizing Pursuits and the Nationalist Quest for Origins in the Birth of the Art History of Thailand', in *The Allure of the West and the Making of Thai Identities*, ed. Rachel Harrison and Peter A. Jackson (forthcoming).

6 Maurizio Peleggi, *The Politics of Ruins and the Business of Nostalgia* (Bangkok, 2002), chapter 1.

7 James Chamberlain, ed., *The Ramkhamhaeng Controversy: Collected Papers* (Bangkok, 1991). The claim of fabrication of the stone inscription was first made by art historian Piriya Krairiksh in 1987 from the pages of the archaeological magazine, *Muang boran*. Also, Peleggi, *The Politics of Ruins*, pp. 41–2.

8 Smitthi Siribhandra and Elisabeth Moore, *Palaces of the Gods: Khmer Art and Architecture in Thailand* (London, 1992).

9 Marc Askew, *Bangkok: Place, Practice, Representation* (London, 2002), pp. 289–304.

10 Maurizio Peleggi, *Lords of Things: The Fashioning of the Siamese Monarchy's Modern Public Image* (Honolulu, 2002), pp. 104–8.

11 Nithi Aeosiwong, *Latthiphiti sadet pho 5* ['The Cult of Rama V'] (Bangkok, 1993).

12 Walter Vella, *Chaiyo! King Vajiravudh and the Origins of Thai Nationalism* (Honolulu, 1978), pp. 137–40, 118–21, 142.

13 See Maurice Agulhon, 'La statuomanie et l'historie', *Ethnologie française*, 2–3 (1978), pp. 145–72.

14 Charles F. Keyes, 'National Heroine or Local Spirit? The Struggle over Memory in the Case of Thao Suranari of Nakhon Ratchasima', in *Cultural Crisis and Social Memory: Modernity and Identity in Thailand and Laos*, ed. Charles F. Keyes and Shigeharu Tanabe (Honolulu, 2002), pp. 113–36. The original study on Thao Suranari is by Saiphin Kaeo-ngarmprasert, *Kanmuang nai anusaori thao suranari* ['The Politics

of the Monument of Thao Suranari'] (Bangkok, 1995).

15 Craig J. Reynolds, 'The Plot of Thai History: Theory and Practice' in *Patterns and Illusions: Thai History and Thought*, ed. Gehan Wijeyewardene and E. C. Chapman (Canberra, 1993), p. 316.

16 Apinan Poshyananda, *Modern Art in Thailand: Nineteenth and Twentieth Centuries* (Singapore, 1992), pp. 36–41.

17 Ibid., p. 46.

18 Thongchai Winichakul, 'Remembering/Silencing the Traumatic Past: The Ambivalent Memories of the October 1976 Massacre in Bangkok', in *Cultural Crisis and Social Memory: Modernity and Identity in Thailand and Laos*, ed. Charles F. Keyes and Shigeharu Tanabe (Honolulu, 2002), pp. 276–7.

seven | Others

1 Sunait Chutintaranond and Than Tun, *On Both Sides of the Tenasserim Range: History of Siamese-Burmese Relations* (Bangkok, 1995).

2 Manas Chitakasem, 'Politics and Thai Literature', in *Texts and Contexts: Interactions between Literature and Culture in Southeast Asia*, ed. L. J. Mallari-Hall and Lily R. Tope (Quezon City, 1999), pp. 56–7.

3 B. J. Terwiel, *A History of Modern Thailand 1767–1942* (St Lucia, Queensland, 1983), p. 141. Bangkok's Burmese community is mentioned in Cecil A. Carter, ed., *The Kingdom of Siam* (New York, 1904), p. 111; and Arnold Wright, ed., *Twentieth-Century Impressions of Siam* (London, 1908), p. 244.

4 Rama VI also added: 'When every Siamese shall begin to think and speak as one man, then will the time have arrived when there will be no longer any anxiety for the well-being of our nation.' Walter Vella, *Chaiyo! King Vajiravudh and the Origins of Thai Nationalism* (Honolulu, 1978), pp. 207–8.

5 Chris Baker, 'Editor's Preface', Prince Damrong Rachanuphap, *Our Wars with the Burmese*, trans. U Aung Thein (Bangkok, 2001), pp. xii–xiii.

6 Ibid., pp. 3–9.

7 Craig J. Reynolds, 'Cultural Production and Militarism', unpublished paper, pp. 8–9.

8 Scot Barmé, *Luang Wichit Wathakan and the Creation of a Thai Identity* (Singapore, 1993), pp. 121–3.

9 Statements by the Minister of Interior, Wan Muhammed Nor Matha, as reported in the *Bangkok Post* (25 January 2003) and *The Nation* (15 February 2003); quoted by Pasuk Phongpaichit and Chris Baker, *Thaksin: The Business of Politics in Thailand* (Chiang Mai, 2004), p. 161. Note that 'knights' (*asawin*) was the name of the infamous police corps that carried out political assassinations of leftist activists and

trade unionists in the 1960s and '70s.

10 Ibid., pp. 162–7.

11 G. W. Skinner, *Chinese Society in Thailand: An Analytical History* (Ithaca, NY, 1957), pp. 161–2.

12 Quoted by Kasian Tejapira, 'Imagined Uncommunity: The *Lookjin* Middle Class and Thai Official Nationalism', in *Essential Outsiders: Chinese and Jews in the Modern Transformation of Southeast Asia and Central Europe*, ed. Daniel Chirot and Anthony Reid (Seattle and London, 1997), p. 77.

13 Sino-Thai patronymics are generally longer than the Thai surnames for they compound the Chinese clan's name with a Thai honorific, e.g., Litrakhunwichit, 'Li, the splendid family'.

14 Kasian, 'Imagined Uncommunity', p. 77.

15 Quoted in Benjamin A. Batson, *The End of the Absolute Monarchy in Siam* (Singapore, 1984) p. 294, 304 (original emphasis).

16 Barmé, *Luang Wichit*, pp. 139, 155.

17 Skinner, *Chinese Society in Thailand*, p. 364

18 Botan, *Letters from Thailand*, trans. Susan Fulop (Bangkok, 1986), p. 78.

19 Praphassorn Sewikul, *Lot lai mangkorn* (Bangkok, 1992).

20 Craig J. Reynolds, 'Tycoons and Warlords: Chinese Historical Romance and Thai Social Formation', in *Sojourners and Settlers: Histories of Southeast Asia and the Chinese*, ed. Anthony Reid (London, 1996), pp. 115–47.

21 For some references in this section, I am indebted to Pattana Kitiarsa's essay, 'Farang as a Siamese Occidentalism', in *The Allure of the West and the Making of Thai Identities*, ed. Rachel Harrison and Peter A. Jackson (forthcoming).

22 Vella, *Chaiyo!*, p. 153.

23 See No Na Paknam, *Farang nai sinlapa thai* ['Westerners in Thai art'] (Bangkok, 1985).

24 Narai's reign is the most studied period in the history of pre-modern Siam due to copious contemporary French accounts that were immediately translated into English: Alexandre Chevalier de Chaumont, *Relation de l'ambassade de Mr le chevalier de Chaumont à la cour du roy de Siam* (Paris, 1686); Abbé de Choisy, *Journal of a Voyage to Siam 1685–1686*, trans. Michael Smithies (Kuala Lumpur, 1993 [Paris, 1687]); Guy Tachard, *Relation of the Voyage to Siam Performed by Six Jesuits Sent by the French King to the Indies and China in the year 1685* (Bangkok, 1981 [Paris, 1686; London, 1688]).

25 *Prachum phongsawadan* ['Collected Chronicles'], XX (Bangkok, 1967), p. 109; quoted in Pattana, 'Farang as Occidentalism', p. 14.

26 Prince Dhani Nivat, 'The Inscriptions of Wat Phra Jetubon', in *Collected Articles by H. H. Prince Dhani Nivat* (Bangkok, 1969).

27 Anna Leonowens, *The English Governess at the Siamese Court* (London, 1870) and *Siamese Harem Life* (London, 1872; reprinted as *The Romance of*

the Harem); Margaret Landon, *Anna and the King of Siam* (London, 1944), was made into a film with the same title in 1946, starring Rex Harrison as King Mongkut and Irene Dunne as Anna. Rodgers and Hammerstein's musical *The King and I* opened on Broadway in 1951 and was made into a film in 1956, starring Yul Brynner and Deborah Kerr in the leading roles. A remake of the film without singing, *Anna and the King*, starring Chow Yun-Fat and Jodie Foster, was filmed in 1999; in the same year, Disney Pictures produced a cartoon version of the musical. *Anna and the King* was to be shot in Thailand but, after careful consideration, the Thai National Film Board rejected Twentieth Century Fox's request for locations, alleging the film's script offered a demeaning representation of Rama IV. Also, the release of this latest film was, like the previous ones, banned in Thailand.

28 King Mongkut's letter to Mrs Leonowens (12 May 1864), reproduced in *Sinlapa watthanatham*, XXV/1 (January 2004), pp. 82–5.

29 Thongchai Winichakul, *Siam Mapped: A History of a Nation's Geo-body* (Honolulu, 1994), p. 189.

30 Quoted in M. R. Seni Pramoj and M. R. Kukrit Pramoj, eds, *A King of Siam Speaks* (Bangkok, 1987), p. 143.

31 Eiji Murashima, 'The Origins of Modern Official State Ideology in Thailand', *Journal of South-East Asian Studies*, XIX/1 (1988), p. 84.

32 Akartdamkeung Rapheephat, *The Circus of Life*, trans. Phongdeit Jiangphattanarkit (Bangkok, 1995), p. 68.

33 Stephen Greene, 'King Wachirawuth's Policy of Nationalism', in *In Memoriam Phya Anuman Rajadhon*, ed. Tej Bunnang and Michael Smithies (Bangkok, 1970), pp. 255–6.

34 For a contemporary analysis of this relationship, see Frank C. Darling, *Thailand and the United States* (Washington, DC, 1965); and for a recent reassessment, Daniel Fineman, *A Special Relationship: The United States and Military Government in Thailand, 1947–1958* (Honolulu, 1997). The film *The Ugly American* (1963) dealt with the US involvement in South-east Asia; in it, Thai journalist, author and politician Khukrit Pramot played the role of the prime minister of the fictional country of Sarkan, a thinly disguised representation of South Vietnam.

35 Wanit Jarungkit-anan, 'Michigan Test', in *In the Mirror: Literature and Politics in Siam in the American Era*, ed. and trans. Benedict R. Anderson and Ruchira Mendiones (Bangkok, 1985), pp. 143–53.

36 The phrases cited appear in the titles of the following monographs: Fred W. Riggs, *Thailand: The Modernization of a Bureaucratic Polity* (Honolulu, 1966); Hans-Dieter Evers, ed., *Loosely Structured Social Systems: Thailand in Comparative Perspective* (New Haven, CT, 1969); Norman Jacobs, *Modernization without Development: Thailand as an*

Asian Case Study (New York, 1971). For critiques of the Western schol-
arship on Thailand, see Peter Bell, 'Western Conceptions of Thai
Society: The Politics of American Scholarship', *Journal of
Contemporary Asia*, XII/1 (1982), pp. 61–74; and Eric Wakin,
*Anthropology Goes to War: Professional Ethics and Counterinsurgency in
Thailand* (Madison, WI, 1992).

37 Walter Meyer, *Beyond the Mask: Towards a Transdisciplinary Approach of
Selected Social Problems Related to the Evolution of Tourism in Thailand*
(Saarbrücken, 1988); Erik Cohen, *Thai Tourism: Hill Tribes, Islands and
Open-ended Prostitution* (Bangkok, 1996).

38 Pattana, 'Farang as Occidentalism', p. 26.

39 Quoted in Pasuk Phongpaichit and Chris Baker, *Thaksin: The Business
of Politics in Thailand* (Chiang Mai, 2004), p. 167.

40 Prince Chula Chakrabongse, *The Twain Have Met; or, An Eastern Prince
Came West* (London, 1957).

Select Bibliography

Following standard usage, Thai authors are entered under their first name according to the romanization adopted by the individual author or publisher and not that used in the text. In translated editions, the work's original place and date of publication is given in square parentheses.

Agulhon, Maurice, 'La statuomanie et l'historie', *Ethnologie française*, 1–2 (1978), pp. 145–72
Akartdamkeung Rapheephat, *The Circus of Life*, trans. Phongdeit Jiangphattanarkit (Bangkok, 1995)
Akin Rabibhadana, *The Organization of Thai Society in the Early Bangkok Period, 1782–1873* (Ithaca, NY, 1969)
Anake Nawigamune, ed., *A Century of Thai Graphic Design*, trans. David Smyth (Bangkok, 2000)
Anderson, Benedict R., and Ruchira Mendiones, eds and trans, *In the Mirror: Literature and Politics in Siam in the American Era* (Bangkok, 1985)
Anderson, Benedict R., *Imagined Communities: Reflections on the Origin and Spread of Nationalism*, 2nd edn (London, 1991)
Anek Laothamatas, *Business Associations and the New Political Economy of Thailand: From Bureaucratic Polity to Liberal Corporatism* (Boulder, CO, 1992)
Apinan Poshyananda, *Modern Art in Thailand: Nineteenth and Twentieth Centuries* (Singapore, 1992)
Askew, Marc, *Bangkok: Place, Practice, Representation* (London, 2002)
Atlas of Thailand: Spatial Structures and Development, under the direction of Doryane Kermel-Torrès (Chiang Mai, 2004)
Augé, Marc, *Non-places: An Anthropology of Hyper-Modernity*, trans. J. Howe (London, 1998)

Baker, Chris, 'Editor's Preface', in Prince Damrong Rachanuphap, *Our Wars with the Burmese*, trans. U Aung Thein (Bangkok, 2001)

Barmé, Scot, *Luang Wichit Wathakan and the Creation of a Thai Identity* (Singapore, 1993)

—, *Woman, Man, Bangkok: Love, Sex and Popular Culture in Thailand* (Lanham, MD, 2002)

Batson, Benjamin A., *The End of the Absolute Monarchy in Siam* (Singapore, 1984)

Bayly, C. A., *The Birth of the Modern World 1780–1914* (Oxford, 2004)

Bell, Peter, 'Western Conceptions of Thai Society: The Politics of American Scholarship', *Journal of Contemporary Asia*, XII/1 (1982), pp. 61–74

Bello, Walden, Cunningham Shea and Li Kheng Poh, *A Siamese Tragedy: Development and Disintegration in Modern Thailand* (London, 1998)

Botan, *Letters from Thailand*, trans. Susan Fulop (Bangkok, 1986; reprint edn, Chiang Mai, 2002)

Bowie, Katherine, 'Unraveling the Myth of the Subsistence Economy: Textile Production in Nineteenth Century Northern Thailand', *Journal of Asian Studies*, LI/4 (1992), pp. 797–823

Breckenridge, C. A., 'The Aesthetics and Politics of Colonial Collecting', *Comparative Studies in Societies and History*, XXXI/2 (1989), pp. 195–216

Brown, Ian, 'Economic Thought in Early Twentieth-Century Siam', in *Thai Constructions of Knowledge*, ed. Manas Chitakasem and Andrew Turton (London, 1991), pp. 84–98

Cannadine, David, *Ornamentalism* (London, 2001)

Carter, Cecil A., ed., *The Kingdom of Siam* (New York, 1904; reprint edn Bangkok, 1988)

Chaiyan Rajachagool, *The Rise and Fall of the Thai Absolute Monarchy* (Bangkok, 1994)

Chatsurman Kabilsingh, *Buddhism and Nature Conservation* (Bangkok, 1998)

Chaumont, Alexandre Chevalier de, *Relation de l'ambassade de Mr le chevalier de Chaumont à la cour du roy de Siam* (Paris, 1686)

Chamberlain, James, ed., *The Ramkhamhaeng Controversy: Collected Papers* (Bangkok, 1991)

Charnvit Kasetsiri, 'Thai Historiography from Ancient Times to the Modern Period', in *Perceptions of the Past in Southeast Asia*, ed. Anthony Reid and David Marr (Singapore, 1979), pp. 156–70

—, 'Siam/Civilization–Thailand/Globalization: Things to Come', paper presented at the IAHA Conference, Bangkok, May 1996

Chatthip Nartsupha, *The Thai Village Economy in the Past*, trans. Chris Baker and Pasuk Phongpaichit (Chiang Mai, 1999 [Bangkok, 1984])

Cheyfitz, Eric, *The Poetics of Imperialism: Translation and Colonization from The Tempest to Tarzan* (New York, 1991)

Chit Phumisak, *Sinlapa phua chiwit sinlapa phua prachachon* (Bangkok, 1978)

Choisy, Abbé de, *Journal of a Voyage to Siam 1685–1686*, trans. Michael
    Smithies (Kuala Lumpur, 1993 [Paris, 1687])
Chula Chakrabongse, Prince, *The Twain Have Met; or, An Eastern Prince Came
    West* (London, 1957)
Chulalongkorn, King, *Phraratcha phiti sipsong duan* ['Royal ceremonies of the
    twelve months'] (Bangkok, 1908)
—, 'The Antiquarian Society of Siam Speech', trans. Chris Baker, *Journal of
    the Siam Society*, LXXXIX/1–2 (2001), pp. 95–9
Cœdès, George, *The Indianized States of Southeast Asia*, ed. Walter Vella, trans.
    Susan Brown Cowing (Honolulu, 1968 [Paris, 1964])
—, *Recueil des inscriptions du Siam. Première partie: inscriptions de Sukhodaya*
    (Bangkok, 1924)
—, 'Les collections archéologiques du Musée National de Bangkok', *Ars
    Asiatica*, 12 (1928)
Cohen, Erik, *Thai Tourism: Hill Tribes, Islands and Open-ended Prostitution*
    (Bangkok, 1996)
—, *The Commercialized Crafts of Thailand: Hill Tribes and Lowland Villages*
    (Richmond, Surrey, 2000)
Condominas, Georges, *From Lawa to Mon, from Saa' to Thai: Historical and
    Anthropological Aspects of Southeast Asian Social Spaces*, trans. Stephanie
    Anderson, Maria Magannon and Gehan Wijeyewardene (Canberra,
    1990)
Connors, Michael K., *Democracy and National Identity in Thailand* (London,
    2003)
Cook, Nerida, 'A Tale of Two City Pillars: Mongkut and Thai Astrology on
    the Eve of Modernization', in *Patterns and Illusion: Thai History and
    Thought*, ed. Gehan Wijeywardene and E. C. Chapman (Canberra,
    1992), pp. 276–309
Copeland, Matthew P., 'Contested Nationalism and the 1932 Overthrow of
    the Absolute Monarchy in Siam', PhD diss., Australian National
    University, 1993
Damrong Ratchanuphap, Prince, Damrong, 'Wat Benchamabophit and its
    Collection of Images of the Buddha', *Journal of the Siam Society*, XXII/1
    (1928), pp. 19–28
—, *Laksana kanpokkhrong prathet sayam tae boran* ['The nature of government
    in Siam since antiquity'] (Bangkok, 1927)
—, *Monuments of the Buddha in Siam*, trans. Sulak Sivaraksa and A. B.
    Griswold, 2nd edn (Bangkok, 1973)
Darling, Frank C., *Thailand and the United States* (Washington, DC, 1965)
Davis, Bonnie, *The Siam Society under Five Reigns* (Bangkok, 1989)
Dhani Nivat, Prince, 'The Old Siamese Conception of the Monarchy', in
    Selected Articles from the Journal of the Siam Society 1929–53 (Bangkok,
    1954), pp. 160–75

—, 'The Inscriptions of Wat Phra Jetubon', in *Collected Articles by H.H. Prince Dhani Nivat* (Bangkok, 1969)

Dhida Saraya, *Tamnan and Tamnan History: A Study of Local History* (Bangkok, 1982)

Diller, Anthony, 'What Makes Central Thai a National Language?', in *National Identity and Its Defenders: Thailand Today*, ed. Craig J. Reynolds (Chiang Mai, 2002), pp. 71–107.

Dodd, William Clifton, *The Thai Race: Elder Brother of the Chinese*, reprint edn (Bangkok, 1996).

Evers, Hans-Dieter, ed., *Loosely Structured Social Systems: Thailand in Comparative Perspective* (New Haven, CT, 1969)

Fineman, Daniel, *A Special Relationship: The United States and Military Government in Thailand, 1947–1958* (Honolulu, 1997)

Girling, John, *Thailand: Society and Politics* (Ithaca, NY, 1981)

—, 'Thailand in Gramscian Perspective', *Pacific Affairs*, LVII/3 (1984), pp. 385–403

—, *Interpreting Development: Capitalism, Democracy and the Middle Class in Thailand* (Ithaca, NY, 1996)

Greene, Stephen, 'King Wachirawuth's Policy of Nationalism', in *In Memoriam Phya Anuman Rajadhon*, ed. Tej Bunnang and Michael Smithies (Bangkok, 1970), pp. 245–62.

Grow, Mary Louise, 'Laughter for Spirits, A Vow Fulfilled: The Comic Performance of Thailand's *Lakhon Chatri* Dance-Drama', PhD diss., University of Wisconsin-Madison, 1991

Herzfeld, Michael, 'The Absent Presence: Discourses of Crypto-Colonialism', *South Atlantic Quarterly*, CI/4 (2002), pp. 899–926

Hewison, Kevin, *Power and Politics in Thailand* (Manila, 1989)

—, 'Crafting a New Social Contract: Domestic Capitalist Responses to the Challenge of Neo-Liberalism', in *Radicalizing Thailand: New Political Perspectives*, ed. Ji Giles Ungpakorn (Bangkok, 2003), pp. 120–151

Higham, Charles, and Rachanie Thorasat, *Prehistoric Thailand: From Early Settlement to Sukhothai* (London, 1998)

Hobsbawm, E. J., *Nations and Nationalism since 1780: Programme, Myth, Reality* (Cambridge, 1980)

—, *Age of Extremes: The Short Twentieth Century, 1914–1991* (London, 1994)

Hong Lysa, 'Twenty Years of *Sinlapa watthanatham*: Cultural Politics in Thailand in the 1980s and 1990s', *Journal of Southeast Asian Studies*, XXXI/1 (2000), pp. 26–47

—, '"Stranger within the Gates": Knowing Semi-Colonial Siam as Extraterritorials', *Modern Asian Studies*, XXXVIII/2 (2004), pp. 327–54

Howland, D. R., *Borders of Chinese Civilization: Geography and History at Empire's End* (Durham, NC, 1996)

Ingram, James C., *Economic Change in Thailand, 1850–1970* (Stanford, CA, 1971)

Ivarsson, Sören, 'Making Laos "Our" Space: Thai Discourse on History and Race, 1900–1941', in *Contesting Visions of the Lao Past: Lao Historiography at the Crossroads*, ed. C. E. Goscha and S. Ivarsson (Copenhagen, 2003), pp. 239–64

Jacobs, Norman, *Modernization without Development: Thailand as an Asian Case Study* (New York, 1971)

Jackson, Peter A., *Buddhadasa: A Buddhist Thinker for the Modern World* (Bangkok, 1988)

—, *Buddhism, Legitimation, and Conflict: The Political Function of Urban Thai Buddhism* (Singapore, 1989)

—, 'Kathoey < > Gay < > Man: The Historical Emergence of Gay Male Identity in Thailand', in *Sites of Desire/Economies of Pleasure: Sexuality in Asia and the Pacific*, ed. Lenore Manderson and Margaret Jolly (Chicago, 1997), pp. 166–90

—, 'The Enchanting Spirit of Thai Capitalism: The Cult of Luang Phor Khoon and the Post-Modernization of Thai Buddhism', *Southeast Asia Research*, VII/1 (1999), pp. 5–60

Jiraporn Wilayasakpan, 'Nationalism and the Transformation of Aesthetic Concepts: Theatre in Thailand during the Phibun Period', PhD diss., Cornell University, 1992

Jory, Patrick, 'Thai Identity, Globalization and Advertising Culture', *Asian Studies Review*, XXIII/4 (1999), pp. 461–87

—, 'Problems in Contemporary Thai Nationalist Historiography', *Kyoto Review of Southeast Asia*, 3 (2003), web publication

Jottrand, Émile, *In Siam*, trans. E. J. Tips (Bangkok, 1996 [Paris, 1905])

Kasian Tejapira, 'Imagined Uncommunity: The *Lookjin* Middle Class and Thai Official Nationalism', in *Essential Outsiders: Chinese and Jews in the Modern Transformation of Southeast Asia and Central Europe*, ed. Daniel Chirot and Anthony Reid (Seattle and London, 1997), pp. 75–98

—, *Commodifying Marxism: The Formation of Modern Thai Radical Culture, 1927–1958* (Kyoto and Melbourne, 2001)

Kemp, Jeremy, 'The Dialectic of Village and State in Modern Thailand', *Journal of Southeast Asian Studies*, XXII/2 (1991), pp. 312–26

Kepner, Susan Fulop, *Lioness in Bloom: Modern Thai Fiction about Women* (Berkeley, CA, 1996)

Kershaw, Roger, *Monarchy in South-East Asia: The Faces of Tradition in Transition* (London, 2001)

Keyes, Charles F., *Thailand: Buddhist Kingdom as Modern Nation-State* (Boulder, CO, 1989)

—, 'National Heroine or Local Spirit? The Struggle over Memory in the Case of Thao Suranari of Nakhon Ratchasima', in *Cultural Crisis and Social Memory: Modernity and Identity in Thailand and Laos*, ed. C. F. Keyes and Shigeharu Tanabe (Honolulu, 2002), pp. 113–36.

Khamsing Srinawk, *The Politician and Other Stories*, trans. Domnern Garden, 3rd edn (Chiang Mai, 2000)

Kho Surangkhanang, *The Prostitute*, trans. David Smyth (Kuala Lumpur, 1994)

Kiernan, Ben, *How Pol Pot Came to Power* 2nd edn (New Haven, CT, 2004)

Kukrit Pramoj, *Four Reigns*, trans. Thulachandra (Bangkok, 1987)

Koizumi, Junko, 'From a Water Buffalo to a Human Being: Women and the Family in Siamese History', in *Other Pasts: Women, Gender and History in Early Modern Southeast Asia*, ed. Barbara Watson Andaya (Honolulu, 2000), pp. 254–68

Landon, Margaret, *Anna and the King of Siam* (London, 1944)

Leitch LePoer, Barbara, ed., *Thailand: A Country Study* (Washington, DC, 1989)

Leonowens, Anna, *The English Governess at the Siamese Court* (London, 1870)

—, *Siamese Harem Life* (London, 1872; reprinted as *The Romance of the Harem*, Charlottesville, VA, 1991)

Lévi-Strauss, Claude, *The Savage Mind* (Chicago, 1966 [Paris, 1962])

Likhit Dhiravegin, *Political Attitude of the Bureaucratic Elite and Modernization in Thailand* (Bangkok, 1973)

Loos, Tamara, *Subject Siam: Family, Law, and Colonial Modernity in Thailand* (Ithaca, NY, 2006)

Loubère, Simon de la, *The Kingdom of Siam* (Singapore, 1969 [London, 1693])

Manas Chitakasem, 'Politics and Thai Literature', in *Texts and Contexts: Interactions between Literature and Culture in Southeast Asia*, ed. L. J. Mallari-Hall and Lily R. Tope (Quezon City, 1999), pp. 42–68

Marx, Karl, 'The Eighteenth Brumaire of Louis Bonaparte', in *The Marx-Engels Reader*, ed. Robert C. Tucker (New York, 1972), pp. 436–525

Mattani Rutnin, *Modern Thai Literature: The Process of Modernization and the Transformation of Values* (Bangkok, 1988)

McCargo, Duncan, and Ukrist Pathmanand, *The Thaksinization of Thailand* (Copenhagen, 2005)

McCoy, Alfred, *The Politics of Heroin in Southeast Asia* (New York, 1972)

Meyer, Walter, *Beyond the Mask: Towards a Transdisciplinary Approach of Selected Social Problems Related to the Evolution of Tourism in Thailand* (Saarbrücken, 1988)

Morell, David and Chai-anan Samutvanija, *Political Conflict in Thailand: Reform, Reaction, Revolution* (Cambridge, MA, 1981)

Morris, Rosalind, 'Three Sexes and Four Sexualities: Redressing the Discourse on Gender and Sexuality in Contemporary Thailand', *Positions*, II/1 (1994), pp. 15–43

Murashima, Eiji, 'The Origins of Modern Official State Ideology in Thailand', *Journal of South-East Asian Studies*, XIX/1 (1988), pp. 80–96

Nidhi Eoseewong, *Latthiphiti sadet pho 5* ['The Cult of Rama V'] (Bangkok, 1993)

—, *Pen and Sail: Literature and History in Early Bangkok*, ed. and trans. Chris Baker and Benedict Anderson (Chiang Mai, 2005 [Bangkok, 1982])

No Na Paknam, *Farang nai sinlapa thai* ['Westerners in Thai Art'] (Bangkok, 1985)

Nora, Pierre, 'General Introduction: Between Memory and History', in *Realms of Memory*, ed. P. Nora, trans. Arthur Goldhammer (New York, 1996), I, pp. 1–23

Ockey, James S., 'Creating the Thai Middle Class', in *Culture and Privilege in Capitalist Asia*, ed. Michael Pinches (London, 1999), pp. 230–50

—, 'Thailand: The Struggle to Redefine Civil-Military Relations', in *Coercion and Governance: The Declining Political Role of the Military in Asia*, ed. Muthiah Alagappa (Stanford, 2001), pp. 187–208

Owen, Norman, 'The Rice Industry of Mainland South-East Asia, 1850–1914', *Journal of the Siam Society*, LIX/2 (1971), pp. 75–143.

Pattana Kitiarsa, '*Farang* as a Siamese Occidentalism', in *The Allure of the West and the Making of Thai Identities*, ed. Rachel Harrison and Peter A. Jackson (forthcoming).

Paritta Chalermpow Koanantakul and Askew, Marc, *Urban Life and Urban People in Transition* (Bangkok, 1993)

Pasuk Phongpaichit, *From Peasant Girls to Bangkok Masseuses* (Geneva, 1982)

Pasuk Phongpaichit and Chris Baker, *Thailand: Economy and Politics* (Oxford, 1995)

—, *Thaksin: The Business of Politics in Thailand* (Chiang Mai, 2004)

Peleggi, Maurizio, *Lords of Things: The Fashioning of the Siamese Monarchy's Modern Image* (Honolulu, 2002)

—, *The Politics of Ruins and the Business of Nostalgia* (Bangkok, 2002)

—, 'Royal Antiquarianism, European Orientalism and the Production of Archaeological Knowledge in Modern Siam', in *Asia in Europe, Europe in Asia*, ed. Srilata Ravi, Mario Rutten and Beng-Lan Goh (Leiden and Singapore, 2004), pp. 133–62

—, 'From Buddhist Icons to National Antiquities: Civilizing Pursuits and the Nationalist Quest for Origins in the Birth of the Art History of Thailand', in *The Allure of the West and the Making of Thai Identities*, ed. Rachel Harrison and Peter A. Jackson (forthcoming)

Pinkaew Laungramsri, 'Ethnicity and the Politics of Ethnic Classification in Thailand', in *Ethnicity in Asia*, ed. Colin Mackerras (London, 2003), pp. 157–63

Praphassorn Sewikul, *Lot lai mangkorn* ['Through the Dragon Design'] (Bangkok, 1992)

Quaritch Wales, H. G., *Siamese State Ceremonies: Their History and Function* (London, 1931)

—, *Ancient Siamese Government and Administration* (London, 1935)

—, *Ancient South-East Asian Warfare* (London, 1952)

Rafael, Vicente, *Contracting Colonialism: Translation and Christian Conversion in Tagalog Society under Early Spanish Rule* (Durham, NC, 1992)

Reid, Anthony, *Southeast Asia in the Age of Commerce, 1450–1680*, 2 vols (New Haven, CT, 1988–93)

Reynolds, Craig J., 'The Case of K. S. R. Kulap: A Challenge to Royal Historical Writing in Late Nineteenth-Century Siam', *Journal of the Siam Society*, LXI/2 (1973), pp. 63–90; reprinted in *Seditious Histories: Contesting Thai and Southeast Asian Pasts* (Seattle and Singapore, 2006)

—, 'A Nineteenth-Century Thai Buddhist Defence of Polygamy and Some Remarks on the Social History of Women in Thailand', Proceedings of the Seventh IAHA Conference (Bangkok, 1979), II, pp. 927–70; reprinted in *Seditious Histories* (Seattle and Singapore, 2006)

—, *Thai Radical Discourse: The Real Face of Thai Feudalism Today* (Ithaca, NY, 1987)

—, 'The Plot of Thai History: Theory and Practice', in *Patterns and Illusions: Thai History and Thought*, ed. Gehan Wijeyawardene and E. C. Chapman (Canberra, 1991), pp. 313–32

—, 'Tycoons and Warlords: Chinese Historical Romance and Thai Social Formation', in *Sojourners and Settlers: Histories of Southeast Asia and the Chinese*, ed. Anthony Reid (London, 1996), pp. 115–47

—, 'Globalizers vs. Communitarians: Public Intellectuals Debate Thailand's Future', *Singapore Journal of Tropical Geography*, XXII/3 (2001), pp. 252–69

—, 'Introduction', in *National Identity and its Defenders: Thailand Today*, ed. C. J. Reynolds (Chiang Mai, 2002), pp. 1–32

—, 'Cultural Production and Militarism' (unpublished paper)

—, ed. and trans., *Autobiography: The Life of Prince-Patriarch Vajiranana of Siam* (Athens, OH, 1979)

Reynolds, Craig J., and Hong Lysa, 'Marxism in Thai Historical Studies', *Journal of Asian Studies*, XLIII/1 (1983), pp. 77–104

Rigg, Jonathan, *Southeast Asia: The Human Landscape of Modernization and Development*, 2nd edn (London, 2003)

Riggs, Fred W., *Thailand: The Modernization of a Bureaucratic Polity* (Honolulu, 1966)

Saiphin Kaeo-ngarmprasert, *Kanmuang nai anusaori thao suranari* ['The Politics of the Monument of Thao Suranari'] (Bangkok, 1995)

Sanitsuda Ekachai, *Behind the Smile: Voices of Thailand* (Bangkok, 1990)

Schur Narula, Karen, *Voyage of the Emerald Buddha* (Kuala Lumpur, 1994)

Seni Pramoj, M. R., and M. R. Kukrit Pramot, eds, *A King of Siam Speaks* (Bangkok, 1987)

Siburapha (Kulap Saipradit), *Behind the Painting and Other Stories*, trans. David Smyth (Singapore, 1990)

Siffin, W. J., *The Thai Bureaucracy: Institutional Change and Development* (Honolulu, 1966)

Skinner, G. W., *Chinese Society in Thailand: An Analytical History* (Ithaca, NY, 1957)

Smitthi Siribhandra and Elisabeth Moore, *Palaces of the Gods: Khmer Art and Architecture in Thailand* (London, 1992)

Smyth, Malcolm, *A Physician at the Court of Siam* (Kuala Lumpur, 1982)

Stowe, Judy, *Siam Becomes Thailand: A Story of Intrigue* (London, 1991)

Streckfuss, David, 'The Mixed Colonial Legacy in Siam: Origins of Thai Racialist Thought, 1890–1910', in *Autonomous Histories, Particular Truths: Essays in Honor of John R. W. Smail*, ed. Laurie J. Sears, Centre for Southeast Asian Studies, Monograph no. 11 (Madison, WI, 1993), pp. 123–53

—, 'Kings in the Age of Nations: The Paradox of Lese-Majeste as Political Crime', *Comparative Studies in Society and History*, XXXVII/3 (1995), pp. 445–75

Sulak Sivaraksa, 'The Crisis of Siamese Identity', in *National Identity and its Defenders: Thailand Today*, ed. Craig J. Reynolds (Chiang Mai, 2002), pp. 33–48

Sumalee Bumroongsook, *Love and Marriage: Mate Selection in Twentieth-Century Central Thailand* (Bangkok, 1995)

Sunait Chutintaranond and Than Tun, *On Both Sides of the Tenasserim Range: History of Siamese-Burmese Relations* (Bangkok, 1995)

Tachard, Guy, *Relation of the Voyage to Siam Performed by Six Jesuits Sent by the French King to the Indies and China in the year 1685* (Bangkok, 1981 [Paris, 1686; London, 1688])

Tarlo, Emma, *Clothing Matters: Dress and Identity in Modern India* (Chicago, 1996)

Taylor, J. L., *Forest Monks and the Nation-State: An Anthropological and Historical Study in Northeastern Thailand* (Singapore, 1993)

Terwiel, B. J., *A History of Modern Thailand 1767–1942* (St Lucia, Queensland, 1983)

—, 'Thai Nationalism and Identity: Popular Themes of the 1930s', in *National Identity and its Defenders: Thailand Today*, ed. Craig J. Reynolds (Chiang Mai, 2002), pp. 108–25

Thailand in Brief 2004 (Bangkok, 2004)

Thak Chaloemtiarana, *Thailand: The Politics of Despotic Paternalism* (Bangkok, 1979)

Thak Chaloemtiarana, ed., *Thai Politics: Extracts and Documents 1932–1957* (Bangkok, 1978)

Thamsok Numnonda, 'When Thailand Followed the Leader', *Social Sciences Review* 4 (1977), pp. 197–223

Thipakorawong, Chaophraya, *The Dynastic Chronicles, Bangkok Era: The Fourth Reign*, ed. and trans. Chadin Flood, 5 vols (Tokyo, 1965–74)

Thongchai Winichakul, *Siam Mapped: A History of the Geo-body of a Nation* (Honolulu, 1994)

—, 'The Changing Landscape of the Past: New Histories in Thailand since 1973', *Journal of Southeast Asian Studies*, XXVI/1 (1995), pp. 99–120

—, 'The Quest for "Siwilai": A Geographical Discourse of Civilizational Thinking in Late 19th and Early 20th Century Siam', *Journal of Asian Studies*, LIX/3 (2000), pp. 528–49

—, 'Remembering/Silencing the Traumatic Past: The Ambivalent Memories of the October 1976 Massacre in Bangkok', in *Cultural Crisis and Social Memory: Modernity and Identity in Thailand and Laos,* ed. Charles F. Keyes and Shigeharu Tanabe (Honolulu, 2002), pp. 243–83

Three Worlds According to the King Ruang: A Thai Buddhist Cosmology, trans. Frank E. Reynolds and Mani Reynolds (Berkeley, CA, 1982)

Van Esterick, Penny, *Materializing Thailand* (Oxford, 2001)

Vella, Walter F., *The Impact of the West on Government in Thailand* (Berkeley, CA, 1955)

—, *Chaiyo! King Vajiravudh and the Origins of Thai Nationalism* (Honolulu, 1978)

—, 'Thianwan of Siam: A Man who Fought Giants', in *Anuson Walter Vella*, ed. R. D. Renard, (Chiang Mai and Honolulu, 1986), pp. 78–91

Vichitvong Na Pombhejara, *Pridi Banomyong and the Making of Thailand's Modern History* (Bangkok, n.d.)

Vickery, Michael, 'Thai Regional Elites and the Reform of King Chulalongkorn', *Journal of Asian Studies*, XXIX/4 (1970), pp. 863–81

Wakin, Eric, *Anthropology Goes to War: Professional Ethics and Counterinsurgency in Thailand* (Madison, WI, 1992)

Wathinee Boonchalaksi and Philip Guest, *Prostitution in Thailand* (Bangkok, 1994)

Wenk, Klaus, *Thai Literature: An Introduction* (Bangkok, 1995)

Williams, Raymond, *Keywords* (New York, 1976)

Wolters, O. W., *History, Culture and Region in Southeast Asian Perspective*, 2nd edn (Ithaca, NY, 1999)

Wright, Arnold, ed., *Twentieth-Century Impressions of Siam* (London, 1908)

Wyatt, David K., 'The "Subtle Revolution" of King Rama I of Siam', in *Moral Order and the Question of Change: Essays on Southeast Asian Thought*, ed. D. K. Wyatt and Alexander Woodside (New Haven, CT, 1982), pp. 9–52

—, *Reading Thai Murals* (Chiang Mai, 2004)

Yuangrat Wedel, *The Thai Radicals and the Communist Party* (Singapore, 1983)

Acknowledgements

Most of this book was written during a sabbatical semester at the Southeast Asia Program of Cornell University, which was generously supported by the National University of Singapore. My thanks go to: Audrey Kahin, Rick Ruth, Benny Widyono, John Wolff, Wendy Treat, Nancy Loncto, Thak Chaloemtiarana, Tamara Loos, Andrew Johnson and Daena Funahashi in Ithaca for their help and hospitality as well as Michael Hertzfeld in Boston; Khairudin Aljuned for invaluable suggestions in the initial stage of writing, Michael Montesano, Steve Keck, Greg Clancey, Yong Mun Cheong and Hong Lysa in Singapore; Craig Reynolds in Canberra for his continuous advice and support over the years; the press's two readers, whose insightful comments were of great help in revising the manuscript for publication; and my family and friends in Rome; and Tania Roy. The bibliography can be read as an acknowledgement of the many scholars of Thailand without whose work my interpretive synthesis could not have been attempted.

Photo Acknowledgements

The author and publishers wish to express their thanks to the following sources of illustrative material and/or permission to reproduce it.

From John Anderson, *English Intercourse with Siam in the Seventeenth Century* (London, 1890), p. 15; Archive of Thammasat University: pp. 125 (foot), 138, 190; photos by the author: pp. 179, 181, 183; from J.G.D. Campbell, *Siam in the 20th century* (London, 1904): pp. 31, 33, 93, 146, 149; from A. Cecil Carter, *Kingdom of Siam* (New York, 1904): pp. 27, 82, 105; from Karl Dohring, *Siam*, vol. I: *Land und Volk* (Darmstadt, 1923): pp. 41, 42 (top); Fine Arts Department, Thailand: p. 175; from Reginald le May, *An Asian Arcady: The Land and Peoples of Northern Siam* (Cambridge, 1926): p. 42 (foot); from Martin Hurliman, *Bangkok* (Zürich: Atlantis Verlag, 1962): pp. 203, 207; photo Library of Congress, Washington, DC: p. 174 (Prints and Photographs Division, Frank and Frances Carpenter Collection; LC-USZ62-5322); National Archives, Thailand: pp. 148, 159, 185; National Identity Office, Office of the Prime Minister: pp. 98, 102, 152; photo National Museum, Bangkok: p. 206; from J. B. Pallegoix, *Description du Royaume Thai ou Siam*, vol. I (Paris, 1854): p. 32; Public Relations Department, Office of the Prime Minister: pp. 56, 99; from Capitaine Seauve, *Les Rélations de la France et du Siam (1680–1907)* (Paris, 1907): p. 62. Special thanks to Kieran Ball for permission to reproduce his photograph on p. 142.

Index